POLITICS, INNOCENCE, AND THE LIMITS OF GOODNESS

POLITICS, INNOCENCE, AND THE LIMITS OF GOODNESS

PETER JOHNSON
Lecturer in Politics, University of Southampton

ROUTLEDGE
LONDON AND NEW YORK

First published in 1988 by
Routledge
a division of Routledge, Chapman and Hall
11 New Fetter Lane, London EC4P 4EE

Published in the USA by
Routledge
a division of Routledge, Chapman and Hall, Inc.
29 West 35th Street, New York NY 10001

© 1988 Peter Johnson

Set by Hope Services, Abingdon
Printed in Great Britain by
TJ Press (Padstow) Ltd, Padstow, Cornwall

British Library Cataloguing in Publication Data

Johnson, Peter, 1943–
Politics, innocence, and the limits of goodness.
1. Politics. Ethical aspects
I. Title
172

ISBN 0–415–01046–2

Library of Congress Cataloging in Publication Data

Johnson, Peter, 1943–
Politics, innocence, and the limits of goodness/by Peter Johnson.
p.   cm.
Bibliography: p.
Includes index.
ISBN 0–415–01046–2
1. Political ethics.   2. Innocence (Psychology)
3. Politics in literature. I. Title.

JA79.J64 1988   172–dc19

IN MEMORY OF MY FATHER
THOMAS WILLIAM JOHNSON
1916–1943

. . . he who loves a person or a thing without knowing him or it falls prey to something that he would not love if he could see it. Whenever experience, caution and measured steps are needed, it is the innocent person who will be most thoroughly ruined, for he has blindly to drink the dregs and the bottommost poison of everything. (Friedrich Nietzsche, *Daybreak, Thoughts on the Prejudices of Morality*)

Innocence . . . to the extent that it is more than 'not guilty', cannot be proved but must be accepted on faith, whereby the trouble is that this faith cannot be supported by the given word, which can be a lie.

(Hannah Arendt, *On Revolution*)

CONTENTS

Preface   ix

1 INNOCENCE AND POLITICS   1

2 PUBLIC AND PRIVATE VIRTUE   18

3 POLITICAL AUTONOMY   68

4 ABSOLUTE VIRTUE AND POLITICS   100

5 THE DISPLACEMENT OF VIRTUE   125

6 POLITICAL PHILOSOPHY AND LITERATURE   166

7 POLITICS AND INNOCENT INTENT   184

8 MORAL PURITY AND POLITICS   198

9 INNOCENT IDEALISM   218

10 INNOCENCE AND EXPERIENCE   235

11 CONCLUSION   249

Notes   258

References   272

Index   281

PREFACE

In his *Essay on Cruelty*, Montaigne refers to those who are 'innocent, but not virtuous': in what follows I explore the political implications of this remark. Perceptive readers will identify the texts of modern political philosophy which have provided most guidance, and I have been conscious too of Sophocles' powerful and elusive statement that nothing tests moral character better than 'the practice of authority and rule'.

For specific assistance I am grateful to Professor Raymond Plant who was the first to risk reading my original draft; to Janet Coleman, whose detailed and thoughtful comments on it raised more questions than I could hope to answer; to Geraint Williams who provided help at a difficult stage; and to Professor Peter Calvert who, on behalf of the Department of Politics at Southampton University, eased the practical difficulties of preparing a manuscript for publication. Thanks, too, are due to Mrs Jean Ballard who efficiently transformed my handwritten material into legible typescript. Finally, I must thank my wife, Sue. Without her encouragement and assistance an unwieldy manuscript would never have become a book. Of course, for the form it takes here I am responsible.

Chapter One

INNOCENCE AND POLITICS

What are the marks of innocence? Candour – a beautiful word – truthfulness, simplicity, a quite involuntary bearing of witness.

(Iris Murdoch, *The Bell*)

A man who wishes to make a profession of goodness in everything must necessarily come to grief among so many who are not good. Therefore it is necessary for a prince, who wishes to maintain himself, to learn how not to be good, and to use this knowledge and not to use it, according to the necessity of the case.

(Machiavelli, *The Prince*)

My theme is the place of moral innocence in politics. My aim is to analyse its nature, and to explain why it is that it may threaten politics. Innocence is a neglected concept in recent moral and political philosophy.[1] It eludes the net of both consequentialist and rights-based moral theories which seek to establish formal grounds for moral obligation. My central intellectual problem is the paradox of innocence. We are familiar with the idea of innocence being harmed or destroyed, and we know what is meant when innocents are victims of circumstance, policy, or outrage. We are not so clear, however, about the nature of the human harm and damage which can result from innocence.

In an imperfect and frequently duplicitous world we often speak of innocence as something which is lost. But this neglects the active sense of innocence. It implies that innocence is of moral significance only for the person who possesses it and who may have to suffer its loss. In politics this is not so. The public nature of political action means that innocence has a wider moral reference than simply the person in whose life it features. One of the victims of innocence may

1

be the political community itself. Innocence can produce political dismemberment, resulting in political suffering and disintegration. The role of innocence in war and civil war raises moral dilemmas and conflicts of an acute kind. We are made aware in these circumstances of the dangers of innocence and the reactions of its victims. But how can this be so? The values associated with innocence – truthfulness, candour, and compassion – have traditionally been seen as crucial to a rapprochement between morality and politics. How can the same values render this rapprochement impossible? The conjunction of innocence and politics, therefore, represents a challenge to moral and political philosophy which ranges across a broad front of ideas. It is my contention that there is a closer connection between moral disposition and political outcome than that allowed by consequentialism: what characterizes moral innocence disqualifies it from constructive political engagement.

Innocence is a concept marked by great complexity, found in a variety of different human contexts. It can mean the absence of sin, guilt or blame. Sometimes it refers to moral purity, lack of guile, wordly wisdom or cunning, lack of knowledge or commonsense.

My primary focus is on those senses of innocence which have a bearing on the relation between morality and politics. So the philosophical and literary texts I feature deal specifically with the way individual lives display meaning and find identity in situations of supreme political intensity; individuals like Melville's Billy Budd whose nature 'had in its simplicity never willed malice', like Henry VI, Shakespeare's 'easy-melting King', like Pyle, Greene's 'very quiet American', 'too innocent to live' ('"God save us always . . . from the innocent and the good"').

Modern moral philosophy has been sceptical of such notions as absolute goodness, its metaphysical foundations, and the air of certainty which surrounds it. In the main it has followed Hume's maxim:

> that no action can be virtuous, or morally good, unless there be in human nature some motive to produce it, distinct from the sense of its morality.[2]

Thus, Philippa Foot writes:

> it seems clear that virtues are, in some general way, beneficial. Human beings do not get on well without them. Nobody can get

2

on well if he lacks courage, and does not have some measure of temperance and wisdom, while communities where justice and charity are lacking are apt to be wretched places to live.[3]

Similarly Peter Geach:

We need prudence or practical wisdom for any large-scale planning. We need justice to secure cooperation and mutual trust among men, without which our lives would be nasty, brutish, and short. We need temperance in order not to be deflected from our long-term and large-scale goals by seeking short-term satisfactions. And we need courage in order to persevere in face of set-backs, wearinesses, difficulties and dangers.[4]

Human beings have the moral values they do because they benefit from them. Moral values are prized not for their own sake but for the individual and social purposes they are intended to fulfil. They are based on minimal altruism; which implies that their choice is rational because it enables agents to pursue their ends so as to maximize their achievement and minimize personal cost and the risk of personal loss.

The attempt to base moral obligation on minimal altruism is common to many ethical systems. Utilitarianism and contractualism may give crucially different accounts of justice in political communities, but they both rely heavily on individualist premises and both include minimal altruism in their derivation of moral obligation. Such views have failed to persuade all moral philosophers. Some have argued that utilitarianism diminishes the importance of moral considerations. Values – truth-telling for example – are not dependent on the benefits which may accrue from them and are a necessary feature of any human society irrespective of their social utility. Some have rejected the attempt to connect morality and self-interest, if not in the full sense of unlimited reward then at least in respect of minimizing the costs. A non-moral justification for morality blurs the essential distinction between morality and prudence. D. Z. Phillips believes:

It is not the case that a thousand tough characters who care for no one but themselves can be shown, on their own terms, that they have a reason to be just. A rogue is not a man who has miscalculated his self-interest. The indifferent cannot be made to care for moral considerations by showing the latter to be founded on what all men want.[5]

Moral considerations have nothing to do with the wants or desires an individual may have or the advantages he may wish to obtain. Morality has nothing to do with costs or advantage, interest or profit. The value in morality is intrinsic, not established extrinsically by any further good or purpose. Morality concerns the disinterested pursuit of the good, which is brought out by a critic of Philippa Foot:

> [she] assumes that if a man's just actions bring about his death, they have ended in disaster. She fails to see that for anyone concerned about justice, death for the sake of justice is not a disaster. The disaster for him would be to be found wanting in the face of death, and to seek the path of injustice and compromise.[6]

The attempt to tie morality to moderate self-interest cannot explain why someone would be prepared to sacrifice his life rather than compromise with tyranny. For Phillips, the meaning of such a choice has to be found in terms other than profit or advantage.

> Death cannot be profitable, since that in terms of which profitableness is to be assessed, namely, myself, no longer exists.[7]

Utilitarian and contract theories see absolute goodness as irrelevant to the derivation of a just society on the grounds that it is unreasonable to expect comprehensive altruism to be shown by all individuals. So the rules of justice have to be derived from a more limited benevolence if they are to have prescriptive force. It is noteworthy that Kant rejects the utilitarian attempt to link morality and interest and yet tries to find a conceptual place for the 'thousand tough characters'.

> As hard as it may sound, the problem of setting up a state can be solved even by a nation of devils (so long as they possess understanding).[8]

Kant's strategy is to employ the idea of practical reason to generate principles of justice. In so doing he hopes to avoid the obvious criticism of his republicanism.

> Now the republican constitution is the only one entirely fitting to the rights of man. But it is the most difficult to establish and even harder to preserve, so that many say a republic would have to be a

nation of angels, because men with their selfish inclinations are not capable of a constitution of such sublime form.[9]

Kant may have had Rousseau in mind, particularly his remark in *The Social Contract*:

Were there a people of gods, their government would be democratic. So perfect government is not for men.[10]

Rousseau thought that the loss of innocence was inevitable and that its full restoration was impossible even in mature and just political communities. For Kant this can be avoided by grounding moral and political principles in formal considerations of reason. At this stage I simply suggest that Kant's attempt to justify republicanism to 'a race of devils' leaves obscure a variety of relations beween politics and absolute virtue.

Those who support the view that moral values are justified by the benefits they bring to the world are not necessarily committed to full consequentialism. They may not claim that the morality of an action is decided by reference to its consequences alone. But they do have a particular conception of moral agency. The idea that morality pays places a high value on individuals who are experienced in the ways of the world. Such individuals know exactly when to act morally. They never do more than morality requires of them, and they are careful never to allow their charitable inclinations to lead them to act unjustly. They act on specific obligations in particular circumstances, and they are proud of the wisdom which enables them to do so. For them, moral knowledge serves to define moral expectations. Such individuals always know in advance the moral price attached to any decision or course of action, and it is usually a low one. In the words of one recent writer:

if it is in our power to prevent something bad from happening, without thereby sacrificing anything of comparable moral importance, we ought, morally, to do it.[11]

Moral agency has the function of perfecting the exercise of practical reason. In Aristotelian language, the twin virtues are practical wisdom and self-control, to be found in a man of justifiable pride. He is the magnanimous man who has no cause to be humble. He exercises virtue confident in the belief that he is both benefiting the world and safeguarding his own moral superiority. Having no fear of doing wrong he requires neither forgiveness nor repentance. In Jowett's famous phrase, he never explains and never apologises because he is never in a position to have to do either.[12]

Surely this picture of the moral individual is of little real value in understanding moral innocence and its place in the world. The morally innocent are ignorant of the benefits which morality may produce. Their goodness does not depend on intellectual premises or on a system of ethical thought and they are indifferent to moral refinements. Incapable of calculating the rewards of morality they are unaware of their own integrity. A major problem occurs when moral innocence and politics overlap, because in political life actions are not just of significance for the agent who performs them. For the morally innocent the importance of morality lies in its connection not with human goods or needs but with the idea of absolute virtue.

We speak about morality having an absolute claim. First, we may wish to distinguish absolute virtues from those which are relative to some further end which is then deemed to be morally desirable. Second, virtues may be seen as absolute in the sense that they completely exclude certain kinds of conduct. Wittgenstein writes:

> 'Supposing that I could play tennis and one of you saw me playing and said 'Well, you play pretty badly' and suppose I answered 'I know, I'm playing badly but I don't want to play any better', all the other man could say would be 'Ah then that's all right'. But suppose I had told one of you a preposterous lie and he came up to me and said 'You're behaving like a beast' and then I were to say 'I know I behave badly, but then I don't want to behave any better', could he then say 'Ah, then that's all right'? Certainly not; he would say 'Well you *ought* to want to behave better'. Here you have an absolute judgement of value, whereas the first instance was one of a relative judgement.'[13]

Third, absolute virtue may require us to do more for others than a minimal statement of our obligations would compel. Fourth, absolute virtue means the exclusion of negotiation or compromise with virtue. This rules out both trading between virtue and interest and deals between virtues.

What place does absolute virtue have in our account of politics? Are the demands of politics such that absolute virtue cannot survive? Are the demands of compassion and truthfulness such that no political life which tried to include them would be possible? These are the central themes of this book. They are traditional preoccupations of political philosophy. Those major attempts to provide a rational basis for justice as the first virtue of political communities encompass such questions and try to answer them. Theories like utilitarianism and contractualism try to show in different ways that justice is to our advantage. But, from the standpoint of absolute virtue, moral actions are not performed for the sake of advantage. We reach the same position if we approach the problem in a different way. Political morality signifies a public world, not simply an aggregate of private individuals. Effective action in this world often seems to require that we put aside moral considerations which we would otherwise respect. However, from the perspective of absolute virtue nothing could override morality. Morality is itself overriding.

Does this make the contrast between morality and politics too stark? Political conduct may be governed by principles of fairness which apply to individuals on a consensual or representational basis and which may result in a justifiable sense of the public good. And there are occasions where even acting well requires that one value is sacrificed to protect another: moral dilemmas are not restricted to political morality. Often moral courage is needed when morally difficult decisions are taken in politics. Could absolute virtue ever countenance such moral compromise? It is one thing to choose death before dishonour, but the deaths of others, e.g. assassination for the public good, as honourable conduct? (Brutus is an 'honourable' man!) So the gap between morality and politics re-opens. My aim in this book is to analyse these dilemmas and paradoxes of political morality, to examine critically the relation between moral character, political decision, and political outcome.

In liberal jurisprudence innocence means the absence of particular guilt. In other words, innocence is lost when particular guilt is present. The establishment of guilt is dependent on the existence of a set of legal rules which enable the identification of agents and the actions which, it is claimed, they are guilty of performing. To be innocent in this sense is to be not guilty of that with which you are charged. This means that the agent does not deserve punishment or forgiveness. Innocence in this sense is understood in the light of a framework of legal rules, against the background of past conduct, and it has a close connection with the ideas of responsibility, blame-worthiness, and the honesty or dishonesty of the accused. Punishment, therefore, presupposes guilt, although if the innocent are punished then this is often rather strangely described as wrongful punishment. Adam Smith has written perceptively about the state of mind of those who are punished for crimes they did not commit. In *The Theory of Moral Sentiments*, he writes:

> an innocent man . . . is often, not only shocked, but most severely mortified by the serious, though false, imputation of a crime; especially when that imputation happens unfortunately to be supported by some circumstances which gave it an air of probability.[14]

Later in the same passage we find:

> The innocent man . . . over and above the uneasiness which this fear may occasion, is tormented by his own indignation at the injustice which has been done to him.[15]

This is an important point to note. Innocents who are harmed, as in the case of those who are punished for crimes they did not commit, are indignant, as Smith puts it, at the 'injustice which has been done to [them]'. The proper stress here is on what is done to the innocent.

There is a different use of innocence which has a strong bearing on the argument. Here the meaning of innocence does not depend on the absence of particular legal guilt: it is conditional, not necessarily on legal rules, but on the existence of moral values and beliefs. We speak of individuals manipulated for political advantage who are innocent of involvement or complicity. This conception of innocence plays an important part in moral and political argument. In just war theory, for example, it provides the foundation for the crucial distinction between combatant and non-combatant, a distinction which both permits and prohibits specific forms of warfare. The moral prohibition on policies and weapons which would endanger the lives of non-combatants depends, in the first instance, on our acceptance of non-combatants as innocent of any military involvement. The moral embargo is again at work against actions which harm or damage the innocent. What is philosophically important about this sense of innocence is that it is both specific and conditional. It has, therefore, an affinity with the legal notion of innocence as absence of particular guilt.

In both cases, innocence is morally important because it signifies the absence of something. What this is varies. It may, for example, be responsibility for a crime or participation in weapon production during a war. This sense of innocence is conditional on the identification of certain characteristics, i.e. lack of specific guilt or responsibility, and is obviously limited to these. Someone who is innocent of a crime may not be innocent in the sense of being 'open' or 'candid'. Innocence becomes a passive virtue – one is innocent simply because one has not done something. To discover how innocence can have an active sense we need to understand it, not as the simple absence of blameable features, but as the presence of a particular kind of moral disposition.

Innocence of this kind will be one of the central concerns of this book. It is the state of being blameless, without stain or moral blemish. It discloses moral purity. In the history of ideas this condition has often been associated with pre-social existence. Rousseau was one among many eighteenth-century writers who contemplated an ideal state of nature in which life was peaceful, innocent, and harmonious. For Rousseau this condition could not endure: human consciousness is instinctive and not mediated by self-awareness. Like childhood, it appears to the present as an ideal, but not as a recoverable stage of life. Its claim to self-sufficiency is an illusion. In religious language, too, the myth of a Golden Age appears as pre-lapsarian; moral innocence in the imperfect human world as holiness or sanctity. It is similar to, but not identical with, images of childhood in the life of an individual and in the early existence of a society or a civilization. Perhaps the most dramatic secular expression of destruction of innocence in this sense is the Childermas, the slaughter by Herod of 'all the children that were in Bethlehem, and in all the coasts thereof, from two years old and under, according to the time which he had diligently inquired of the wise men.'[16]

In the final act of Shakespeare's *Henry VI (Part 3)* when Gloucester asks the King if he thinks he is an executioner, Henry replies:

> A persecutor, I am sure, thou art:
> If murdering innocents be executing,
> Why, then, thou art an executioner.[17]

Gloucester has killed Henry's son. Later he will murder the boy Princes in the Tower. There is a double meaning of innocence in this passage, its impact strengthened by Henry's speaking conditionally.

9

How can the murder of the innocent be an execution when the innocent are without blame?

Innocence as moral purity implies an inability to inflict harm. It trusts in its vision of the world as good and pure. More significantly, the innocent are ignorant of their moral insight. They are unaware of their own goodness, and they behave well not from an astute recognition of the virtue of doing so, but because they are incapable of envisaging moral conduct in any other way. This means that the morally innocent are forgetful of self. But their actions are not merely unselfish. They spring from an obliteration of self which places them on the edge of saintliness. Innocence in this sense implies a kind of ignorance, an absence of knowledge and experience. Yet this is not artlessness in the ways of the world. Moral innocence is not simply freedom from guile or cunning. It is not mere inexperience in which someone may be 'too innocent for his own good', or innocent of the consequences of his actions.

An inattention to moral qualities and virtues does not mean that moral innocence must be unassertive. In contrast to innocence as the absence of particular guilt or responsibility it possesses a substantive vision of the moral good which is intrinsic to its nature. Far from being passively content with its inactivity – we are innocent when we have not done something – moral innocence requires the disclosure of its nature to the world. One of the characters in Iris Murdoch's novel, *The Bell*, says:

> Virtue, innocence, should be valued whatever its history. It has a radiance which enlightens and purifies and which is not dimmed by foolish talk about the worth of experience.[18]

The revelation of innocence can take the form of a test. In Dostoevsky's *The Idiot*, Myshkin's moral simplicity is found to be vulnerable when confronted with the passions and interests of the world. This challenge, however, may work the opposite way. J. P. Stern refers to the world of political institutions as 'the kingdom of the Leviathan, where men are bound not by love but contract, not by worship of Nature or the Divine but by mutual agreement.'[19] What impact does the disclosure of moral innocence have on such a realm, its imperatives, rules and powers?

Innocence as inexperience is found in someone about to enter a social institution or who is on the point of learning the rules of a mode of conduct. An amateur, say, a novice, or an apprentice are all innocent of activity they will in time understand and appreciate. This is an important feature of ordinary moral thinking, but by itself it is not sufficient. Moral innocence refers not to a self requiring experience for its fulfilment and completion, but to a moral character praiseworthy on its own terms. We are not simply talking of a manner of acting. Our primary focus is personal moral identity and disposition.

This raises a problem. We often speak of moral conduct as admirable in one sense but not in another. An action may be benevolent without being brave. An individual may be honest but not considerate. However, in the case of moral innocence the unity of virtue is central. That innocence is not open to transfer between actions. We speak of someone being too innocent for his own good. But if moral innocence refers to a sort of integrity or perfectibility then this must be resisted. The difficulty about moral innocence is that it is hard to think of its being improved upon or bettered. It represents a purity of virtue which cannot be modified in the way in which we might ordinarily reflect on our moral experience.

Moral existence contains a diversity of values which both extend and limit one another. The attribution of rights to individuals justifies both the extension and the restriction of welfare provision. Considerations of promise-keeping and truth-telling limit the actions which may be performed on the grounds of benevolence and the alleviation of need. Moral requirements often pull in different directions. Emphasis is on moral wisdom and experience; it is certainly true that action in the face of often severe moral and political conflict requires judgement of a mature and refined kind, a preparedness to face moral compromise if any morally desirable outcome is to be achieved at all. However, moral innocence excludes the negotiation between values which such compromises involve. In this sense, moral innocence conceives virtue as absolute, and not relative either to any other virtue or to any other human need, want, preference, or interest.

In Michael Slote's provocative work, *Goods and Virtues*,[20] he writes:

> There is something equally passive about the traditional virtue of innocence, and . . . an individual's perfect honesty may precisely *consist* in his freedom from certain temptations.[21]

Slote makes this point in the course of his discussion of time-relative virtues. He argues that a virtue like prudence has little point in the

11

context, say, of a child's trust, but makes sense in a world in which trust may be misplaced or individuals may be too trusting for their own good. Slote applies this time-relative argument to innocence.

> Perhaps one should find innocence absurd, pathetic, or gratuitous in an adult, but desirable, admirable, or possibly even enviable in children, and such an attitude finds its natural expression in the thought that innocence is a virtue in [relation to] childhood, but the opposite of a virtue in [relation to] adulthood.[22]

Slote's position is a compromise between those who wish to reject innocence as a virtue and those who accept it as such in all contexts. He says:

> Some will undoubtedly wish to reject this compromise, holding either that innocence is a virtue, and perhaps especially precious in adulthood, or else that there is nothing particularly desirable even about childhood innocence.[23]

I want to take issue with Slote's claim that innocence is a passive virtue. It is certainly true that we speak of innocence being corrupted, perverted, or tainted. The honesty of the innocent may simply be unawareness of temptation. But there is no necessity that these should be its only manifestations, and certainly not its most important ones. These may be identified by stressing a feature which Slote neglects. Moral innocence is not simply a state which is acted on as opposed to acting itself. Where the worldly see ingratiation and hypocrisy, the innocent see kindness and friendship. Moral innocence may see the world as better than it is, but this does not by itself explain why it is vulnerable simply to whatever experience it may encounter. All Slote has shown is that the sense of innocence betrayed is only one of its meanings. A second difficulty concerns the relation between innocence and the world. Suppose someone wished to assert against Slote that innocence was a particularly admirable virtue in adulthood. This would mean that moral innocence makes a difference both to the individuals in whose character it exists and to the political world of which they are a part. It is impossible for Slote to conceive of this because for him innocence is a state which exists only to be lost, to be gradually displaced by the mature virtue of prudence.

Michael Oakeshott has expressed similar views in his essay, 'On being conservative':

Everybody's young days are a dream, a delightful insanity, a sweet solipsism. Nothing in them has a fixed shape, nothing a fixed price; everything is a possibility, and we live happily on credit. There are no obligations to be observed; there are no accounts to be kept. . . . These, in my opinion, are among our virtues when we are young; but how remote they are from the disposition appropriate for participating in the style of government I have been describing. . . . Some unfortunate people, like Pitt (laughably called 'the Younger'), are born old, and are eligible to engage in politics almost in their cradles; others, perhaps more fortunate, belie the saying that one is young only once, they never grow up. But these are exceptions. For most there is what Conrad called the 'shadow line' which, when we pass it, discloses a solid world of things, each with its fixed shape, each with its own point of balance, each with its price.[24]

Once past Conrad's 'shadow line' any encounter with moral innocence can only be with an impostor, with vanity posing as innocence or with the experienced playing the innocent for what they can get. For Oakeshott, the morally innocent are exceptions; but what of their moral nature and its effect on politics?

George Steiner writes:

Innocence is irreconcilable with human action; but only in action is there moral identity.[25]

It is true that moral and political beliefs characteristically issue in action. Such beliefs are informed by experience, judgement, and the capacity for reflection both on oneself and others. Steiner emphasizes that innocence lacks these crucial features of human conduct. However, he overlooks important aspects of innocence in its political expression by assuming that innocence is always something which is acted on or affected by. Seeing innocence as emblematic, Steiner does not raise questions concerning its substance. Moral innocence, for example, may consist in an uncritical belief in the application of moral principle to practice. It may be a belief in the impregnability of personal virtue, or the holding on trust of a code of honour. It can be found in an attachment to a way of life, irrespective of cultural or moral diversity. We see it, too, expressed more dramatically in politics, not just in the belief that people are better than they are or that their motives are more altruistic than we should expect them to

13

be, but crucially in the assumption that morality can enter the political world in relatively simple ways.

Moral innocence is not adequately understood as a passive virtue, merely being acted upon and not itself acting on the moral and political fabric of the world. Recent discussions of moral integrity have rightly emphasized the difficulties involved in speaking about it in consequentialist terms or by reference to Kantian maxims of duty.[26] It has been argued that the utilitarian idea of morality as a device for the achievement of purposes fails to explain how morality can be an obstacle to such achievement. Uncritical allegiance to moral principle may exhibit a kind of moral corruption. Integrity in morality, therefore, is not equivalent to perfectibility. Virtue is not expressed without struggle.

Peter Winch asks us to consider the case of an Elder in a religious community committed to the ideals of non-violence who kills a gangster who is about to murder a young girl member of that community.[27] Winch argues persuasively that the Elder feels both that he has done something wrong *and* that he would not have been able to forgive himself if he had not done it. Moral integrity is shown in his willingness to forgo his own moral perfectibility for the sake of another's life. Morality, therefore, cannot be construed as a series of guidelines for the achievement of a set of ends or purposes.

A similar example is introduced by Shirley Robin Letwin in her admirable discussion of the virtues appropriate to a gentleman. Like Winch, she accepts that integrity does not reside in conformity with a handbook of moral instructions, and she asks us to consider the relation between integrity and honesty. She says:

> A gentleman feels obliged to recognise that a literal truth can deceive even more effectively than a bold falsehood, and to notice with precision whom he is addressing, for what purpose, in what time and place. He does not excuse a disregard for the contingent human world by pleading a saint's or a philosopher's absorption in a 'higher' reality or in universal abstractions. To discern and to take into account the personal identities and particular circumstances that constitute the reality of human life is for him always a duty. His honesty leads him to speak differently to friends and to strangers, in private and in public. He will lie to a murderer in order to save his friend, though his honesty will keep him from pretending, to himself or others, that he has not lied.[28]

For both Winch and Letwin moral integrity *can* be consistent with killing and lying. It is true that these actions are performed with great reluctance and for morally admirable purposes. In both cases, too, the agents are aware of the character of what they have done. We see why moral integrity and moral innocence part company at this point. Winch's claim is 'that there is *no* general kind of behaviour of which we have to say that it is good without qualification.'[29] But surely moral innocence consists precisely in the belief that moral goodness does not compromise. Integrity requires a self-knowledge which innocence cannot possess.

The problems and dilemmas which trouble someone of moral integrity elude the innocent pursuer of the good. Would such a moral innocent enter into negotiation with virtue? How would the actions of such an individual affect the political world? These questions are not so divorced from what Letwin calls 'the contingent human world' as it might appear. First, there is a common tendency to diminish the innocent devotion to the good and to reinterpret it in ways which make it easier to understand. Kierkegaard writes:

> If he does acknowledge [his virtue], they will at once raise against him the cry that he wants to make himself important, wants to make out that he is better than others.[30]

Such considerations need not figure in the kind of goodness I have in mind. Second, moral innocence expresses unqualified virtue in a way which moral integrity does not. This sense of virtue may be described as absolute or pure, as we might speak of the way a saint is virtuous. How is this moral disposition to be understood? What is its relation to the world?

I am not suggesting that those for whom virtue has an absolute importance are for that reason alone morally innocent: innocence may play little or no part in their character and conduct. The virtues of the morally innocent are absolute and it is only on this basis that we can fully understand their character and the dilemmas they encounter. Politics involves the exercise of practical wisdom, of judgement in imperfect circumstances, and the capacity to assess the consequences of actions and policies for human beings and their political communities. This emphasis on prudence fits in with Slote's account of it as a time-relative virtue. Lack of prudence would then explain why moral innocence can lead to political catastrophe. This line of argument will not do, partly because it neglects the variety of forms taken by moral innocence in a political context, but mainly because it construes innocence either as incompetence or as immaturity.

A graphic illustration of the problem of political morality which is the subject of this book is found in passages from *Henry VI (Part 3)*, and *Henry VI (Part 2)*. The first is from the end of *Henry VI (3)*, when his kingdom and his rule have disintegrated, and the second is from *Henry VI (2)*, clearly locating the source of this tragic disintegration in his moral character. At the point of his defeat in battle, Margaret says of her king:

> Henry, your sovereign,
> Is prisoner to the foe; his state usurp'd,
> His realm a slaughter house, his subjects slain,
> His statutes cancelled, and his treasure spent,
> And yonder is the wolf that makes this spoil.[31]

In the second part of the trilogy she finds the explanation for this in Henry's character:

> Henry my lord is cold in great affairs,
> Too full of foolish pity.[32]

Now what is the connection between these two quotations? What is the connection between the judgement 'too full of foolish pity' and the political chaos and defeat which are the outcome? It is tempting to answer that Shakespeare is making the Machiavellian point that in the calculation of power there is no place for pity. But legitimate rule matters to the king not merely as a rhetorical elaboration of power but as an authentic political aspiration. It is also tempting to answer that we are talking not about pity in politics but about a parody of the genuine article, namely 'foolish pity'. On this view, King Henry's innocence would be incompetence or immaturity. But this will not do. Henry is a compassionate man. 'Foolish', therefore, must refer to a conjunction of pity and politics which cannot be explained in utilitarian or Machiavellian terms.

My problem is the nature of the relation between moral innocence and political disaster. The sense of moral innocence which is causing the difficulty is not absence of particular guilt but is more akin to absolute virtue or purity of heart. This has an active and not simply a passive sense and its moral significance cannot be explained in terms of its benefits. Moral innocence and moral integrity are not the same. Persons of moral principle may refuse to compromise their moral beliefs for the sake of political advantage but their knowledge is of the kind lacked by the morally innocent.

> an innocent person is not innocent merely by virtue of being a person not guilty of wrongdoing or not morally guilty of wrongdoing, but a person absent of a certain kind of knowledge.[33]

Moral innocence is marked by the presence of a specific kind of virtue *and* the absence of a specific kind of knowledge. These conceptual marks make moral innocence an unstable state which provokes reflection on its relation with politics. 'Foolish pity' and politics then is the most concise expression of the theme of this book.

Chapter Two

PUBLIC AND PRIVATE VIRTUE

... disaster and even greater degradation can ensue from trying to maintain a level of moral purity which the political life of the time cannot sustain.

(Charles Taylor, 'Ethics and politics')

And ignorance of vice, makes vertue lesse.

(John Donne, *To the Countesse of Bedford*)

Moral innocence contains two seemingly incompatible features – a knowledge of virtue and an ignorance of the capacity for evil in oneself and in others. Can we describe the innocent as virtuous, therefore, when they are ignorant of the evil which morality resists and when they do not understand the temptation which evil offers?

Socratic moral thinking provides a natural starting-point for such a question. Socrates' understanding of morality contains a strong intellectual element and he was very much aware of the dilemmas generated by political morality.

Fifth-century Athenian thought generally held that knowledge in politics is gained by experience – of what power is necessary, of what aims are practicable, of how far deception needs to be carried, to what extent we should trust others, to what degree we should persuade, force or coerce them for our own purposes. The Sophists paid little attention to moral innocence. A distinction central to their thought is between nature and convention, between a natural state in which individuals are free to follow their nature and a social one in which conduct is restricted by the artificial compact of politics and the laws and moral rules which it creates. While some Sophists, like Callicles, describe human motivation as pure egotism, others, such as Antiphon, describe it in terms of enlightened self-interest, but none portrays

18

the pre-social state as a condition of natural moral innocence. Their subjectivism means that as individuals are confined within private mental worlds certain knowledge is impossible. We are left with merely opinion or belief. There is no absolute moral or political knowledge, which means that on the Sophistic view the morally innocent lack experience of the tricks, deceptions and cruelties of morals and politics. In the context of Athenian *realpolitik* such ignorance would be seen as devastating. The Greek familiarity with war, imperialist expansion, decline, and the economic needs of a volatile, democratic city-state placed a high value on realism. The Sophistic ideas of morality as a cloak for self-interest, or of right as a disguise for might, were representative. In such times moral innocence endangers the city more than the individual: it is artless in politics where cunning is required; it is simple when circumstances require guile. Innocence gives trust when we should be suspicious, and it has confidence in honesty and respect when the interests of state demand that rights be ignored or breached. For some Sophists innocence has the character of play, a stage to be enjoyed in children but looked at with scorn and ridicule if it persists into adulthood. This emphasis on escape from innocence and acquisition of experience is found in a long speech by Callicles in the *Gorgias*.

> For philosophy, you know, Socrates, is a pretty thing if you engage in it moderately in your youth; but if you continue in it longer than you should, it is the ruin of any man. For if a man is exceptionally gifted and yet pursues philosophy far on in life, he must prove entirely unacquainted with all the accomplishments requisite for a gentleman and a man of distinction. Such men know nothing of the laws in their cities, or of the language they should use in their business associations both public and private with other men, or of human pleasures and appetites, and in a word they are completely without experience of men's characters. And so when they enter upon any activity public or private they appear ridiculous, just as public men, I suppose, appear ridiculous when they take part in your discussions and arguments. ... It is a good thing to engage in philosophy just so far as it is an aid to education, and it is no disgrace for a youth to study it: but when a man who is now growing older still studies philosophy, the situation becomes ridiculous, Socrates, and I feel towards philosophers very much as I do towards those who lisp and play the child.[1]

Callicles' general preoccupation is with the complex nature of human ignorance, first in relation to the young who, in the process of growing old, replace their inexperience with knowledge of the world and its ways; second in relation to philosophy whose study by the old is seen by Callicles as absurd; and third in relation to the philosopher whose philosophy disqualifies him from knowledge of the world.

How does Socrates defend himself against Callicles' arguments? Callicles emphasizes the impossibility of certain knowledge and it is this which Socrates is concerned to refute. He affirms that there is moral knowledge and a true political art, and that it is teachable by reference not to experience but to knowledge itself. But what kind of knowledge could this be?

In the course of his conversation with three of his friends who are trying to persuade him to evade the sentence of death passed on him at his trial, Socrates refers to 'the greatest good that can befall a man' . . .

> to discourse every day about goodness and those other subjects about which you hear me conversing and examining myself and others . . . the life unexamined is not worth living.[2]

There is considerable irony in the fact that the advice Socrates knows he must reject comes from his friends. Socrates is drawing attention to what it means to live a philosophical life. For him it involves the exercise of thought, bringing thought to bear on human life and the values which inform it – goodness, truth, justice, and obligation. Socrates argues that the contemplative life stands in opposition to the pragmatic urgencies of practical politics. In addition there may be circumstances, as his life shows, where thought even undermines the demands of friendship. In other words, the obligations imposed by thinking are great. In Socrates' case they required that he accept his own death. The contemplative intelligence has often found itself in social and political contexts which endanger it. Intellectual obligations may clash with the demands of political necessity. Socrates was well aware of the external threats to contemplation. He was charged with impiety and corrupting the youth of Athens: he understood from personal experience the pressing character of political imperatives, and his death indicates that when the needs of the city are most urgent then contemplation is most endangered. Socrates also realized that not all challenges to thought are external. Some are internal in the sense that they are found within individual character and disposition. We are familiar with the intellectual who collaborates with evil; to Socrates this would have been unintelligible.

Socrates has argued that 'the life unexamined is not worth living'. In the words of one modern critic: 'the good life must have reflection as part of its goodness'.[3] This has a direct bearing on moral innocence. The morally innocent act well but in a manner which is unreflective. We describe their honesty as candour. Their goodness is disinterested not because they have understood that morality requires the sacrifice of personal advantage: it would not occur to them to act otherwise. For the Sophists such ignorance is a mark of weakness because the innocent are blind to the selfishness of human nature and the experience necessary to survive in the world. For Socrates this lack of knowledge diminishes virtue. It does not eradicate it completely, but it renders it unstable and untested.

Socrates distinguishes sharply between knowledge and belief. Knowledge is the recognition of truth. We cannot know that which is false, but beliefs and opinions can be mistaken. For Socrates, knowing what virtue is necessarily means being virtuous. The claim to be good does not establish the existence of goodness. Thus, someone who believes himself to be charitable may not be. In order to be charitable it is necessary to know what charity is.

The craft analogy and the use of definition both strongly influence the reasons which Socrates gives for the value of this moral knowledge. Unlike belief or opinion it involves standards of judgement which enable the rational scrutiny of moral change, provide grounds for decision in cases where moral rules do not apply, and form a basis of conviction against the temptation to act badly. Such knowledge means that moral principles can be stated and justified in a manner which can clarify and resolve moral disagreement.

> The reasoned conviction of someone who can give a Socratic account of virtue is not just intellectually desirable; unless moral situations are predictable and decisions easy, the justification a man can offer himself for his beliefs may well affect his practice.[4]

Socrates' distinction between moral knowledge and belief enables us to make sense of some important aspects of moral experience. There is a moral difference between someone who believes in honesty because it pays and someone who behaves honestly irrespective of the benefits which may follow. There is a difference between someone who believes in honesty because this gains approval and someone whose honesty is intrinsic, regarded as admirable for its own sake. In Socratic terms, to believe in honesty because it pays material benefits or because it is the conventional thing to do is to be ignorant of the kind of value honesty is. Those whose virtue is based on belief cannot be virtuous.

Can Socrates account for moral innocence in terms of this argument? The morally innocent are ignorant of their capacity for evil and of immorality in others. They are unaware of the possibility of acting badly. However, this does not mean that they hold beliefs about virtue which are mistaken. Their ignorance is not that of the man who believes that honesty pays. We cannot say, therefore, that the morally innocent do not know what morality is because they hold false beliefs about it. On the other hand, their virtue cannot be described as disinterested. Their ignorance of evil means that they have no conception of having interests to protect or advance. In Socratic terms, moral innocence does not consist in beliefs about the nature of virtue, but neither does it know what it is. From the standpoint of Socrates' claim that virtue is knowledge, therefore, moral innocence is an enigma.

Examination of other Socratic paradoxes confirms this conclusion. If virtue is knowledge then evil is due to ignorance and must be involuntary. A tyrant such as Archelaus does not will his evil acts: he is ignorant of the source of his wickedness. Evil excludes knowledge of itself.

This is a highly intellectual account of wickedness, and most philosophers have followed Aristotle in his charge that it fails to understand the nature of moral weakness.[5] The root difficulty is Socrates' dichotomy between knowledge and ignorance. We could redescribe the moral ignorance of the tyrant as a lack of knowledge of the good. But this does not work with moral innocence. The difference is between evil due to ignorance and an ignorance of evil.

When Socrates examines the connection between virtue, harm, and happiness his arguments have a closer bearing on moral innocence. He is speaking about the more familiar sense of innocence as something lost or wronged. The proposition that the good man cannot be harmed leads Socrates in the *Gorgias* to assert its corollaries – it is better to suffer wrong than to commit it, and it is better to submit to punishment than to avoid it. The paradoxical character of these maxims is well brought out by Polus who responds to them in a typically realistic way:

> What do you mean? If a man is caught in a criminal plot to make himself tyrant, and when caught is put to the rack and mutilated and has his eyes burnt out and after himself suffering and seeing his wife and children suffer many other signal outrages of various kinds is finally impaled or burned in a coat of pitch, will he be happier than if he escaped arrest, established himself as a tyrant, and lived the rest of his life a sovereign in his state, doing what he pleased, an object of envy and felicitation among citizens and strangers alike? Is this what you say is impossible to refute?[6]

For Socrates the goodness of virtuous individuals does not consist in the material benefits which may result. Their goodness is not harmed, therefore, if such benefits are endangered or removed. Socrates specifically states that it is preferable to be an innocent person who is wronged than to wrong others.

> Polus: 'Then you would wish rather to suffer than to do wrong?'
> Socrates: 'I would not wish either: but if I had either to do or to suffer wrong, I would choose rather to suffer than to do it.'[7]

Socrates does not fully appreciate that the innocent who are wronged may respond in a number of ways. Individuals who are punished for a crime they did not commit are different from those who are guilty and are punished and also from those who are made to suffer for their beliefs. The guilty may gain redemption for their wrong-doing by coming to recognize its blameworthy character. This is not open to the innocent who have nothing to redeem and nothing to exchange for a reduction in suffering. The fuller reaction of moral innocence in such a context preoccupies Melville in *Billy Budd, Sailor*:

> a young seafarer of the disposition of our athletic foretopman is much of a child-man. And yet a child's utter innocence is but its blank ignorance, and the innocence more or less wanes as intelligence waxes. But in Billy Budd intelligence, such as it was, had advanced while yet his simple-mindedness remained for the most part unaffected.[8]

At what point does moral innocence identify its tormentor? Socrates cannot answer this question because he cannot admit the manifold nature of moral disposition. His assertion that virtue is knowledge is one reason for this; another is his defence of the unity of the virtues. By this Socrates means a number of different things. To be virtuous it is necessary to possess, not just some, but all the virtues. There is no conflict between the virtues. There is a single source of virtue which grounds or substantiates the great variety of moral terms. This is wisdom, a state of spiritual harmony which achieves its fullest rational expression in philosophy.

In the *Gorgias* Socrates connects virtue with happiness, arguing that the good are most happy, those who understand that their evil must be admonished and punished discover happiness, but that the man who is most unhappy is:

> the man who does the greatest wrong and indulges in the greatest injustice and yet contrives to escape admonition, correction or punishment – the very condition you describe as achieved by Archelaus and other tyrants . . .[9]

Socrates has argued that:

> happiness . . . consists not in a release from evil but in never having contracted it.[10]

Later:

> the happiest of men is he who has no evil in his soul . . .[11]

These statements are ambiguous in that they apply both to the morally innocent and to those who have resisted the temptation of evil. Socrates' emphasis on virtue as knowledge means that for him the morally innocent possess an illusory happiness. Their morality is a dream. We see this, too, in Socrates' grading of the most admirable lives in the *Phaedrus*:

> the soul which has seen most of truth shall come to the birth as a philosopher, or artist, or some musical and loving nature; that which has seen truth in the second degree shall be some righteous king or warrior chief; the soul which is of the third class shall be a politician, or economist, or trader; the fourth shall be a lover of gymnastic toils or a physician; the fifth shall lead the life of a prophet or hierophant; to the sixth the character of a poet or some other imitative artist will be assigned; to the seventh the life of an artisan or husbandman; to the eighth that of a Sophist or demagogue; to the ninth that of a tyrant . . .[12]

Socrates explicitly describes these states of human aspiration as requiring probationary periods. They are different forms of human knowledge, philosophic, artistic, and practical, and each involves the supersession of ignorance.

Socrates' moral concerns affect our understanding of moral innocence in a political context. For Guthrie, Socrates' philosophy of virtue included:

> the conviction that not only wealth, but power, reputation and honour were as nothing compared to the well-being of one's soul, that the unexamined life was not worth living because goodness, or the right state of the soul, depended on knowledge, especially self-knowledge, and that to suffer any injury, even death, was better than to commit one, because wrong-doing harmed the soul.[13]

It is not surprising that someone who held such principles should come into conflict with political imperatives. It is true that Socrates was not a supporter of Athenian democracy, but not all anti-democrats exhibited Socrates' integrity or posed the same intractable problems for the state. Athens had been a polis at war, wracked by plague, imperial expansion abroad, and internal dissension at home. Athenian politics were marked by passion, appetite, and fear. Debates over the conduct of the war were conducted on the basis of self-interest, uncertainty of the outcome of agreed expeditions, policies, or strategies, and with an increasing neglect of a rational assessment of the public good. Socrates well understood the nature of political imperatives. He had undertaken military service patriotically and he had opposed specific orders during the rule of the Thirty Tyrants. In his trial he refuses to compromise his speech to make a good impression on the jury; he chooses death against banishment; and he rejects manoeuvres to get him off lightly by the payment of a small fine. The arguments he employs to defend his position to his friends in the *Crito* do not depend solely on the importance of his private moral integrity. They have a public bearing, too, in that they reflect Socrates' conviction that Athenian politics expressed (usually false) belief, not knowledge, and that it is only through philosophical enquiry that such knowledge can be acquired. It is for this reason that Socrates spends so much of the trial explaining the connection between philosophy and ignorance. Only through knowledge can justice in the individual and the city be achieved. It is precisely because of the importance of this consideration that Socrates will not be deflected from it, even by fear of his own death.

Some have described Socrates here as having regained the moral purity of the innocent.

> There are individuals who may appear to have regained, at least in part, their innocence . . . such persons – perhaps Socrates and Father Zossima may serve as examples – regain, without self-deception, some of their lost childlike innocence. This extraordinary achievement appears in their cases to come about through disarming evil, by overcoming what it is in one that accounts for the inclination to do evil and by overcoming, too, what it is that accounts for fearing the evil that might be done one.[14]

Socrates' moral position implies integrity of an uncompromising kind, not only in relation to the moral values which have guided his life, but also in philosophy. But this is not the integrity of moral innocence, although there are certain common features which Morris brings out by describing Socrates as having recaptured the certainty displayed by innocent virtue. Both refuse to negotiate with virtue and both appear impregnable in the eyes of the world. Socrates, it is true, professes ignorance, but this is not the ignorance of the innocent. As Kierkegaard points out:

> The Socratic ignorance was not an empirical ignorance, for he was in possession of much information, had read a great many poets as well as philosophers, and was highly experienced in the affairs of life. No, he was not ignorant in any empirical sense. He was, however, ignorant in a philosophic sense.[15]

Socratic ignorance does not consist in not knowing certain facts about the world. In his trial he was innocent of the charges brought against him, but not of the temptation to avoid death by sacrificing his beliefs. His ignorance is an essential part of his philosophy. The logic of question and answer, the attempt to establish truth and falsity by dialectic refutation, and the interrogative method which provokes contradiction are essential to philosophy because it is through them that ignorance is revealed. It is therefore incumbent on philosophy to follow the logos wherever it leads.

But is Socrates as ignorant as he sometimes presents himself to be? His manner of argument is ironic in that he pretends to an ignorance he does not possess and plays at seeking enlightenment from those who have none. Socratic irony is not merely a deception to trick his opponents. It is a form of mediation between himself and the world, a deliberate device which he maintained to the end of his life. By stressing it Socrates functions as a gadfly, stinging others and himself into a recognition of their own ignorance. This enables us to see Socrates' self-mastery as a mature virtue, a trait which is possible only as the result of a long process of self-enquiry and not before. Irony serves to distance Socrates from moral innocence. For those who are devoted to it, philosophy involves learning how to die, a point exemplified in the *Apology* where Socrates argues that the greater shame is to fear death and leave the obligations of philosophy unfulfilled.

The proposition that virtue is knowledge and his commitment to philosophy mean that for Socrates moral innocence is the starting-point for human self-awareness. It means, too, that a perpetual tension exists between philosophy and politics; the demands of the spirit and the imperatives of the city exist in a state of permanent imbalance. In Plato we see a dramatic attempt to restore the unity which Socrates sees as irretrievably displaced, and we see further how moral innocence is minimized as a true pursuit of virtue.

Plato transfers Socratic concerns to a broader intellectual canvas. Philosophical reason has an active, transforming character. It is architectonic; through its exercise society can be remoulded in such a way as to make a secure life for the reflective intelligence in a world that is both stable and just. In the *Republic* Plato describes the philosopher who:

> . . . has watched the frenzy of the multitude and seen that there is no soundness in the conduct of public life, nowhere an ally at whose side a champion of justice could hope to escape destruction; but that, like a man fallen among wild beasts, if he should refuse to take part in their misdeeds and could not hold out alone against the fury of all, he would be destined, before he could be of any service to his country or his friends, to perish, having done no good to himself or to anyone else – one who has weighed all this keeps quiet and goes his own way, like the traveller who takes shelter under a wall from a driving storm of dust and hail; and seeing lawlessness spreading on all sides is content if he can keep his hands clean from iniquity while this life lasts . . .[16]

Plato presents a series of startling choices. The philosopher can stand firm in his allegiance to reason, in which case he may have to sacrifice his life before he can do any good, or he can retreat from politics and keep his hands clean. It is impossible to act politically and retain virtue uncompromised. So he attempts in the *Republic* a comprehensive reconstruction of human justice in which, as he says to Adeimantus, the individual character is – 'cast in a society congenial to his nature, where he could grow to his full height and save his country as well as himself.'[17]

One choice available to the philosopher is withdrawal from the world, but for Plato the problem of contemplation in an alien society requires a radical solution. Nothing less than the total transformation of society is sufficient. This elevates the intellect and severely circumscribes the political. What place is there in such a world for moral innocence?

Plato's object is the creation of a political society in which it is impossible for the just man to be treated unjustly. Philosophy must become sovereign if such a society is to come into existence, and, by a dialectical argument which stresses the analogy between the soul and the city, Plato claims to show how this can be. Both the aim and the method involve implications for our understanding of the relation between public and private. Socrates' commitment to philosophy means a necessary tension between the private individual and the public world. For some this is an essential feature of political morality; it constitutes its characteristic dilemmas and difficulties. But for Plato it is a tension which has to be overcome if philosophy is to have a place in the world and if that world is to be just. The gap between private and public, the idea that there can be an ethic of one which the other lacks, is for Plato a source of political strife and an inconsistency not to be tolerated in a rational political community. Plato explicitly conceives the split between private and public as a kind of disunion:

> disunion comes about when the words 'mine' and 'not mine',
> 'another's' and 'not another's' are not applied to the same things
> throughout the community. The best ordered state will be the one
> in which the largest number of persons use these terms in the
> same sense, and which accordingly most nearly resembles a single
> person.[18]

The public world can easily degenerate into a squabble of competing private interests in which the public good, if it emerges at all, is achieved only by accident. In such a world philosophy is useless, an assertion which is explained by the parable of the Ship of State.[19] The craft analogy is once again at work between the knowledge provided by navigation and the art of governing a political community. Plato consistently presents actual politicians as dealing in opinion and belief. They are calculating and manipulative, concerned with the fatal arithmetic of political power. The philosopher, on the other hand, represents unity, cohesion, and stability. Reason for Plato provides a foundation for politics at odds with the idea of the conciliation of opinion. Political philosophy is a search for fixity and this requires the abolition of the distinction between public and private.

For Plato it is the role of philosophy to transfigure politics. Reconstruction requires a *tabula rasa*; the political world is open to complete conceptual revision.

> He will take society and human character as his canvas, and begin by scraping it clean. That is no easy matter; but, as you know, unlike other reformers, he will not consent to take in hand either an individual or a state or to draft laws, until he is given a clean surface to work on or has cleansed it himself.[20]

Politics requires harsh methods if philosophy is to obtain the clean sheet which Plato thinks it needs, and in the *Republic* it is proposed that all over the age of 10 be banished to initiate the just society.

Plato is aware of the political meaning of the acquisition of knowledge and much of the *Republic* is concerned with the system of education which is necessary for a just society to persist. The tripartite division of the soul into reason, spirit, and appetite is expressed politically in terms of the structure of Guardians, Auxiliaries, and Producers. This is not a static conception. Plato's state is an organic community which exists in time. It is therefore vulnerable to change. Philosophy as a search for universal truth, the Forms which are eternal and unchanging, requires that development is severely scrutinized and controlled. The advocacy of eugenics in the *Republic* is a part of this; another is Plato's philosophy of education. Here Plato follows Socrates' argument that virtue is knowledge and its corollary that moral conflict, weakness, and evil are due to ignorance. We saw that this Socratic maxim did nothing to dispel the mystery which surrounds moral innocence and a similar point holds for Plato.

The education of new generations involves the formation of

character and not the mere assemblage of information; it is the means by which the continuity of the just society is ensured. Plato is not concerned with education as a method for the achievement of personal autonomy. Rather it is seen as the initiation of the young into a set of rules and values which are in a very strong sense not open to question. The young are innocent in the sense of being ignorant of their nature and the world. But this ignorance is not that of someone who holds false beliefs about a particular state of affairs. As they are undeveloped, the young are not yet in a position consciously to hold true or false beliefs about anything. Education ensures that the young acquire knowledge and not false beliefs or opinions.

Plato is right to imply that loss of innocence cannot be understood simply in terms of the acquisition of experience. This tells us nothing about how such experience is acquired, whether vicariously or through participation. Experience without understanding means that the distinction between true belief and knowledge is left obscure. Someone may acquire experience and be unable to give an account of it, in which case they may have true belief but they do not have knowledge. Plato is right, too, to imply that it matters deeply to a society how innocence is lost and how it can endure. This is why Plato considers that his refutation of the Sophists is a matter of practical and not just intellectual importance. On the Sophistic view a political innocent is someone ignorant of political reality and its imperatives and necessities. To lose innocence is to realize that in politics it may be necessary to deceive or to bribe opponents in order to achieve results. But to Plato this would simply replace one ignorance with another more dangerous kind. Not any political experience is desirable to displace innocence.

Plato's account of education stresses an understanding of virtue which identifies the temptations offered by passions and appetites. Reason as the controlling element in the soul has this function in adult life but, for those unaware of it, initiation has to be mediated by precept and example. The loss of innocence is less significant than its manner and this requires a public virtue to negate the exchange rate of private interest and will. W. B. Yeats:

> And may her bridegroom bring her to a house
> Where all's accustomed, ceremonious;
> For arrogance and hatred are the wares

Peddled in the thoroughfares.
How but in custom and in ceremony
Are innocence and beauty born?[21]

But Plato's account of education is too monolithic to allow a plurality of moral experience. Anything which tells against the rule of reason in morality and politics is an object of suspicion. Plato is much concerned with what he sees as the dangers of irrationality, which serves to nourish the soul with falsehood and illusion. This is his basic ground for banning imitative art from the *Republic*. The imaginative power of literature, painting, and poetry to communicate tragedy and conflict is dangerous because it distracts from the basic Platonic idea that moral and political problems admit of a rational solution if we see them from the right standpoint. Literature encourages us to see moral conflict from the point of view of the participants. We see how their morality makes sense to them. They do not represent a partial view of the whole or lack sufficient rationality to perceive a solution to the problems which trouble them. Their moral position is not an inadequate version of a deeper reality but an expression of personal character and identity. Plato's insistent rationalism neglects this.

Moral innocence falls outside the Platonic classification of knowledge, ignorance, and false belief. Can it be described as a kind of true belief? Moral innocence would then consist of beliefs about virtue which fall short of knowledge but which are nevertheless true. Plato does not underestimate the significance of true belief and in the *Republic* he discusses the sight-lovers who argue that moral knowledge consists in the identification of the properties of the various kinds of moral action. We might say that repayment of a debt is just conduct. The assertion is true, but the repayment of a debt does not exhaust the concept of justice. Irwin writes:

> If a sight lover had knowledge of justice, his view that justice is debt-paying would be always true; since it is not, he has only belief.[22]

True belief, then, is partly true and partly false. It presents only a part of the whole. It is therefore unstable and cannot be transmitted. True belief is a kind of awareness, but it is not fully reflective. Do these considerations apply to moral innocence? First, true belief in relation to virtue is not consistent with ignorance of evil. Someone

31

who thinks justice is repayment of a debt must understand the possibility of deliberate non-payment. But this is precisely the understanding which is absent in moral innocence, and so it cannot be a kind of true belief. Second, if moral innocence does not consist in true beliefs about virtue because they are not consistent with ignorance of evil, can we still say it is a form of true belief because, unreflective, it does not possess knowledge of virtue? But true belief is only partially unreflective. There is nothing in Plato's account to prevent someone who believed that justice meant the repayment of debts giving a justification for that belief. Plato's view only requires that such a defence does not constitute knowledge. Moral innocence, however, excludes arguments in its own support. It cannot, therefore, be described as true belief because there is no respect in which it is partly true and partly false.

Nevertheless, it may be argued that while moral innocence is not true belief it does have some features in common with it. It is unreflective and unstable. It lacks the awareness of the complexity of virtue possessed by the morally mature. We have seen that its moral content cannot be described in Plato's terms as either knowledge or true belief; equally, its unawareness cannot be described as ignorance or false belief. From Plato's standpoint, however, it should not be thought that moral innocence remains completely inexplicable. Might it not be seen as a kind of deficiency? In the *Republic* Plato argues that virtue assumes the presence of normal physical and mental capacities. It follows from this that different human defects may be obstacles to virtue. Crime is understood as a disease, a deviation from morality; the chronically ill cannot live a worthwhile life; and the disabled are both individually and socially disqualified from virtue. Plato is perfectly consistent in drawing these conclusions. Once human moral autonomy has been defined in terms of the presence of certain essential features it follows that, unless special reasons are given, those who lack these features cannot be described as human, moral, and autonomous. There are, of course, a number of routes out of this difficulty but it remains a problem for many moral theories, particularly moral egalitarianism and rights-based accounts. Haksar challenges these in a way reminiscent of Plato:

> The congenital idiot is a parasite; for people claim for him privileges because he is a member of the human species, yet he does not (unlike normal people) contribute to the true grandeur of

32

the human species, neither now nor (as normal babies will) in the future. He is a degenerate specimen, so why should this not be reflected in his status *vis-à-vis* the normal specimens? Why should the doctrine of equal respect apply to him?[23]

Can moral innocence be described as a deficiency? One immediate problem is that the physically defective and the terminally ill are often, although not always, aware of their condition. The morally innocent, however, possess no self-understanding. They have no conception of the world being different from the way they picture it and they do not see their perceptions as defective. This means that we cannot describe the morally innocent as akin to the chained prisoners in Plato's cave analogy because it is not a simple lack of education which characterizes them. The moral vision of innocence precludes our thinking of it as deficient. In Platonic terms a sense of this vision is found in those moral beliefs derived from a musical education. Plato stresses the importance of music in the education of the young; it establishes harmony, pattern, and order. By itself it is insufficient to the foundation of virtue and it has no place in the higher education of the philosopher. Music without an additional training in mathematics and dialectic creates a particular type of virtuous person who will see virtue as honourable in itself and will pursue it disinterestedly, but who is incapable of providing a rational account of this. For Plato the soul of such a person is not simply deficient. It is confined within the realm of particular beliefs and so cannot attain to knowledge of the form of virtue and the eternal. Music, therefore, is important for the young but debilitating and stunting for the mature who have the capacity to transcend it. By this token, the moral innocent is like Plato's virtuous person of musical education. They value virtue for its own sake but do not know why. This brings out a crucial feature of innocence. Melville describes Billy Budd:

> He was illiterate; he could not read, but he could sing, and like the illiterate nightingale was sometimes the composer of his own song.[24]

Plato's intellectualism casts too wide a net to catch the precise character of moral innocence. The musically educated moral agent is myopic; he does not fully see virtue. Plato's insistence on knowledge leads him to the idea of philosopher-rulers. The morally innocent, from Plato's perspective, must be seen in this light – they are as a result unfit to rule. Does this mean that the morally innocent are too good to rule?

Plato is saying that the good must rule, but although the morally innocent are good their innocence disqualifies them because they lack self-awareness and a full rational appreciation of the nature of virtue. There is a further difficulty in relation to goodness and ruling. Plato argues that the Guardians rule by virtue of their philosophical natures. This inclines them towards goodness, truth, and beauty and away from evil, lying, and ugliness. However, in the *Republic* Plato says explicitly that there are occasions when the Guardians may lie nobly. What are we to make of this? These are not innocent lies in the sense of untruths of no great moment. They are serious and they are intended to deceive. It should not be thought, however, that Plato is talking about lying in politics as a problem in political morality. The 'Noble Lie' is uttered in the context of the just society of the *Republic* and not in the actual, imperfect political world. The lie is told not by self-seeking politicians or by well-intentioned rulers attempting to minimize harm or suffering but by Guardians whose nature Plato informs us is to love virtue and justice. There are two defences of this apparent paradox in the *Republic*. First, the lie is a kind of treatment (myth as fable). We may lie to someone for his own good or to deceive an enemy. Our motives in both cases are honourable; lying is therefore like a medicine in that it is in the long-term interests of the patient. Second, Plato argues that if there are situations in politics where lying is necessary for the general benefit it is preferable that those of virtuous natures, the Guardians, decide what these are and when lies should be told. It is better for the virtuous to do this than the self-seeking, and it is an essential feature of their moral integrity that they are willing to shoulder the moral burden. But the 'Noble Lie' could not be told by the morally innocent. It would not occur to them to entertain the deceit. There is a strong sense, therefore, in which moral innocence is unfit for rule because, in Platonic terms, it is too good.

While Plato's moral epistemology fails to capture the complete sense of moral innocence it does illustrate some of its salient features. In politics, however, Plato's unwavering commitment to the idea that all but philosophers are incapable of just rule means that he cannot isolate precisely what it is about moral innocence which can make it so damaging in certain political contexts.

Aristotle shares with Socrates and Plato a number of characteristically Greek assumptions regarding ethics, but he departs from them in ways which, on first sight, offer a more fruitful understanding of moral innocence. His account of reason in ethics is more intricate than Plato's and avoids the worst consequences of its rationalism. Aristotle distinguishes between theoretical and practical reason, the former exercised in the contemplative realms of philosophy and science, the latter in the practical activities of morality and political life. Virtue is expressed in praxis and requires the exercise of practical reason. So virtue has an aspect which is not intellectual, but is, as it were, a feature of character. We can describe this as a disposition to the right desires. For Aristotle, to be virtuous means to have the capacity to engage in practical reasoning but it also requires a disposition to act well. Equally, this disposition cannot guarantee virtue if the capacity for practical reasoning is absent. The virtuous disposition is intelligent, and this means the exercise of deliberation, judgement, and choice. Morality requires the capacity to assess the character of oneself and others in the light of the idea of human flourishing or well-being which Aristotle takes to be the end of human life, a view which apparently leaves moral innocence ambiguous and mysterious.

Aristotle's emphasis on virtue as a disposition places initial attention on the idea of character. Prior to the introduction of practical wisdom, part of the rational element of the soul, he stresses that natural virtue is a disposition devoid of reason. It is an unreflective disposition with respect to certain feelings and desires which resemble full virtue but are not the same because they lack practical wisdom, deliberation, and choice. As such, natural virtue is prey to passion, vulnerable to misunderstanding and error, and lacks the capacity to translate the desire for the good into action. It is based not on a full understanding of its own virtue, but on an unreflective, unknowing feeling for goodness. It represents for Aristotle the morality of the undeveloped self.

Full virtue requires both practical wisdom and desire for its completion. The aim is not an abstract code of conduct but the gradual acquisition of the capacity for judgement in, first, the full identification of the end of life, which is to live well or virtuously, and, second, the ability to find the means for the achievement of that end. Aristotle does not see ethics as being concerned with the discovery of the principles of right conduct, so he releases the virtuous disposition from its imprisonment in a mesh of moral rules and regulations. Does this mean a clearer idea of moral innocence as a feature of character?

Aristotle's emphasis on judgement as a central ingredient of practical wisdom seems to exclude moral innocence. Bernard Williams has argued that there is no necessary connection between having an admirable disposition and having a capacity to judge or assess others. This overlooks 'a conception of innocence, the image of a virtue that is entirely unselfconscious and lacking the contrast with self that is implied by judgement of others.'[25] For Aristotle, the prudent man is the man of practical wisdom who understands the requirements of moral situations, knows which virtues are involved, and to what degree. It is impossible to imagine the exercise of prudence without self-reflection. To be fully virtuous is to have a fixed and permanent disposition to choose virtue for its own sake. But not all those who are virtuous for its own sake are fully virtuous. Aristotle admits that a good action may be performed not from choice but from natural virtue. This means that natural virtue lacks the intellectual capacity for self-awareness which is an essential feature of practical wisdom. It does not contain the deliberative element which Aristotle sees as necessary to moral choice. Does this mean that moral innocence is a natural virtue? Obviously the absence of practical wisdom does not transform moral innocence into wrong-doing, and the morally innocent do not act well for the wrong reason. But not all those who lack practical wisdom are morally innocent. An unyielding commitment to moral principle, for example, may cause misunderstanding and harm but we would not describe it as a case of moral innocence.

Is moral innocence a kind of ignorance and how is it related to moral understanding? Aristotle argues that youth is incapable of virtue because it is inexperienced, lacks judgement, and is too much under the influence of passion.

> he who lives as passion directs will not hear argument that dissuades him, nor understand it if he does; and how can we persuade one in such a state to change his ways? And in general passion seems to yield not to argument but to force. The character, then, must somehow be there already with a kinship to virtue, loving what is noble and hating what is base.[26]

Aristotle pictures moral development as emerging from an unconsidered disposition to virtue and through the gradual acquisition of experience, mediated by habit and training, to the attainment of practical wisdom. Some will fail to achieve full moral initiation and moral understanding. These are conceptual and not merely temporal possibilities. They are examples of natural but not full virtue, and while the two may resemble one another Aristotle is firm in his belief that there is a difference between them.

> It is not merely the state in accordance with the right rule, but the state that implies the *presence* of the right rule, that is virtue; and practical wisdom is a right rule about such matters.[27]

There are two respects in which natural virtue is ignorant. First, it is unable to account for its own virtue. A child may not understand why its kindness is praised. A generous person may not be able to explain why his generosity is directed towards one rather than another when both are equally in need. Aristotle tends to assume that practical wisdom completes virtue in the sense that it is only then capable of full articulation. The morally innocent are those who act well but do not know why. They are morally inarticulate, incapable of communicating either their virtue or their feelings when they are wronged. But it is not only the morally innocent who are deficient in full moral expression. Ignorance of virtue is a matter of degree, and so Aristotle is pushed towards the philosophical or contemplative life as the only source of full knowledge of the good. He is ambiguous as to the priority between the speculative and the practical realms, but the point is that Aristotle assumes that moral inarticulation can be removed either by upbringing or by knowledge. This is too broad to bring out the specific character of moral innocence. Billy Budd, in Melville's story, is illiterate and he has a speech impediment, but he is not inarticulate in the same sense as a child or someone who cannot fully explain his generosity. Billy's innocence cannot survive communication with the world. The child must enter and understand the world to grow and develop. Judgement is an art to be learned and perfected, but it is superfluous to moral innocence. Second, Aristotle's natural virtue is a feature of a personality as yet unformed. The child's identity is undeveloped, not yet fixed, untouched by the world and the gradual acquisition of experience. Moral innocence would be childhood which has never been outgrown, the moral innocent a simpleton faced with experience which he has never acquired and which is incomprehensible to him. The comic aspect of this is well portrayed in Waugh's *Decline and Fall* when the innocent Paul Pennyfeather enquires of the titled society lady who has been interviewing prospective employees for her chain of South American brothels:

> 'I say, Margot, there was one thing I couldn't understand. Why was it that the less experience those chorus-girls had, the more you seemed to want them? You offered much higher wages to the ones who said they'd never had a job before?'
>
> 'Did I, darling? I expect it was because I feel so absurdly happy.'
>
> At the time this seemed quite a reasonable explanation, but, thinking the matter over, Paul had to admit to himself that there had been nothing noticeably light-hearted in Margot's conduct of her business.[28]

But there is a moral difference between simplicity and the simpleton. In Paul Pennyfeather innocence manifests itself as naivety, his unawareness of people's true motives simply absurd. Is moral innocence moral retardation, its indifference to wickedness a casual oversight? Aristotle's emphasis on deliberative rationality means that he tends to discard all those kinds of virtuous character and conduct which fall short of it. This means that the non-deliberative love of the good which moral innocence involves cannot be seen in Aristotelian terms as the simple lack of practical wisdom or ignorance. In other words, moral innocence falls outside Aristotle's classification of virtue.

> When, therefore, have we the just, and when not? Generally speaking, when one acts in accordance with purpose and voluntarily, and when one does so knowing the person, the means, and the end, those are the conditions of a just act. In the very same way the unjust man will be he who knows the person, the means, and the end. But when without knowing any of these things one has done something that is unjust, one is not unjust oneself, but unfortunate.[29]

Aristotle adds a second distinction to establish the kind of ignorance which results in injustice:

> When the ignorance is the cause, he does not do this voluntarily, so that he does not commit injustice; but when he is himself the

cause of his ignorance and does something in accordance with the ignorance of which he is himself the cause, then he is guilty of injustice, and such a person will justly be called unjust.[30]

Someone who is so drunk that he does not know that he is beating his father is unjust, whereas a child who beats his father out of ignorance cannot be called unjust. For Aristotle the moral innocent is like a child who does not know what he is doing. He is therefore doubly unfortunate: first he has not attained the level of self-understanding which enables him to be responsible for what he does; second he has no control over the outcomes of his actions. His lack of experience means that any virtues he seems to possess will be defective. On courage, for example, Aristotle writes:

> there are some who are brave from the opposite of experience. For those who have no experience of the probable results are free from fear owing to their inexperience. Neither, then, must we call these brave.[31]

Nevertheless, there are passages in Aristotle's ethical writings where he seems to allow for non-deliberative, inspirational virtue. In a manner reminiscent of Plato he refers to the man who has a natural musical talent but who is unable to teach music. Such individuals

> are called fortunate who, whatever they start on, succeed in it without being good at reasoning. And deliberation is of no advantage to them, for they have in them a principle that is better than intellect and deliberation, while the others have not this but have intellect; they have inspiration, but they cannot deliberate. For, though lacking reason, they attain the attribute of the prudent and wise – that their divination is speedy; and we must mark off as including in it all but the judgement that comes from reasoning.[32]

However, lack of rational judgement means that virtue in such individuals is uncertain; although Aristotle has parted company with Plato's rationalism he has not left it completely. The man of inspirational virtue may find his life is erratic and unpredictable but this does not entirely diminish it. Natural song has a sweetness which the trained voice lacks but its incidence and duration may be unreliable. Similarly, with inspirational virtue we may find it highly admirable but be unable to depend on it when the need is greatest. So how can the difference between it and the virtue of practical wisdom be characterized? Can we describe moral innocence as an inspirational virtue, performed for its own sake, but derived not from ratiocination but from a vision of moral goodness?

Aristotle assumes that virtues exist in the context of a rational system and that they have to be in harmony for there to be a properly ethical life, a requirement which will be met by prudence, not a feature of inspirational virtue. Inspirational and natural virtue are very close in Aristotle's thought. There is a kind of virtue which Aristotle says is sometimes found in excess, but not an obsessive concern with honour which is consistent with a dishonourable character. Supererogation does not capture its full sense because it involves something more than action in excess of duty. Aristotle sometimes describes it as superhuman, heroic, or godlike virtue, and he often talks as if the goodness of the godlike man goes beyond virtue. He does not analyse its nature in detail but it involves a natural perfectibility which seems particularly appropriate to moral innocence. Excess may also be found in the way someone ignores specific qualifications to moral conduct. They may be excessively trusting in their dealings with others. Aristotle has an ambivalent attitude to this kind of moral excess. He seems to think of it as a defect, a characteristic of youth which exists prior to the acquisition of practical wisdom and before habit and training affect personality. But there is a sense in which he finds this kind of virtue admirable. Trust is not hedged with the caution which experience of betrayal conveys. Openness is natural and unsuspecting. In this moral world everything is as it appears to be, and if over time we learn that this is not the case, for Aristotle this is a cause for regret. Aristotle seems to be saying that the spontaneous quality of natural or inspirational virtue should never be completely lost and if we cannot wholly recapture it then practical wisdom is a dependable alternative guide.

Virtue in excess is found, too, in a political form where Aristotle is concerned with what he calls 'pre-eminent virtue' and its place in a political community. In his examination of democracy he considers the practice of banishing those whose natural moral inequality leads them to predominate in the affairs of the city, giving the example of Periander's counsel which was to 'cut off the tallest ears of corn till he had brought the field to a level'.[33] This discussion takes place against the background of Aristotle's view that the structure of the constitution determines the nature of political equality, although it is clear that he intends the point to have a wider bearing. He describes the problem as universal, found in the perfect state as well as in those states which fall short of perfection. Of ostracism he writes:

> In the perfect state there would be great doubts about the use of it, not when applied to excess in strength, wealth, popularity, or the like, but when used against someone who is pre-eminent in virtue – what is to be done with him? Mankind will not say that such a one is to be expelled and exiled; on the other hand, he ought not to be a subject – that would be as if mankind should claim to rule over Zeus.[34]

This interesting passage considers the relation between excess of virtue and politics. Is such virtue beyond incorporation in a political community? Aristotle's most profound political values would seem to suggest so. Politics is a realm of public virtue. Its guiding conception is justice construed not as absolute, complete in itself, but as plural, capable of generating distinguishable ideas of equality and inequality which will thereby have a significance for the diversities that political life contains. Aristotle's emphasis is on political agreement, on a civic harmony achieved not by force or unthinking conformity but by rational discussion between men of moderation whose guiding values are generated by practical wisdom. The over-riding objective is the avoidance of extremes, the minimizing of civic disruption and the risk of revolution, strife, and war. Aristotle's political values stress stability not at any cost but through the exercise of prudence and moderation. The temper of his political thought is to reduce political excess in the extremes of aristocracy, oligarchy, and democracy as well as the more obviously brutal regimes of dictatorship and tyranny. It is one of Aristotle's deepest political beliefs that a state which is both just and stable will be most capable of surviving the catastrophes which political life contains. War and loss of political freedom, enslavement and insurrection were familiar to the Greeks, and Aristotle attempts to construe politics so that the risk of their occurrence is reduced, a testimony to his belief in the creative power of reason.

Aristotle is concerned also with sources of internal damage. Interest and passion are obvious examples but they are not the only ones. In the *Eudemian Ethics* he writes:

Agreement is only found in the case of good men; at least, bad men when they choose and desire the same things harm one another. Agreement, like friendship, does not appear to have a single meaning; but still in its primary and natural form it is morally good, and so the bad cannot agree.[35]

Internal damage to politics arises from the nature of character. Moral scepticism is connected with political disorder and decay; by contrast, Aristotle asserts, virtue involves agreement, a shared ground for judgement and deliberation about the moral ends of a political community. Such ends are not to be regarded instrumentally. They are not simply external to the activity but constitute it in the sense of being a part of its nature. It should not be assumed from this that Aristotle has an uncomplicated view of the relation between morality and politics. His distinction between the good man and the good citizen indicates that not all good citizens are good men. Complete identification between the two is only possible in the ideal state, whilst among those states which fall short of the ideal it is constitutional states which come closest to bringing the two together. Moral education and the exercise of virtue in ruling are essential if the transition from private virtue to public ethic is to be achieved. For Aristotle, private and civic friendship presuppose agreement and share a common moral basis for judgement. But this does not mean that they are identical. Aristotle speaks of friendship based on virtue, utility and pleasantness. Civic friendship is based on utility, legal and moral.

> Civic friendship, then, looks to the agreement and the thing, moral friendship to the purpose; here then we have more truly justice, and a friendly justice.[36]

Aristotle is aware of the complicated distinctions between good man and good citizen, moral and civic friendship, but one powerful belief persists – that practical wisdom excludes excess and that excess of virtue represents a profound threat to the political. Why should this be so?

Aristotle criticizes those who argue that virtue is self-sufficient. Virtue issues in action, which means that moral agents are necessarily faced with the diverse circumstances of the world. They may experience defeat or failure for reasons which are often completely outside their control. Friendship may result in rebuff and betrayal, trust may be broken, policy may be challenged and defeated. Withdrawal into private consolation and stoic self-sufficiency is not, for Aristotle, a natural or a morally desirable course to take. Goodness requires the assaults of the world if moral character is to be formed and if the virtues of courage, steadfastness in the face of misfortune, and magnanimity are to be developed. Aristotle largely considers that such internal and external threats to virtue can be successfully overcome by the exercise of prudence, though there are some areas, tragic or of great moral difficulty, outside its scrutiny and control. Generally, however, it is prudence which counters excess and which makes the individual and the city less vulnerable to bad luck, disaster, and the freedom of action of other individuals and states. This places great emphasis on the moral value of foresight, an aspect of prudence which above all the innocent lack. The inexperience of the morally innocent means that they have no need of prudence; their innocence separates them from the world and they are a source of great danger to it.

The prudent learn foresight because they are aware of the possibility of reverse. Their actions are often surrounded by the secondary strategies of insurance, qualification, and caution. The mad, the naturally gay, the reckless, and the innocent share an unselfconscious ignorance of such tactics. Unlike the mature they are separated from the world by a natural enclosure of character. The innocent face the future neither with foresight nor with trust in good luck. Their inexperience means they have no conception of the need for either. Against those who are naturally open, generous, and trusting and who realize that their altruism is incautious the morally innocent do not consider acting otherwise and are unaware of the moral risks which will ensue. Aristotle in the *Rhetoric*[37] charts the connections between time of life, moral character, and the world. The young and the old exhibit excess in different ways, the former in their being sanguine, ardent, high-minded, and credulous, the latter in being cautious, timid, suspicious, and querulous. It is the mature who display in their conduct the moderation appropriate to practical wisdom and who are best placed to avoid the dangers which arise from the circumstances of the world and from defect of character. On this view, moral innocence is such a defect, and those who exhibit it are, as Aristotle writes of the youthful character,

. . . likewise prone to pity, from their conceiving everyone to be good, and more worthy than in fact he is; for they measure others by the standard of their own guiltlessness; so that they conceive them to be suffering what they do not deserve.[38]

A virtuous disposition must be balanced, an essential feature of his account of human flourishing.

Those who are in their prime will be . . . neither rash in too great a degree, . . . nor too much given to fear, but keeping themselves right in respect to both. Neither placing confidence in all, nor distrusting all, but judging rather in conformity to the truth. Neither living with a view solely to what is honourable, nor with a view only to expediency, but with a respect to both.[39]

The exclusive concern for virtue shown by moral innocence seems an imbalance, a distortion in the harmony of the moral psyche, a danger to the soul and to the world. Moral innocents exist in the world in the sense that they are a part of its customs and rituals, they participate with others, take part in its ceremonies, and occupy its offices. But their innocence means that their involvement must be incomplete. A disposition severed from the life of the polis will be defective and unfulfilled. For Aristotle, the moral life and the political life are lived in association. Friendship, citizenship, and political allegiance cannot be expressed in isolation. They require a human context for their full meaning to exist and become apparent. The political community, therefore, is not an artificial invention, alien and opposed to human nature, a device constructed to accommodate interest. It is intrinsic to our understanding of human possibilities and flourishing, and while it includes a degree of instrumentality it cannot be reduced to it. Political association is necessary as an expression of political education and development. Its agreement is between citizens whose goodness has been acquired and asserted in the context of the uncertainties and limitations of the moral and political world. Courage in war knows the risk of defeat; famine and shortage give sense to self-denial and self-assertion alike. It is in this specifically imperfect human context of association that the human excellences are struggled for, achieved, or lost. For Aristotle it is practical wisdom which is necessary for the realization of such excellences. But moral innocence belongs only fitfully to this world, an entertaining distraction, a diversion from the hard compromises of practical life, a disposition to distrust. Its unwavering confidence in the goodness of the world implies that it cannot be fully accommodated in the political community until it is lost. Politics excludes moral self-sufficiency. Virtue cannot be achieved by talking to oneself. How then do the morally innocent communicate with the world?

Virtuous conduct exists in a public world and is expressed in language. Practical wisdom embodies deliberation, judgement, and choice, activities which can take place only in the context of discourse. Friendship, debate between citizens, and political argument all presuppose articulation. Aristotle's emphasis on rhetoric highlights the close logical connection between articulation and agreement. Moral language conveys its ideas in the context of the challenges they face and the external and internal limitations they struggle with. Moral innocence, however, does not share this conception of virtue. It cannot communicate with others in terms of their moral vocabulary stressing moral difficulties, compromises, misfortunes, and disavowals. Moral innocence is as a consequence inarticulate in the face of the world. Its incapacity for speech reveals its incomprehension of the world.

The central features of Aristotle's moral and political teleology identify moral innocence as excluded from the full range of moral experience. This comes about through its moral imbalance, its isolation, and its inarticulation. His ambivalent description of the relation between practical wisdom and contemplative truth makes him uncertain as to which is the more complete account of human perfectibility, but moral innocence does not fit into either category. It lacks the experience of the world necessary for prudence and it does not possess a capacity for rational speculation. Practical wisdom embodies composite human nature; it expresses and makes manifest the desire for the good. Reason, as Aristotle remarks, is a thing apart. But is an innocent vision of goodness philosophically unintelligible? Must goodness exist either in the practical world or as a focus for pure rational speculation and analysis? Aristotle also has difficulty explaining the connection between the natural desire for virtue and practical wisdom. Moral innocence as a natural virtue is seen as childlike, a state uncontaminated by knowledge of the world, an unreflective innocence which has never been outgrown. But it does not always have this character. It can be an attempt to hold experience and development at bay, which would keep a distance between purity of heart and the compromises and corruptions of the world. This possibility is found in the beliefs of Maggie Verver and her father in Henry James' *The Golden Bowl*:

They knew, it might have appeared in these lights, absolutely
nothing on earth worth speaking of – whether beautifully or
cynically; and they would perhaps sometimes be a little less trying
if they would only once for all peacefully admit that knowledge
wasn't one of their needs and that they were in fact
constitutionally inaccessible to it. They were good children, bless
their hearts, and the children of good children.[40]

Such a moral stance is puzzling not simply for an Aristotelian
account of the virtues. It seems to picture innocence as both unreflective
and active. It is a state of unselfconscious purity and refusal to know
the world.

Finally, it can be argued that moral innocence escapes Aristotle's
distinction between human and divine value. Aristotle links natural
goods with dispositions:

For the goods men fight for and think the greatest – honour,
wealth, bodily excellences, good fortune, and power – are
naturally good, but may be to some hurtful because of their
dispositions.[41]

Innocence is not the noble disposition which possesses such natural
goods for their own sake and which exercises them in accordance
with practical wisdom. Nevertheless, the disjunction between virtue
and disposition which Aristotle is investigating is valuable; if moral
innocence is not a human disposition in relation to either character
or virtue is it godlike? We have already noticed that Aristotle refers
to superhuman virtue. He refers to the virtues of the gods:

what sort of actions must we assign to them? Acts of justice? Will
not the gods seem absurd if they make contracts and return
deposits, and so on? Acts of a brave man, then, confronting
dangers and running risks because it is noble to do so? Or liberal
acts? To whom will they give? It will be strange if they are really
to have money or anything of the kind. And what would their
temperate acts be? Is not such praise tasteless, since they have no
bad appetites?[42]

The innocent exchanging business contracts and making commercial
agreements do present an absurd picture. It is odd to praise innocence
or admire the risks it runs. Its goodness does seem beyond temperance
and generosity. But the innocent are not needless in the way of the

gods. Their innocence is found in the world – and their love of the good faces certain challenge if their innocence is lost.

In Greek ethics, virtue is conceived as an excellence whose perfection can be achieved by skill and training. Both Plato and Aristotle stress the function of reason in controlling the passions and facilitating a virtuous life. Both argue that the individual apart from a moral and political community lives a deficient and attenuated existence. Self-knowledge in concert with others is a fundamental principle in Greek ethics. Judged by these criteria, moral innocence is incomplete and dangerous. Its lack of self-knowledge means that its goodness is unstable. Inexperience and a stubborn belief in the goodness of the world make it an insecure foundation for political rule. Plato's rationalistic ethics overlooks specific features of moral innocence by including it in the general category of moral incapacity. Aristotle's emphasis on community membership as a necessary feature of moral identity helps us see moral innocence as an attribute of a moral self not fully disclosed to the world, but we need to show the political sense of moral innocence not just for the Aristotelian moral universe but for our own. Moral innocence must be understood not against an intellectual background in which the unity of the virtues is presupposed, but in a context which recognizes that moral and political considerations often pull in different directions.

Classical ethics takes as its basic concepts the ideas of virtue and goodness: its concern is to outline the substantive nature of human development and well-being. By contrast, an equally powerful tradition of thinking about ethics is concerned with the formal or structural principles of morality where the guiding ideas are duty, obligation, and right. The aim is not a substantive moral and political teleology but the formulation of a pattern of inter-personal moral rules. To what extent does this ethical thinking elucidate the character of moral innocence?

The construction of rules of moral conduct is an essential feature of utilitarianism. In its most basic form this means that the morality of actions is decided by reference to their outcomes or consequences. Here I shall raise three difficulties in relation to moral innocence. First, utilitarianism is concerned with the production of states of affairs which are seen to be generally beneficial. The primary moral focus ceases to be the agent and becomes the changes in the world which the agent is praised or blamed for bringing about. As moral innocence is a feature of moral character, utilitarianism by its very nature seems not to be able to explain it. Second, utilitarianism cannot exclude negotiation between morality and expediency because of the means/ends split which is built into its basic structure. Moral innocence is a belief in the goodness of the world in the sense not that things will turn out for the best but that the motives of others are benign. It sees the value of goodness as both intrinsic and sufficient, neither recognizing the claims of expediency for what they are nor seeing the necessity to accommodate them. Third, utilitarianism displaces the agent in favour of states of affairs as the centre of ethical attention. Consider someone who innocently seeks to do good by helping another. Is the generosity of the morally innocent the same as the utilitarian displacement of self? In both the self plays no part in the goodness of the act, but there are important differences. The innocent act of generosity is unselfconscious; it is blind to considerations of self. The morally innocent have no pride in their acts of virtue and they do not calculate the consequences of their actions. Utilitarianism, however, is indifferent to agency not because the self is placed in the moral background but because it does not matter to utilitarianism which self produces desirable states of affairs. As long as these are achieved it is ethically unimportant whether the agent who achieves them is motivated by pride, altruism, or self-interest.

To overcome these difficulties I want to examine an ethical system which concentrates on the derivation of formal moral rules but which does not exclude agency. Its main emphasis is not on virtue as a disposition or on the production of beneficial consequences but on the idea of humanity as rational and autonomous. Morality is valuable not because it leads to other things generally regarded as advantageous but because it is grounded in the rational capacity of all moral agents. This is the moral philosophy of Kant. How does it bear on moral innocence?

Kant does not discuss moral innocence explicitly in his ethical writings although there are passages where the notion is explored in different ways. The first discussion comes from Kant's *Lectures on Ethics*, delivered between 1775 and 1781, which predate the major ethical treatises. Kant begins by contrasting legal and moral guilt; the former refers to actual transgression of right while the latter includes the thought of such transgression.

a man who harbours evil dispositions and does nothing to reform them, is ethically guilty of the offences he might have, but has not, committed; the intentions are there, but he lacks the opportunity of giving effect to them and it is only circumstances which force him to abstain.[43]

The fact that someone has not acted badly does not mean that he did not have the intention to do so. He may have been disposed to act badly but been prevented by threat of revenge or fear of discovery. To confirm this Kant writes:

We are innocent of moral transgression only if our dispositions are pure.[44]

But how is purity of disposition to be established? Kant gives a number of answers to this question which take us to the heart of his moral and political philosophy. Initially Kant argues that purity of heart is dependent on the extent to which it overcomes temptation. It is impossible to conceive of a life of virtue which is not imperilled in various ways by evil.

No virtue is so strong that it can never be tempted, and we have no proper acquaintance with our own dispositions until we have been placed in circumstances where they might have passed into action.[45]

Virtuous action requires a capacity to resist temptation. Those who have never been tempted and therefore regard themselves as morally innocent do not know the strength of their moral convictions. They do not know by what token they hold them to be important and they are unaware of how easily their principles may be overcome. Moral innocence is an illusory virtue if it involves ignorance of temptation.

We are morally innocent if we prove in practice on every occasion the purity of our dispositions.[46]

Virtuous action issues not from the ignorance of, but from the understanding of, temptation.

This interpretation of Kant's point fits with his general ethical strategy, which is to understand virtue as overcoming vice. C. C. J. Webb makes this point in the context of Kant's discussion of evil:

Kant always tends to suppose that goodness can only be

warranted pure when it goes against interest and inclination – in endurance of suffering, even to a bitter death, for the sake of the world's advantage and even for that of his own enemies.[47]

For Kant an innocent disposition in ethics is a state of inner moral worth, a condition of blamelessness in the face of great temptation and sometimes unjustly inflicted suffering. Such a moral condition requires acts of considerable sacrifice if it is not to be compromised and it entails that a greater value is placed on living virtuously than on the preservation of life. This Socratic injunction is expressed by Kant in the form of an example in the *Lectures*.

> Assume that a number of persons are innocently accused of treachery, and that whilst some of them are truly honourable, others, although innocent of the particular accusation levelled against them, are contemptible and of no real worth; assume further that they are all sentenced together, and that each of them has to choose between death and penal servitude for life; it is certain that the honourable amongst them would choose death, and the vile ones the galleys. A man of inner worth does not shrink from death; he would die rather than live as an object of contempt, a member of a gang of scoundrels in the galleys; but the worthless man prefers the galleys, almost as if they were his proper place.[48]

Moral innocence in this sense is consistent with self-sacrifice, though inner moral worth is not faced with this challenge on every occasion. For Kant innocence does not refer simply to a temporal state which is historically traceable or scripturally expressed and which rests on an unprovable postulate of innate or natural goodness. Its moral nature excludes weakness, actions performed for mixed motives, and, of course, actions which are intrinsically evil. It further excludes acting well for the sake of profit, reputation, or happiness. Such considerations are for Kant heteronomous; the moral will is governed by criteria outside itself. Within the conception of heteronomy Kant considers most objectionable the view that it is the private or individual will which establishes the nature of moral imperatives.

> *Empirical principles* are wholly incapable of serving as a foundation for moral laws.[49]

The appeal to private moral feeling is superficial

when those who cannot *think* believe that *feeling* will help them
out, even in what concerns general laws: and besides, feelings
which naturally differ infinitely in degree cannot furnish a
uniform standard of good and evil, nor has anyone a right to form
judgements for others by his own feelings.[50]

Moral innocence avoids the excesses of heteronomy by its commitment
to virtue, but it expresses this in an unreflective and direct way.
Kant describes it as paying

> virtue the honour of ascribing to her *immediately* the satisfaction
> and esteem we have for her, and does not as it were, tell her to her
> face that we are not attached to her by her beauty but by profit.[51]

Moral innocence has the appearance but not the substance of virtue
and may draw close to authentic virtue, but Kant recognizes that its
condition is incoherent and unstable.

> Innocence is indeed a glorious thing, only . . . it is very sad that it
> cannot well maintain itself, and is easily seduced.[52]

For Kant it is unsurprising that innocence is lost, but it is also
insufficient to say it is lost by the realization that the world is not as
good as it was thought to be or by the gradual acquisition of moral
experience. The virtuous disposition requires a formal grounding in
reason if it is to be permanent and if it is to have a universal
significance. So Kant argues for a man to be morally good, not
privately regard himself as good, or be seen as good in the eyes of the
world, or unselfconsciously act well, he

> should become not merely a *legally* but a *morally* good man, that is,
> virtuous in his intelligible character (virtus noumenon), a man
> who, when he recognises a thing as his duty, needs no other spring
> than this conception of duty itself; this is not to be effected by
> gradual *reform*, as long as the principle of his maxims remains
> impure, but requires a *revolution* in the mind, and he can only
> become a new man by a kind of new birth, as it were by a new
> creation and a change of heart.[53]

The primacy of reason is a characteristic Enlightenment assumption, but Kant parts company with Aristotelian assumptions
regarding practical wisdom. Moral considerations for Kant are

derived not from experience but from a conception of reason which is *a priori* in character. Kant excludes prudence from moral conduct because it is gained from experience, it issues in judgements which can be mistaken, and it is open to conclusions which are not morally singular but diverse. Kant argues that reason, as against prudence, will establish the nature of moral duty and this can never be in error. Kant thinks of morality as formal because this is the only way of resisting heteronomy. For Kant, actions are rigidly divided into those which are moral and those which are self-interested. This sharp distinction implies in Kant a dualism between morality and nature including human desires, needs, and interests. This may reflect a metaphysical gap between the noumenal and the phenomenal worlds, but in any case it suggests that, compared with the idea of duty established by reason, moral innocence is defective and lacks certain moral direction and foundation. We must now consider whether or not this conclusion is justified.

Kant considers that in ethics what he calls the 'revolution in the mind' can only be achieved by a theory which is formal and rigorous. Key terms are reason, morality, and freedom. Reason is the distinguishing feature of human conduct and, by contrast with merely empirical considerations, the universality of reason provides the basis for the derivation of principles which will govern moral and political life. It establishes the only firm foundation for human freedom. On the basis of reason, human agency is separated from nature and is poised to achieve realization and its own autonomy. Freedom is distinguished from inclination and the satisfaction of material wants and is placed firmly within the moral realm. The universal character of reason means that it is logically impossible to assert that my will is free but the wills of others are not. Freedom is a common human attribute because human rationality entails the impossibility of it being otherwise. Autonomy appears not as absence of restraint or the pursuit of private desires but as a freedom of choice which exclusively expresses the rational wills of all human beings. It is not based on contingent capacities and abilities and it does not apply arbitrary distinctions. Its logical driving force is its basis in universal human reason.

Autonomy has two functions in relation to the character of morality: one, moral agency presupposes an agent who is free and rational; two, autonomy constrains morality by setting limits to the principles and actions it contains. How does moral duty present itself? It appears neither as consequential benefit nor as natural virtue but as conformity with a universal moral law.

> An action done from duty has its moral worth, *not in the purpose* to be attained by it, but in the maxim in accordance with which it is decided upon; it depends, therefore, not on the realisation of the object of the action, but solely on the *principle* of *volition* in accordance with which, irrespective of all objects of the faculty of desire, action has been performed.[54]

Kant's concern is with the formal character of morality, with the establishment of moral rules by which actions can be judged, motives evaluated, and the contrast between the moral and non-moral maintained. Such rules have the form of imperatives, either hypothetical or categorical in kind. Hypothetical imperatives are maxims of prudence and Kant considers they assume but do not prove the rational basis of their ends. These are the staple ingredients of utilitarianism but do not capture the full sense of moral obligation. For Kant, moral imperatives are categorical in nature. They have the status of commands or obligations, the force of moral necessity, and are never optional. A moral imperative requires obedience but, as the source of this command is not external to reason, actions in conformity with such imperatives are consistent with both human agency and freedom. Kant asserts that this conception generates three formulations:

(1) Act only according to that maxim by which you can at the same time will that it should become a universal law.
(2) Act only that humanity is considered as an end, and never merely as a means.
(3) Such actions are to conform with a possible kingdom of ends.

The moral and political vision incorporated by these maxims constitutes the basic intellectual framework of liberalism. Kant pictures a society in which individuals treat each other as ends in themselves, a community of mutual respect in which the moral dynamic is found not in subjective preference or intuition but in the nature of human rationality. Kant's moral principles are formal and tend towards equality and perfectionism.

The formulation of the categorical imperative implies the need for a theory of politics. Human action takes place not in a vacuum but in the context of relations with others. If such relations are not to be based on contingent or accidental considerations of geography, psychology, or history they must involve rational agreement. This may be termed the publicity requirement. Kant's moral principles operate as a framework for politics and this enables individuals to create a community which is both just and consistent with human nature. Such principles will be autonomous when they adequately express humanity as free and rational. They are not adopted because of social position, individual wants, or natural endowments, which for Kant are heteronomous considerations. The rules apply publicly to all free and rational beings. So a theory of politics is inevitably an intrinsic part of a theory of morality. It is concerned with criteria which control conflicts of interest. The universality principle requires that this should be in a universal manner. It is law which expresses universality in politics.

Kant's political philosophy is juridical in form, but this does not mean that morality and politics are coextensive. Kant distinguishes between internal and external duties which may be either perfect or imperfect. A duty is imperfect if no one is in a position to demand compliance by right. A perfect duty is one where compliance can be rightfully claimed. Political duties are properly only concerned with perfect duties to others. These are the proper objects of coercion by a legally constituted authority. Both moral and political duties must be in accordance with the categorical imperative, but in the case of political duty external compulsion is justified so as to supplement the deficiency in individual will. These distinctions do not represent a conflict between moral and political considerations. They must be understood in the light of the general structure of Kant's moral philosophy, which provides a basis for the reconciliation of conflicting moral demands by reference to the ideas of universality and rational agency. But are these ideas sufficient to cover the complete scope of political morality?

Kant accepts that in politics there may be a case for performing actions which would otherwise be regarded as morally objectionable. But to avoid the obvious consequentialist weaknesses in such a concession he argues that such actions must be limited by the rules of his general theory of political right. Kant's famous distinction in *Perpetual Peace* between the moral politician and the political moralist exemplifies this. Expediency and pragmatism are not completely excluded by Kant from his account of politics but are tolerated provided they are within the law and are necessary for the achievement of a just society. Unlike the political moralist, the moral politician is aware of the need to keep a moral distance between himself and the ambition and selfishness which politics sometimes involves. It is open to him to form alliances with those who disagree with his motives and he may on occasion have to negotiate with the evil and the base, but in so doing his actions are morally informed with the principles of right, which establish that there is a limit beyond which he cannot go, and a teleological conception of history, which implies that however complicated his strategies and alliances the moral end will be served. The moral politician is an emblem of the Enlightenment. He is mature, rational, and wise. He prefers reform and gradual progress to revolutionary upheaval. By contrast with Machiavelli, his metaphysics enables him to refute moral and political scepticism. His aim, as Kant puts it, is to unite the political precept 'be ye therefore wise as serpents' with the moral injunction to be 'as harmless as doves'.[55] However, this belief in the harmony of morality and politics is unconvincing. Kant's acceptance that there may be occasions where a juridical state has to act in a way which is less than morally acceptable conflicts with his prime ethical require-ment that individuals should never be treated as means, and it is no intellectual consolation to be told that history has a just society as its ultimate end. Kant writes:

> A true system of politics cannot therefore take a single step without first paying tribute to morality . . . all politics must bend the knee before right, although politics may hope in return to arrive, however slowly, at a stage of lasting brilliance.[56]

Kant's moral structuralism affects the way he understands the relation between morality and politics in that politics is construed simply as a field of application for the rules already arrived at and taken to be true in morality. This assumption ignores the possibility of moral conflict between moral and political demands and it cannot make sense of the idea of a morally admirable character damaging the political world. Kant's ethical formalism means that he mis-understands integrity. For an action to be moral it is not sufficient, Kant believes, simply to display good or charitable inclinations.

> It is not this kindliness of heart and temper which the moralist should seek to cultivate, but good-will from principles. For the former is grounded in inclination and a natural necessity, giving rise to unregulated conduct. Such a man will be charitable, by

inclination, to all and sundry; and then, if someone takes advantage of his kind heart, in sheer disgust he will decide from then onwards to give up doing good to others. He has no principle by which to calculate his behaviour. Therefore, the moralist must establish principles, and commend and inculcate benevolence from obligation.[57]

But to describe an act of benevolence as deficient because it is not based on rational principle is to say nothing about the moral integrity of the individual who performs it. His intentions may be pure and he may not give up benevolence if others take advantage of him. This may be not because he grasps the rational basis of benevolence but rather because of the importance it has for him. Equally it is possible to understand the rational foundation for acts of charity but to lack the moral disposition to perform them. Integrity can be displayed in particular actions, in the context of a specific moral character rather than a set of abstract rules. Even if we grant that someone sees morality as acting in accordance with moral principle this is not a guarantee of integrity. On the contrary, it is perfectly consistent with the presence of moral corruption.

Innocence is a disposition of character. Its goodness does not require a grounding in reason and its actions are not performed as duties. Kant's conditions for an action to be described as moral – obligatoriness, universalizability, and duty – exclude supererogatory acts from the realm of morality. For Kant, a moral act is not optional. Its obligatory nature refers to its moral necessity. But supererogatory acts, such as volunteering, are acts which would not be blameworthy if we failed to perform them. Thus they lie outside Kant's classification and cannot have moral value. The universality test points to the same conclusion. It refers to the exclusion of proposed courses of action from morality rather than a positive account of moral virtue. Equally, Kant tends to dismiss acts which go beyond duty as arising from pride or self-regard. Even where these motives are absent Kant attaches value to supererogatory acts only if they are performed in difficult circumstances or where they go against our deepest inclinations. Kant's formal distinction between acts which it is our duty to perform and acts which it is not, overlooks those moral outlooks which are neither duties nor inclinations. Sanctity is identified with fanaticism and innocence reduced to the ignorance of risk.

Similar problems arise if we examine moral innocence in the context of the idea of publicity. Kant refers to this as 'a transcendental concept of public right', by which he means that it is a function of rationality that any political principle which cannot be made public is incompatible with justice. Thus principles of justice must be based on agreement between rational agents in abstraction from all material and empirical aspects of their relations. This provides the transcendental formula of public right:

> All actions affecting the rights of other human beings are wrong if their maxim is not compatible with their being made public.[58]

Kant considers that this principle is both ethical and juridical in character. Its importance lies in its providing a necessary foundation for principles of justice which will be public and open to all. Each individual will know where they stand in relation to the moral rules of a just society, and each will accord every other equal respect. Obligations and duties cannot be private in nature. It is, therefore, essential that any proposed ethical maxim satisfy the publicity requirement. If it fails to do so it will be self-refuting.

There are problems associated with this idea, particularly in the need for secrecy and concealment in policies which depend on such strategies for their success, but in relation to moral innocence publicity produces striking weaknesses. Kant's publicity requirement is, in part, a search for principles which will be impartial between all rational agents. It is from this standpoint that features of personality are regarded as accidental or arbitrary. Kant assumes that this process of reasoning will generate the same conclusions whoever participates in it. But moral thinking is not indifferent to the character of the agent, which cannot be arbitrarily brushed aside. Moral innocence and its loss are shared human experiences but they do not depend upon reason and we do not understand them better by placing them in the context of principles arrived at by all rational agents. In terms of the derivation of the publicity requirement, moral innocence is a puzzle. It is open and candid in the way that Kant argues that mutual respect requires, but its openness is not based on rational agreement and its candour does not depend on others doing likewise. For moral innocence, trust does not depend on reciprocity and its goodness does not derive from mutually agreed principles.

This point becomes clearer if we turn to the substance rather than the derivation of Kant's publicity requirement. Kant contrasts openness and secrecy, public and private in a simple way. Either a maxim is capable of being expressed openly or it is not. Either it can be incorporated in a public vocabulary, available to all, or it cannot. But not all undisclosed states of mind threaten justice. Moral innocence is not fully part of a public world; it is unformed, lacking experience in the duplicities of life. However, it does not face the world as a spy concealing its true motives and ambitions. Its honesty is based not on duty but on a private perception of the world. For Kant this means that it is a subjective ethical condition which cannot serve as a foundation for public right.

Confirmation of this Kantian view of moral innocence is found in the theme of ignorance. Kant posits a moral agent as a kind of rational spectator standing outside the self and its desires to consent to rational principles which confirm his freedom. Self-knowledge involves a standing apart from the self and the world, followed in logic by a reconstruction of both self and world on the basis of rational principles. Moral innocence falls short of this human autonomy. Its lack of experience does not disqualify it. The substance of its morality does not disqualify it. For Kant it is excluded because it is ignorant of the rational basis of its own activity. It is not fully conscious of the rationality of its virtue and as such is defective. Kantian ethics lacks a developmental morality which could construe moral innocence as natural and spontaneous, resisting capture in terms of either reason or inclination.

> Rationalism seems in the end to overlay with pure metaphysics the very moral point of righteousness itself. We ought indeed to pursue righteousness, but for righteousness sake, or, to be precise, for the sake of the values that it serves.[59]

Kant's metaphysic of morals involves a dualism between reason and nature which vitiates his account of moral character and weakens his grasp of the problems of political morality. His formalist emphasis on duty means that many features of moral experience are seen either as subjective or as part of a rational belief in human progress and well-being. This shapes his account of political morality and means that substantive problems are misconstrued as political expediency. Further, a formalist moral theory has serious difficulty with moral dilemmas and conflicting moral demands. In the realm of political morality such situations are common. Kant's method for dealing with these is to place his account of political right in the context of moral theory based on reason. But, as we have seen, this rests on an unpersuasive picture of the self as rational agent and an uncritical belief in the priority of virtue.

An influential modern work of political philosophy which may high-light the difficulties involved in too readily accepting the Kantian tactic is Ronald Dworkin's *Law's Empire*. For Dworkin, integrity is the basis for a civilized political community; he would find it incon-ceivable that there might be circumstances where it was morally desirable to sacrifice it or where it could be responsible for great political damage and harm. Political integrity expresses the virtues of justice, fairness, and due process. It shares with moral integrity the belief that even where individuals disagree in their moral and political convictions they express these in a way which is coherent, consistent, and not capricious or wilful. Integrity, therefore, refers not to the content of moral and political beliefs (although certain beliefs may be excluded from the start on this count), but to the manner in which these beliefs are acted upon. Integrity has an obvious manifestation in the requirement that law be coherent in principle, and in the adjudication of legal rules and social policies in a way that is public, responsible, and fair. Dworkin is fully aware that his three component virtues may pull against one another on occasion.

> Justice . . . is a matter of the right outcome of the political system: the right distribution of goods, opportunities, and other resources. Fairness is a matter of the right structure for that system, the structure that distributes influence over political decisions in the right way. Procedural due process is a matter of the right procedures for enforcing rules and regulations the system has produced.[60]

He tends to think of political philosophy as being either axiomatic, constructing abstract and formal rules of conduct, or evolutionary, that is, not fully manifesting the formal rules of justice but in the process of moving towards a just and fair society. From this perspective it is easy to dismiss formal objections to his account of integrity as merely temporary moral setbacks which will be overcome when the full framework of justice is historically instantiated.

For Dworkin, political integrity gives a moral authority to

governments which act in accordance with its ideals, and protects citizens against deceit and partial treatment. It further encourages the belief in self-government and the mutual recognition of rights, and through its stress on publicity and consistency it facilitates the process of law, claims for redress of grievance, and the recognition and restitution of rights. Through its concern with fidelity and the mutual acceptance of obligation it discourages both exploitation and free-riding. Such claims are far-reaching but there are respects in which they appear deficient.

It may be doubted that integrity is an exclusive guarantee either of morally admirable conduct by an individual or of the political behaviour of states. It is insufficient because there may be occasions where an individual or a state has to sacrifice principles otherwise regarded as moral for the sake of the achievement of a morally desirable end. In political morality it is not unusual to find hard moral conflicts in which difficult choices have to be made. It seems inadequate to say that whatever the decision in such situations integrity is undisturbed. Equally, we cannot take the consequentialist line and argue that integrity is normally sufficient, except in cases where conflict can only be resolved by reference to the outcomes of the alternative policies. The whole point of the introduction of integrity was to establish a framework of moral rules where obligation was prior to the assessment of consequences. It might be argued that it is always open to the individual of moral integrity to hold fast to his moral beliefs and face the consequences of doing so. It certainly does not follow that such a course of action always has a single moral sense. It may be motivated by a refusal to accommodate principle to the demands of a morally complex situation; it may indicate a willingness to do more than is required by a statement of minimal obligation; it may indicate a prepardness for self-sacrifice. Or we may have here the presence of moral innocence. These elaborations of integrity – and certainly the special character of moral innocence – take no account of the complications of political morality. However, they do indicate that such considerations are not merely logical irritants on the fringe of Dworkin's account, but rather penetrate its central assumptions. If integrity exhibits moral complexity it cannot act as the singular underpinning of political virtue. In which case we must either examine the detailed ways in which various forms of moral character have a political bearing or establish a more satisfactory theoretical starting-point from which we can reconstruct the relation between morality and politics, something which John Rawls' contractualist theory of justice attempts to do.

It is not my intention to provide an exhaustive criticism of Rawls' views, as expressed either in *A Theory of Justice* or in his important later articles,[61] and I will not comment on the critical debate which Rawls' position has stimulated. It should be noticed that the problems of political morality have little place in Rawls' theory. There is a good reason for this. Political morality may be said to involve conflicts of moral principle; we may see such conflicts as being open to some kind of utilitarian resolution or as dilemmas which are intrinsically irresolvable. Rawls' contractualist starting-point claims to establish a structure of rational agreement which not only will generate the basic principles of a just society but will also remove serious moral and political dispute. Rawls attempts to connect politics with morality and to express the basis of morality in terms of an initial choice made by rational and moderately self-interested individuals who are ignorant of their place in society and history, their natural assets, and their conception of the good. I do not intend to examine the process by which Rawls claims such individuals will choose the principles of justice as a basis for a just society except to say that it is intended to remove conflicts of various kinds in its essential construction. The clash between principle and interest is removed, Rawls claims, by the thin theory of the good, in which the role of primary goods is crucial; the conflict between principles is removed by the device of lexically ordering the agreed principles of justice; and any disagreement between competing loyalties is removed by assuming that individuals, families, states, and generations have the same logical identity and function in relation to the original position. Further, it must be stressed that justice is only a part of Rawls' enquiry. His aim is the construction of a comprehensive, coherent, contractualist theory of virtue, and it is with the relations between the parts of this theory that I shall be mainly concerned.

Unlike Dworkin, Rawls does not place such great weight on the concept of integrity. Indeed, he says explicitly that:

> the virtues of integrity are virtues, and among the excellences of
> free persons. Yet while necessary, they are not sufficient, for their
> definition allows for most any content . . . It is impossible to
> construct a moral view from these virtues alone; being virtues of

61

form they are in a sense secondary. But joined to the appropriate conception of justice, one that allows for autonomy and objectivity correctly understood, they come into their own.[62]

In this passage Rawls gives an example which fits his argument neatly. A tyrant may exhibit all the attributes of integrity in the service of an evil end. We require the principles of justice to exclude such a possibility. As someone may pursue an immoral course of action with a degree of moral diligence it seems obvious to Rawls that we need something more than moral diligence if the immorality of the action is to be condemned; the principles of justice provide this. But this argument does not fit all cases. Take the case of someone who gives up his integrity to avoid a specific evil. Such a person has not chosen evil against good. His choice does not require supplementing by the principles of justice. His integrity is not employed in the service of a bad end. He has sacrificed it not to evil but for the achievement of good. A possibility of this kind exists outside Rawls' classification. It is not a requirement of obligation derived from principles of fairness. Equally, it is not a manifestation of integrity as a secondary virtue because it is integrity which has been given up.

It is open to Rawls to describe such acts as involving supererogatory virtues. Moral duties on a contractual account are minimal because they are linked to the principles of fairness chosen by rationally self-interested individuals in the original position. But such duties do not exhaust the class of morally desirable actions. Can the sacrifice of integrity be described by Rawls as a supererogatory act? He defines supererogation as including acts which it is morally good to perform but which are not duties or obligations, and he argues that in important respects supererogation is compatible with the morality of justice and fairness agreed in the original position. While supererogation cannot involve rules which would be accepted by rationally self-interested individuals, it does aim for the satisfaction of the same values aspired to by actions based on obligation. Supererogation, therefore, refers to morally admirable actions which go beyond duty in two main ways.

On the one hand, the love of mankind shows itself in advancing the common good in ways that go well beyond our natural duties and obligations. This morality is not one for ordinary persons, and its peculiar virtues are those of benevolence, a heightened

sensitivity to the feelings and wants of others, and a proper
humility and unconcern with self. The morality of self-command,
on the other hand, in its simplest form is manifest in fulfilling with
complete ease and grace the requirements of right and justice. It
. . . displays its characteristic virtues of courage, magnanimity,
and self-control in actions presupposing great discipline and
training.[63]

He argues that supererogation is not discontinuous with the values
derived from the original position and expressed as justice and
fairness.

. . . the moralities of supererogation, those of the saint and the
hero, do not contradict the norms of right and justice; they are
marked by the willing adoption by the self of aims continuous
with these principles but extending beyond what they enjoin.[64]

How does Rawls express the difference between the requirements
of obligation and the permissions of supererogation? First, in terms
of loss or risk, so that someone who performs a supererogatory act
does not invoke exemption on grounds of loss or risk which actions
on the basis of obligation would normally include. Second, in terms
of active benevolence, in which the moral desire to provide some
benefit or good for others is paramount, as compared with acting for
the sake of others out of duty or the impersonal redistribution of
goods which results in actual benefit being achieved. Third, supererogation goes beyond positive but not negative duties. As Heyd
writes in a passage to which I am indebted:

We can be more generous than the duty of mutual aid requires,
but we cannot fulfil our promises more than necessary, nor refrain
more than we ought to from injuring innocent people. . . . For
Rawls, obligations are generally concerned with being fair, but we
cannot be more fair than is required.[65]

If, as Rawls says, negative duties have a lexical priority over positive
duties, then this seems to imply that supererogation comes low down
in the hierarchy on the basis of the binding character of moral
requirements. As Heyd points out, Rawls rejects this because he
does not include supererogation as a part of the agreement reached
in the original position, but it does fit in with his general method for
the resolution of conflict, and his emphasis on moderate self-interest
would suggest that it is rational to place duty before self-sacrifice.

Rawls tends to consider supererogation as including acts which in an ideal world would be classed as duties. This is a consequence of his belief that it is necessary to show that morality is to our advantage. But these assertions collapse if we can show that for some individuals morality has an intrinsic value which exists irrespective of loss, risk, and considerations of duty. Heyd has argued that Rawls' attempt to distinguish supererogation from the claims of obligation in terms of the exemption provided by loss and risk does not work in all cases. Some supererogatory acts, such as mercy, do not necessarily involve loss, and acts of kindness which clearly go beyond duty involve no risk whatsoever, while the fulfilment of certain obligations, on the other hand, can involve a great deal of danger to the person who accepts them. Rawls runs into these problems because of his refusal to understand acts of conspicuous virtue except in terms of his original position and the principles generated by it. This expresses his assumption that morality has to be explained in terms other than itself.

> The doctrine of the purely conscientious act is irrational. This doctrine holds, first, that the highest moral motive is the desire to do what is right and just simply because it is right and just, no other description being appropriate. . . . But on this interpretation the sense of right lacks any apparent reason; it resembles a preference for tea rather than coffee. Although such a preference might exist, to make it regulative of the basic structure of society is utterly capricious; and no less so because it is masked by a fortunate necessary connection with reasonable grounds for judgements of right.[66]

For these reasons Rawls' account of supererogation does not help us understand the sacrifice of integrity for the sake of another. This is not a case of conflicting duties where one can be described as *prima facie* and the other supererogatory. The act of sacrificing integrity does not simply go beyond what is normally required, because we do not know what a normal requirement would be in such circumstances. Equally, it cannot be defined in terms of the loss or risk suffered by the person who makes the sacrifice. There may be no physical risk, but there will be self-reproach if the sacrifice has not been made.

Rawls' basic ethical framework tells against an adequate explanation of such features of moral experience because he takes it as self-evident that justice is the first virtue of a political community and that this can be shown by contractualist argument to be to our advantage. This means that it is difficult for him to appreciate the moral complexity involved in cases where it is virtue which constitutes the obstacle to acting well and where the expression of moral innocence can result in political disaster. Such possibilities represent a total inversion of Rawls' method of argument. From the ascription of the twin moral capacities of a sense of justice and a conception of the good to the idea of a person Rawls constructs a picture of moral and political virtue which aspires to a perfect logical order. From the premises of the original position each successive layer of argument results in specific features of our moral experience being organized one after the other in a coherent, hierarchical formation. Rawls asserts that his search for an Archimedean point is necessary to remove the contingent inequalities of the world. Like Kant, Rawls considers virtue to be capricious unless it is grounded in rationality. But for him rationality is abstract unless it is connected with moderate self-interest. The thin theory of the good and the idea of a rational plan of life have to take the weight of moral agency both for those prepared only to accept modest obligations and for those who are prepared to surpass them. This way of conceiving morality means that it is hard to identify moral differences except by tracing them back to the original position. An innocent pursuit of goodness in which advantage and the needs of the self are unimportant is a moral possibility which is only half-glimpsed by Rawls' argument. We need to see moral virtue as completely distinct from advantage, gain, or the avoidance of loss before we can appreciate its political implications. This is the extent to which Rawls' contractualism has to be overturned.

There are two further points to consider. First, it might be argued that moral innocence lacks knowledge in the same way as individuals in the original position do before the veil of ignorance is progressively lifted. Is a moral innocent a 'bare person'[67] in the sense of lacking information about their place in the world, moral nature, and aptitude? If this was the case it might be open to Rawls to construe innocence as a starting-point, a focus of moral perfectibility prior to its gradual incorporation into the world. On this view, innocence is lost as the veil of ignorance is lifted and the comprehensive structure of rights and obligations, just institutions and practices revealed. But moral innocence is not incompatible with a knowledge of a place in society. It requires that such personal and social attributes are seen as unimportant. It does not stipulate the abolition of the contingencies of life. Indeed, it is seen as admirable because it pays them scant regard. Moral innocence is not lost in the rationally organized way posited by Rawls in the lifting of the veil of ignorance, which overlooks the double moral identity of innocence in human life. We are distraught when it is corrupted or brutally taken away but we often find absurd those who have never lost it. In this respect, Rawls' rationalism links with his moral structuralism, and this combination distracts us from the philosophical significance of particular moral experience. Second, moral value, as Rawls recognizes, exists in a public world. But the relation here is not contractualist. The public context of moral action is not an artificial creation, the result of an agreement between individuals of a particular moral psychology. Rawls assumes that the principles of justice which result from such an agreement, and which govern the lives of individuals in a just political community, will be the same for states and generations. But why should this be so? The credibility of contractualism in this respect rests on its being able to reduce these concepts to a common individual denominator. If this is rejected not only is it impossible that the same principles should apply to all three it is also likely that principles of justice agreed between individuals will conflict with considerations arising from the different character of states and generations. Rawls cannot allow that individuals, states, and generations are different logical animals. If they are, then the space between private and public virtue is re-opened and no amount of contractualist engineering will keep it closed.

In this chapter I have examined different views of moral innocence in the context of a variety of accounts of public and private morality. My choice of moral innocence is not perverse or accidental. It represents a perfectibility which exists on the limit of virtue. In terms of character, it contains elements which some moral theories would see as disqualifying it from virtue. It resists explanation in either Aristotelian or Kantian terminology. Our main aim is to examine its impact on politics. To do so it is necessary to investigate the character of political morality. I have resisted the neo-Kantian attempt to link politics with morality in terms of a formal theory of right. Equally, a utilitarian stress on outcomes does not grasp the autonomous character of moral conduct. Moral innocence needs to be placed not in the context of right or utility but in the context of an attempt to distinguish the demands of the political and the moral worlds. If they are neither mutually exclusive nor reducible to a basic set of moral principles, how can their relations be understood?

Chapter Three

POLITICAL AUTONOMY

O judgment! thou art fled to brutish beasts, And men have lost their reason.'

(Mark Antony, *Julius Caesar*, III. ii)

The great modern crimes are public crimes.

(Thomas Nagel, 'Ruthlessness in public life')

Those who claim that moral considerations have a bearing on politics have often seen morality as a way of establishing the boundaries of politics. Acts which cross these boundaries thereby transgress the rules established by morality. Thus, acts which are regarded as permissible and desirable in politics are regarded as impermissible and undesirable by morality. This position is elegant and powerful. It is from morality that we derive the sustenance to condemn acts such as deceit, corruption, cruelty, torture, and exploitation. More positively, morality establishes the virtues necessary for the flourishing of human communities. Such ideas form the mainstream of thinking about the relation between morality and politics. In different ways they are present in Classical moral and political reflection, in the Natural Law tradition, in Christian moral theology, and in the intellectual changes of the Enlightenment which adapted and extended them. Within these broad bands of thought the human agent is understood as self-conscious and rational, possessing a capacity for knowledge of himself, of others, and of the world. In morality the emphasis is on human autonomy, equality of respect and consideration and, as applied to politics, the primary virtues of justice and fairness.

From this perspective, however, the relation between morality and politics appears over-simple. Morality condemns some political actions but we do not know what it is about politics that establishes

68

the grounds for such condemnation. If the answer is the acquisition and retention of power then the problem posed by political morality is relatively straightforward: how can tyrants be replaced by individuals who possess at least a minimum moral sense? Harriet Martineau recognizes this:

> Under a pure despotism, the morals of politics would make but a very short chapter.[1]

But in political life it is not true that only tyrants act immorally. This means that the problem of political morality is both more complex and more intractable. Immoral acts are performed for political ends not only by political gangsters but by individuals whom we might otherwise describe as morally admirable. Sometimes the good have to behave badly or at least less than well if effective political action is to take place.

The gap between morality and politics is not simply between those who are predisposed to act well and those who are not. This may prompt withdrawal to a life of private virtue. It may inspire an attempt to transform the historical situation in which this problem arises or an heroic determination to pay the moral price that political action involves. Tension between morality and politics exists in the context of the massively disrupting features of modern political experience. In our century the extreme disjunction between thinking and doing would drive to the point of madness anyone unfortunate enough to be both well intentioned and politically ambitious. Orwell saw this clearly. In *Writers and Leviathan*, speaking of the writer and political engagement, he writes:

> we see the need of engaging in politics while also seeing what a dirty, degrading business it is. And most of us still have a lingering belief that every choice, even every political choice, is between good and evil, and that if a thing is necessary it is also right. We should, I think, get rid of this belief, which belongs to the nursery! In politics one can never do more than decide which of two evils is the lesser, and there are some situations from which one can only escape by acting like a devil or a lunatic.[2]

It is the final phrase which exerts the fascination. Orwell was no doubt thinking of the Spanish Civil War, but since his death we have seen and probably will continue to see much worse. Why is it that politics seems to demand the abdication of morality?

Many have taken the view that moral principle can be an obstacle to the achievement of desirable political objectives. For those in politics:

> If they stand arm'd with seely honesty,
> With wishing prayers, and neat integritie,
> Like Indians 'gainst Spanish hosts they bee.

> Suspitious boldnesse to this place belongs,
> And to 'have as many eares as all have tongues;
> Tender to know, tough to acknowledge wrongs.[3]

Donnes's lines exert a powerful and problematic influence. But what establishes the difference between public and private life? The implication is that it is difficult to give an account of the dangers of virtue in politics unless it is in instrumental or consequentialist terms. Trust and honour have to be over-ridden because of the consequences of not doing so. Absolute virtue prohibits negotiation with outcome. Instrumental ethics stresses the cost of moral principle. Resolution of this dilemma requires a release from both the abstract ethics of Kant's deontology and the calculative, production-line morality of utilitarianism. Concentration on the idea of moral innocence enables us to see the impact of absolute virtue in politics and the possibility of giving this impact a non-instrumental moral sense. We need an account of the distinction between public and private which avoids the individualist premises of both contractual and utilitarian political thinking.

The concept of the public has a wider logical bearing than the political. It has a range of important connections with notions of the social, the communal, and the world. But it is in relation to the political that the central problems of political morality are generated. Here I am not specifically concerned with charting the boundaries of politics in relation to the economic or the religious and I will not comment on attempts to identify politics with legislative, administrative, or civil and constitutional thinking and practice. To pursue a deeper grounding for politics is to try to articulate a justification of politics and it is this spirit which has animated the central tradition of political philosophy from Plato onwards. The question being raised concerns the necessity of politics, with how it is that there is such a thing as political existence at all. Here the attempt is to answer Rousseau's question – how is it possible for human beings to be both ruled and free? For Marx, political life is the expression of alienation, from ourselves and from others. For anarchists like Bakunin, politics is an unnatural blight, a disease of the spirit, to be purged from the human condition. Disagreement over the necessity of politics is also to be found in its identity. Is the character of a state to be discerned in its ruler, in the nature of its representation, the form of its legislature, the 'common recognition of the manner of attending to its arrangements' in Oakeshott's phrase, or in the constitution which embodies the spirit of a political community? Again, political language may be distinguished by the specific types of utterance it contains – imperative, emotive, hortatory, rhetorical, persuasive, and inspirational. But none of these manoeuvres fully explains the autonomy of politics in relation to the problems of political morality. One attempt to rectify this is made by Machiavelli and it involves a realist demarcation of the political world. This picture is the dominant influence in thinking about political morality. What does it involve? To what extent is it coherent?

Interpretations of Machiavelli have varied greatly from his being seen as a teacher of evil, an advocate of republicanism, the discoverer of the autonomy of politics, an originator of the scientific study of politics, the author of practical political advice, to a convinced moral sceptic. Not all these interpretations are inconsistent with each other, and it has been the trend of much modern exegesis to try to amalgamate the doctrines of *The Prince* with those of *The Discourses*, showing that the idea that Machiavelli was the apostle of power is an exaggeration and arguing by contrast that his republicanism requires that power be seen as a necessary but not a sufficient condition of good government.

In the context of Renaissance political life and ideas Machiavelli was consciously diverging from both classical and medieval routes to the political good. Both these emphasized to different degrees and in different ways the unity of public and private virtue. Against this, in five remarkable chapters in *The Prince*, Machiavelli describes his political originality. He draws a sharp distinction between public and private conduct. Actions may be justified in private in a way which is not possible in public. Machiavelli is led to an inversion of conventional moral value. In politics meanness is more advantageous than liberality, cruelty is more useful than mercy, it is better to be feared than loved, and it is more beneficial to lie than tell the truth. This reversal of moral value is given an additional elaboration in Machiavelli's doctrine of duplicity. It is necessary to appear just, to wear the clothes of goodness while engaging in deceit and betrayal to gain political advantage. Machiavelli claims to be concerned with the world as it is and not as it ought to be. It follows that the only way to learn about political life is through experience. But political action has the force of necessity. It has outcomes which are often unavoidable. Action in such a world is not to be hindered by such trifles as moral scruple. This view derives from Machiavelli's realistic account of human nature. In *The Prince* humanity is portrayed as naturally selfish, and since men act morally only under constraint they are governed more by fear than genuine love or regard. Human life is greedy, ambitious, and discontented. In such a world political stability can be achieved only through the recognition of necessity. Machiavelli asserts:

> It is necessary for a Prince who wishes to maintain himself, to learn how not to be good, and to use this knowledge and not to use it, according to the necessity of the case.[4]

This returns us to the world of prudence and expediency. It can pay to be evil. The good act may be dissimulation disguising evil motives. While it is true that Machiavelli tends to see the environment of political action as one of struggle between self-regarding individuals who face each other in a posture of aggression and competition, there are three important qualifications to this picture. One is that Machiavelli does not deny the significance of religion in the life of a political community, and even though he regards the religious world as an accessory to politics he appreciates that it represents a common human need which cannot be explained in purely individual terms. Machiavelli's sense of history makes him aware that historical circumstances – whether a state is at war or peace, internally stable or disrupted by civil war or fear of attack – shape the political virtues which a state can exhibit. His support for republicanism may be understood in this light, that political glory is dependent on historical and structural features which individuals to a great extent find beyond their control. Machiavelli's emphasis on power does not commit him to an uncritical adulation of its use in any context. He is quick to condemn tyranny and those who employ power for evil and destructive purposes to create instability and disorder.

Such considerations qualify the force of Machiavelli's realism but they do not eradicate it. For Machiavelli, political action takes place not in an ordered and rational universe but in a hostile and unpredictable world. Fortune is Machiavelli's way of describing the obstacles to political success. It represents the external world over which human conduct has little or no control. Virtue refers to the knowledge required if Fortune is to be overcome, and it is manifested in courage, strength of will, and foresight. On the simplest level the relation between Virtue and Fortune is like that between purpose and choice. While luck and risk cannot be overcome completely, and while there is no guarantee of success, Machiavelli considers that the most determined will keep the spoliations of misfortune to a minimum. The only way to avoid political failure, which almost always means death, is to fit in with the ways of Fortune and this means cultivating the capacity to predict her actions. It is foreknowledge which determines political success, being able to perceive the shape of future events so as to identify the alternative courses of political action available. This process of identification rests on Machiavelli's cyclical theory of history, but it is political virtue which marks off political success from failure in the quickness with which it grasps the movement of events. In what does political virtue consist?

It is important to distinguish moral and political virtue. Humility, charity, and honesty are private virtues but they are useless and sometimes dangerous in politics. Rule requires political virtue, a strong military order, expressed in Machiavelli's admiration for Roman republicanism which embodied a strong constitution, mixed and limited government, rule of law, civil liberty, and patriotism. These ideals are given practical expression in Machiavelli's detailed political maxims regarding mercenaries, spies, and conspiracies. Political virtue involves a state of constant anticipation, most dramatically expressed in political circumstances of severe transformation and disruption in which the fabric of the state is under strain and rule under threat. The most admirable political response is to attack Fortune with boldness and resolution. To reduce the risks it is prudent to employ Fortune to your own advantage, to see what actions the times will allow, to decide whether they demand courage, determination, or patience. What Machiavelli does not admire is facing the political world in deliberate and prolonged resistance to the run of events. This will bring disaster as also will the belief that a ruler can lie low and wait until the storm has passed. But the most reprehensible choice is to confront the political world armed with the private moral virtues and a determination to be loyal to them come what may.

Machiavelli considers political virtue can be made compatible with Fortune, although it cannot be overcome completely. In politics there are no complete or final victories. The most we can expect is that by the exercise of political virtue rulers will anticipate and prepare for the worst. The estimable politician lives in the future, but even he may find that his policies are outwitted by Fortune and his decision and prudence come to nothing. Political knowledge involves the exclusion of private morality. The ruler requires a flexibility not possible in the context of formal moral rules and procedures. This does not simply mean duplicity, the choice of masks to protect identity and motive in hostile political arenas. It does not refer only to the choice of political strategy – to be the 'lion or the fox'. As one commentator puts it:

> The 'reason of state' (ragione di stato) is the cause of morality, and higher moral law in the light of which the seemingly immoral acts necessary to politics are trans-valued.[5]

We should be in no doubt as to the nature of the conduct which Machiavelli considers politically necessary. In *The Discourses* he specifies what may be done in defence of the state:

> where the very safety of the country depends upon the resolution to be taken, no considerations of justice or injustice, humanity or cruelty, nor of glory or of shame, should be allowed to prevail.[6]

In these circumstances, Machiavelli argues, it may be necessary to perform acts which may range from fraud to murder. This is not moral nihilism, for values like integrity and honesty still have importance in private life. In the public realm, however, they may be held in suspension; one must be ready to displace them by political necessities which go beyond them and which Machiavelli considers are primary. This point is grasped by Hegel who comments:

> Machiavelli's fundamental aim of erecting Italy into a state was misunderstood from the start by the blind who took his work as nothing but a foundation of tyranny or a golden mirror for an ambitious oppressor. But even if his aim were accepted, it was

said that the means were detestable, and thus moralising had further room for displaying its platitudes, such as that the end does not justify the means. In this instance, however, there can be no question of any choice of means. Gangrenous limbs cannot be cured with lavender water. A situation in which poison and assassination are common weapons demands remedies of no gentle kind. When life is on the brink of decay it can be reorganized only by a procedure involving the maximum of force.[7]

With these ideas before us we can construct Machiavelli's evaluation of moral innocence and its impact on politics. It represents a life of quietistic virtue, a belief in goodness which Machiavelli considers to be flatly contradicted by the facts of human nature. In politics its characteristic virtues of integrity and charity are an invitation to political exploitation and disorder. Innocent rule lacks the experience necessary to identify those we can trust and those who are our enemies. It has no need to anticipate threats because it is fully confident that none will materialize. Its unrealistic confidence that evil will be overcome by good means that its knowledge of stratagem and device has been retarded. The idea of using immoral means to achieve moral ends has no significance for it and in the political situation which Hegel describes its virtue is empty.

These conclusions are not as irresistible as they appear. They are weakened by a number of difficulties in Machiavelli's analysis of the relation between morality and politics which lacks metaphysical grounding and involves many contradictions and oversights. His sceptical view of human nature undermines his republicanism and vitiates his account of the distinction between public and private. If human beings are naturally selfish then what is the basis of the contrast between morality and politics? Is it an unlimited contrast or are there important moral qualifications of degree? Machiavelli's conceptions of political necessity and political virtue form a realism which pushes him towards an unrestricted contrast between morality and politics. His is an instrumental account of the dangers of moral innocence. He emphasizes its undesirable outcomes for the political community, but he assumes that the displacement of the moral by the political is a consequential matter. It is clear now that we need a non-consequential sense of this displacement. We need an account of political morality more receptive to the idea of moral innocence and the impact it has on politics.

So I wish to consider a work which is neither contractualist nor utilitarian in its assumptions. In a short and neglected section in Bosanquet's *The Philosophical Theory of the State*[8] he examines the morality of public and private action. I shall not consider the extent to which Bosanquet's arguments in this section are logically independent of the general Idealist metaphysic which informs the book, but it is worth emphasizing that I want to give them a slightly different function. Bosanquet sees the problem of political morality not in terms of the conflict between morality and politics but in terms of the morality of public and private action. How does Bosanquet explain the difference between these two concepts? The state as the embodiment of a political community cannot be construed as a private actor. Its ends are public ends and in practical life this means those ends which its institutions, practices, and policies embody. The political world is a public world involving public aims and purposes which cannot be reduced to the aims and purposes of private individuals. The actions of a state are those of an institution which possesses authority and power and which, as Bosanquet puts it, 'has ultimate responsibility for protecting the form of life of which it is the guardian.'[9] There is a logical distinction between acts performed by private individuals and acts performed by public, political bodies.

> A public act which inflicts loss, such as war, confiscation, the repudiation of a debt, is wholly different from murder or theft. It is not the act of a private person. It is not a violation of law. It can hardly be motivated by private malice or cupidity in the strict sense . . .[10]

Does this mean that Bosanquet considers that public acts are immune from moral criticism? On the contrary, they can be criticized morally but not in terms which would apply to the acts of individuals. In part this is because the state is not reducible to the intentions and actions of its agents. There is a danger in this line of argument which Bosanquet recognizes. It suggests that the state remains pure whatever crimes its agents commit. But this risk is not sufficient to alter the logical contrast between public and private acts. This is given further weight in the argument that private beliefs in public contexts can result in persecution and intimidation. This is supplementary to Bosanquet's main point which concerns the moral evaluation of public acts. If they cannot be judged as analogous to private conduct then what is the basis for their moral scrutiny?

In relation to promise-keeping and the upholding of treaty obligations Bosanquet considers that the state is morally bound, but not because they are matters of private honour. Promise-keeping embodies public ends, but even in cases where the decision to uphold a treaty is problematic the question is decided by reference to public and not private considerations. Bosanquet acknowledges that the state cannot be morally indifferent, but to what extent do its public ends justify immorality on their behalf?

> we deny that States can be treated as the actors in private
> immoralities which their agents permit themselves in the alleged
> interest of the State; or, again, can be bound by the private
> honour and conscience of such agents; and we deny, moreover,
> that the avowed public acts of sovereign powers which cause loss
> or injury, can be imputed to individuals under the names of
> private offences; that someone is guilty of murder when a country
> carries on war, or of theft when it adopts the policy of repudiation,
> confiscation or annexation.[11]

Bosanquet's assertions draw our attention to the distinction between office and office-holder and to the importance of the contrast between public and private acts for a morally sophisticated vocabulary. Public immorality does not refer to cases where public officials are corrupted for private gain, and the contrast is with a state which acts out of a selfish and brutal conception of its interests. In this latter case it is the state as such which is acting immorally, and here Bosanquet argues it is to be judged by reference to 'the tribunal of humanity and of history'.[12]

The public/private distinction exists in the context of Bosanquet's doctrine of the state, which depends on Idealist conceptions of logic and the interpretation which Bosanquet gives to Rousseau's idea of the General Will. These features make it difficult for him to consider the state as a subject for moral criticism even in its public persona. So Bosanquet tends to oscillate between the state and the international community as the ultimate court of ethical appeal on such questions, which means that many complex areas of political morality are ignored or approached with philosophically preconceived ideas. Nevertheless, the attempt to draw logical distinctions between public and private is a necessary step in tackling the problems of political morality. Bosanquet gives us no adequate theory for the moral evaluation of public acts, the immoralities they may justify, and the interaction between moral character and public world, between office-holder and office. The contrast between morality and politics is not drawn by Bosanquet in instrumental terms but even so this insight needs to be extended if the autonomy of politics is to be fully appreciated.

Public acts are not analogous to the acts of private individuals, the weakest sense of Bosanquet's non-instrumentalism. Oakeshott, too, denies that civility is a condition of prudence, but neither can it be deduced from any system of moral rules or imperatives.

> Civil relationship is certainly a fiduciary relationship in which faithfulness is not a device for promoting the satisfaction of substantive wants; but it is not the faithfulness of friends.[13]

The absence of a direct line of inference between morality and politics does not deflect Oakeshott from his belief 'that civil desirabilities are unconnected with more intimate moral relationships . . . That it is not necessarily a sign of something amiss if they are not found to be pulling in the same direction . . .'[14]

It is precisely with the non-instrumental nature of such connections that we are concerned. Dissection of the idea of the public enables us to explore how moral character may have its impact. The disanalogy between public and private is the preliminary move in this direction. In modern politics, offices endow rights and obligations which cannot be reduced to matters of individual character and motivation. The special responsibility of public affairs lies in the fact that its policies have consequences for the lives and well-being of great numbers of persons unknown to those forming the policies. Public and private are related through the ideas of accountability and representation which mean that in public life, as Hampshire has pointed out,[15] it is necessary not only to protect interests but also to explain and justify the policies which affect them in a uniquely explicit way.

It is wrong, therefore, to apply to political life the same moral standards that are appropriate in private life. Public violence and its threat have always been in prospect in politics, and in the execution of policy. This introduces moral problems associated with the justice of war and revolution, the occasions of the justifiable use of force both in terms of its weaponry and its legitimate targets, and the sense in which collectivities can be blamed. None of these matters can be discussed by analogy with individual morality. Inevitably this involves the problem of 'Dirty Hands'. If political morality is a consequentialist morality it is wrong to be morally fastidious regarding choice of means. In politics, hands may be stained in various ways ranging from deceit to the murder of political opponents and innocent victims. Hampshire argues:

> The assumption of a political role . . . carries . . . a new
> responsibility, which entails . . . a withholding of some of the
> scruples that in private life would prohibit one from using people
> as a means to an end and also from using force and deceit.[16]

Now which scruples are to be withheld? We need to discover why someone who chooses not to withhold moral scruple can bring about political disaster.

I am concerned with what recent analyses of the 'Dirty Hands' problem[17] say regarding the apparent discrepancy between virtue and politics. Walzer, for example, argues that the problem has to be understood within morality and it exemplifies a particular type of moral dilemma in which the choice is not between the right and the expedient but between alternative actions both of which it would be morally wrong to perform. From the standpoint of utilitarianism such a dilemma is illusory. The right course of action is established by the calculation of consequences. There can be no intrinsic conflict between moral principles which is not open to resolution in this way. But utilitarianism does nothing to prevent the large-scale treatment of individuals as means, and it cannot account for an individual who has made such calculations continuing to feel that he has acted wrongly even though the consequences he hoped for have come about. The importance of this rejection of utilitarianism is that it places the idea of moral character in the centre of the 'Dirty Hands' problem, which means that political morality has to be understood from the perspective of the moral agent and not as the abstract calculation and assessment of impersonal outcomes. But if utilitarian considerations are excluded where lies the contrast with politics which creates the moral difficulty? For Thomas Nagel, for example, it is essential to give a non-utilitarian account of public morality if the limits to ruthlessness in public life are to be cogently established.[18] The attempt to restrict the incidence of 'Dirty Hands' by a tighter specification of the moral rules which govern institutions and offices does not entirely square with the emphasis on moral character in politics. Even so, the institutional rules governing individual moral decisions by office-holders would still have to be scrutinized and applied by individual moral agents and this means that moral character cannot be completely excluded from the dilemmas which may arise.

Is it possible to govern innocently? Walzer's answer is that it is not and, further, it is not desirable that it should be. 'Dirty Hands' problems take the form of moral dilemmas which are intrinsic to engagement in politics. We cannot act well in politics without confronting them and being prepared to pay the moral cost they involve. The moral dilemma is disclosed in politics when we realize that:

> sometimes it is right to try to succeed, and then it must also be
> right to get one's hands dirty. But one's hands get dirty from
> doing what it is wrong to do. And how can it be wrong to do what
> is right? Or, how can we get our hands dirty by doing what we
> ought to do?[19]

Walzer asks us to imagine a politician who 'wants to do good only by doing good'. What are we to make of him when his moral intentions are tested?

> In order to win the election the candidate must make a deal with a
> dishonest ward boss, involving the granting of contracts for school
> construction over the next four years. Should he make the deal?[20]

The problem lies in the candidate's goodness. He holds fast to moral principle and he has done so consistently in the past. It is because he has moral scruples regarding what he should or should not do that we regard him as an admirable candidate. On the other hand, election victory will mean that many desirable political projects can be achieved. A candidate who is thought of as susceptible to corruption will be defeated. The difference is that if the candidate with moral integrity makes the deal he knows that he has acted immorally.

> We know he is doing right when he makes the deal because he
> knows he is doing wrong. I don't mean merely that he will feel
> badly or even very badly after he makes the deal. If he is the good
> man I am imagining him to be, he will feel guilty, that is he will

80

believe himself to be guilty. That is what it means to have dirty hands.[21]

It is important to realize that the moral character of the person who is prepared to dirty his hands in this way is regarded by Walzer as praiseworthy.

> he is not too good for politics and he is good enough. Here is the moral politician: it is by his dirty hands that we know him. If he were a moral man and nothing else, his hands would not be dirty; if he were a politician and nothing else, he would pretend that they were clean.[22]

Further, Walzer's belief in the impossibility of governing innocently is his sense that someone might be described as 'too good for politics'. This does not require any specific belief in the essential corruptibility of politics. Nor does it simply mean that such a person might think that they could achieve morally desirable ends without being tested. Equally, the fact that someone may be morally in advance of a particular practice is often an additional reason for finding their character admirable. Rather Walzer considers that someone who chooses absolute virtue against moral flexibility will not only fail to do the right thing in terms of beneficial outcomes, but may also abdicate from the duties and responsibilities of office. It might be said that one of the great strengths of the absolute position is that it completely refuses to do deals with virtue, but for Walzer 'We would not want to be governed by men who consistently adopted that position.'[23]

This view is shared by many writers. Nagel, for example, refers to 'a loosening of the requirement that one always pursue the best results'.[24] As Nagel realizes, this is a dangerous manoeuvre and he attempts to minimize the risks by increasing specification of the rules which govern the actions of office-holders.

Bernard Williams is another who is prepared to accept a space between moral and political considerations without committing himself to a full-scale consequentialism.

> it is a predictable and probable hazard of public life that there will be these situations in which something morally disagreeable is clearly required. To refuse on moral grounds ever to do anything of that sort is more than likely to mean that one cannot seriously pursue even the moral ends of politics.[25]

Williams accepts this does not mean that the morally objectionable nature of such acts is simply cancelled. Guilt on the part of the moral agent who performs them will prevent this and a further obstacle is the moral reaction of the victims of such acts. Nevertheless, Williams persists in his argument that the space must remain for two reasons. First, that in politics, as in private life, there is no disposition that is correct all the time. Second, that in politics, as in the law, it is necessary to be sensitive to moral costs. This is not to assert a comprehensive utilitarianism but to claim that there are circumstances where the cost of not allowing moral considerations to be over-ridden are too great to bear. Williams concludes that the problem of 'Dirty Hands' will only admit of solution by a narrowing of the gap between the moral and the political, in other words by closing the distance between Plato and Machiavelli.

> . . . allowing both that the good need not be as pure as all that, so long as they retain some active sense of moral costs and moral limits; and that the society has some genuinely settled politics and some expectations of civic respectability.[26]

So this conclusion does not allow for the presence of goodness in circumstances of political upheaval where civic expectations are minimal. Williams' tactic of narrowing the gap from both ends results in a rather bland view of political morality in which moral determination and integrity are sacrificed to a conventional politics.

Martin Hollis[27] accepts that in politics it is sometimes necessary to abandon principle if anything is to be achieved. I assume that Hollis means the abandonment of principle not to advantage but to the satisfaction of a political good. He contrasts this first with an ethic which is not prepared to accept accommodation to consequences in any circumstances. By this standard any counting of the costs, any consideration other than the strict unswerving adherence to moral principle, will be moral treason. The scriptural example he gives is:

> 'Love your enemies, do good to them that hate you, bless them that curse you, and pray for them that despitefully use you'.[28]

For Hollis, it is relatively easy to challenge this kind of absolute ethic on consequentialist lines and he contrasts it with a flexible under-standing of duty in which individuals have to choose which principles apply in a given situation or decide what action a particular principle requires. But these criticisms also apply to the role of moral principle in moral life and do not specify the problematic nature of such principles in a political context. So Hollis outlines the claim that the same integrity which governs private life is applicable to political conduct. It is the notion of private integrity which causes the problem. If moral integrity is expressed as unconditional and unqualified then there is no reason to consider political considerations as exceptions. But for Hollis:

> there are several reasons for thinking that the statesman should not practise the moral consistency of a rhinoceros. The integrity of the martyr is saved at his own expense, whereas the statesman's refusal to compromise is paid for by his people. The martyr concedes nothing to the differing moral opinions of his neighbours, whereas the statesman represents both the martyr and his neighbours . . . . The martyr goes to the stake himself and that we admire. But, let loose with political power, he sends others to the stake with an equal will, and, in shutting his eyes to the moral nuances of political life without thereby abolishing them, he licenses very foul play, provided that it is conducted outside the limits of his simple moral lexicon. This seems to me the result of flatly denying all the presumptions which make the Dirty Hands problem both urgent and difficult.[29]

Hollis emphasizes the moral constrictions of office-holding in politics. To this extent his position is close to Nagel's; he wishes to bring the integrity connected with office within the moral dilemmas of political morality. By so doing he stresses that the generation of some moral dilemmas arises specifically from the moral integrity due to office which cannot be reduced to the beliefs of the individual who contingently happens to occupy it, and that clean hands in politics are not guaranteed by resigning from office or stepping aside from its responsibilities. But what is not so satisfactory is his explanation for the occurrence of 'Dirty Hands'.

> Why, precisely, then, must good men apply principle so deviously that dishonesty becomes a virtue?[30]

His answer is that in the context of diverse conceptions of the good and the plurality of values politics must compromise absolute goodness and find what integrity it can in trimming. Every resolution of the dilemmas of political morality will be partial and incomplete. All political decisions are morally blighted to some degree, and those who make them have to recognize that in political life their character will remain morally incomplete.

Barrie Paskins agrees with the general position that it is not possible to govern guiltlessly, but his conclusion is not that we must compromise with morality, rather that it should be eliminated altogether. If it is moral scruple which prevents the achievement of a morally desirable end then why bother with morality at all? There may be some circumstances where it is morality which is responsible for the problem in which an individual finds himself.

> Healthier, less exploitable and more realistic is the view that morality, which has us inescapably in its grip, shows in some situations the aspect of a destroyer, demanding the deaths of people to whom the good man has nothing but good wishes.[31]

What is not clear is how morality is to be transcended, and it is surely the case that Paskins' argument is directed against not morality as such but particular moral conceptions within it.

All these views share a hostility to the moral character which Walzer describes as 'too good for politics'. Politics would be impossible if such individuals ruled. But what kind of good character do they mean? We must recognize that there is a strong ingredient of paradox involved in the criticism that the good should not rule. It is not as if it is suggested that the bad should rule but rather that if the good ruled they would be blind to the kinds of necessities which the bad deal in day by day. It is because lying comes easily to the bad that we do not want them to rule. We need a strong argument to discover why goodness is disqualified from politics. What view emerges from these discussions of 'Dirty Hands'?

The picture is of a moral character possessing either a particular kind of intractability or a preoccupation with its moral purity. Hollis describes this disposition in terms of duty, principle, or ethical imperative. Morality is conceived as providing a set of guidelines which must be rigidly adhered to. Alternatively, obsession with virtue demands that it remain unblemished whatever the consequences. If it is to survive, morality cannot tolerate deviation. This is a picture of morality as a matter of private integrity, and if this is what absolute virtue amounts to then it means a kind of selfishness, of putting one's moral self above everything else. Hollis exaggerates when he claims that this means ordering others to die for the sake of ethical beliefs or tolerating foul play because preoccupation with personal integrity paralyses one. It is surely a travestied account of goodness which conceives absolute virtue to be a tough, thick-skinned determination to maintain its purity at any cost. Indeed there is considerable equivocation in Hollis' description of the individual of absolute virtue. In one form he embodies the abstract framework of Kant's moral imperatives, in another he is the clear voice of conscience, and in yet another guise the martyr who accepts death rather than betray his public cause. It is not clear that these moral personae can be amalgamated to form the one coherent good character which should not have a place in politics. If this is true, then precisely why goodness and politics are seen as incompatible has not yet been established.

The root difficulty in this view is in its attempts to bring morality and politics together in an over-simple way. It requires that morality be thought of as less pure and politics as less impure than they are commonly thought to be. But the moral end of their relationship is expressed in a way which ignores the standpoint of the agent and neglects important moral differences within virtuous dispositions and a range of connections between morality and political vulnerability. Consider the importance of self-understanding in morality, the contrasting ways in which moral agents may perceive their own virtue. Someone may regard his goodness of character with pride and his virtuous disposition as an admirable achievement, a moral triumph over the temptations and challenges of the world. The man of justifiable pride will be confident in his courage, moral leadership, and capacity to pass the most onerous tests life may place before his virtue. This disposition does not hide itself away but requires a public stage on which its moral exploits can be paraded and applauded. By way of contrast, another may wear his virtue lightly with a spontaneous indifference to its value. He may consider his integrity to be perfectly natural and he may disregard any moral praise his actions elicit. Goodness may be expressed innocent of self and the challenges of the world. Such virtue is unreflective and does not need an additional defence from either the abstract utterance of reason or the self-confirmation of pride. These contrasting dispositions mean that morality may be an obstacle to political judgement in different ways and not simply as a framework of moral principle through which political proposals cannot pass. Moral innocence implies an unaware-ness of self which places it beyond incorporation in politics. Pride involves a preoccupation with self which threatens the political realm in a significantly different way. Analysis of this aspires to a richer conception of the relation between morality and politics than that assumed so far.

Earlier I discussed Williams' view that a total moral embargo on performing morally disagreeable actions would lead to political ineffectiveness even where the moral aims of politics were concerned. For Williams, moral commitment means a refusal to make the moral compromises necessary for political action. But how is it that moral refusal can lead to political catastrophe? We need a tighter explanation of this connection than unintended consequence. In Williams' book *Ethics and the Limits of Philosophy* he refers to Aristotle's discovery of what Williams calls the Coriolanus paradox:

> . . . about people who make the aim of their life political honour [and who] tend to defeat themselves by making themselves dependent on those to whom they aim to be superior.[32]

The element of self-defeat involved in pride is a source of preoccupation for both moral and political philosophy. It forms an essential part of Hobbes' description of human nature and it receives a more explicit political expression in Machiavelli's defence of the public institution of impeachment in *The Discourses*, where he writes of Coriolanus:

> all should reflect on the evils that might have ensued in the Roman republic had he been tumultuously put to death, for this would have been an act of private vengeance, which would have aroused fear; and fear would have led to defensive action; this to the procuring of partisans; partisans would have meant the formation of factions in the city; and factions would have brought about its downfall.[33]

Machiavelli's concern is to identify those moral dispositions which are sources of political dissonance and to construct a framework of public law which will resist the excesses of private self-regard. Pride as a threat to the public realm is perhaps nowhere better explored than in Shakespeare's *Coriolanus*.

In any reading of the character of Coriolanus the idea of his nobility must play a vital part. It dominates both his moral disposition and his political conduct. It rules both his private understanding and his public reputation. But it should not be thought that nobility confers upon Coriolanus the character of the simple good man whose conscience provides his guide to personal and political life. On the contrary, the idea of nobility, of a life lived in accordance with an ideal of heroic virtue, involves a high degree of ambiguity and indeterminacy which first expresses itself as straightforward political disagreement over the merits of Coriolanus as a statesman. Two officers discuss his appointment as Consul:

> *First Officer.* 'That's a brave fellow; but he's vengeance proud, and loves not common people.'
> *Second Officer.* '. . . There have been many great men that have flattered the people, who never loved them; and there be many that they have loved, they know not wherefore; so that if they love they know not why, they hate upon no better a ground.'[34]

These contrasting estimates of Coriolanus raise the question of his exclusive attachment to honour in a way which leaves open the nature of his motivation. Precisely why he acts as he does is left obscure. Aufidius finds it impossible to locate the true source of Coriolanus's character. He attempts to analyse the nature of his dangerous ally:

> whether 'twas pride, which out of daily fortune ever taints the happy man; whether defect of judgement, to fail in the disposing of those chances which he was lord of; or whether nature, not to be other than one thing.[35]

To emphasize pride as a central preoccupation in the drama is to follow a long line of interpretation. When Coriolanus pursues honour he does so as an embodiment of the authority of Rome. Nothing less than perfection will satisfy him in the execution of these public duties, and what guides and controls his conduct are the public virtues of courage, steadfastness, and self-sacrifice. But honour requires a rejection of all forms of human weakness and this becomes something like an attempt to cut free from all human relations. He wishes to:

> Stand,
> As if a man were author of himself,
> And know no other kind.[36]

The attachment to honour as an end in itself becomes quite naturally a source of pride, and this makes it very different from those states of mind which look like it and are often a reason for moral commendation. Virtues such as self-respect or self-regard are transformed into the vice of pride when the agent's attention is fixed on himself as the performer of the action rather than on the worth of the action itself. What distinguishes pride from conceit or vanity is that it regards truly worthwhile actions and capacities as the exclusive property of the person who performs or possesses them. When those actions and capacities refer to achieved moral goodness pride distorts their value by emphasizing not their intrinsic worth but only the self that performs them. It is in this sense that Hume speaks of the object of pride as self. Virtues which were once communal and public in character are transformed through pride into vices of an individualistic and egocentric kind. The pride which Coriolanus has in his own rectitude is seen by the tribunes, either seriously or for reasons of political advantage, as inhuman:

> You speak of the people
> As if you were a god to punish, not
> A man of their infirmity.[37]

Thus Coriolanus may be understood as representing a most profound source of political dissociation. Through his pride the values which sustain the life of a political community are dramatically altered to such a degree that they become the causes of political disintegration and dismemberment. Rome at peace is torn by strife and discord. Rome at war sees victory decline into possible defeat. How is pride destructive of the exercise of judgement, a faculty crucially important to the flourishing of political communities? How is pride, an individual moral defect, connected with political disaster? Within the play, individual character and disposition receive opportunity for political expression in a number of distinct ways. Individuality may be asserted through the formal, public offices of state. The offices of tribune and consul, the inherited description of patrician and plebeian, are logically distinguishable from their bearers. This provides space for freedom of action, a degree of limited contingency which renders possible the development of events. Individual actions are performed in an already existing political context and often involve consequences which were unintended. The political divide between patrician and plebeian, the onset of famine, the state of war between Roman and Volscian, none of these is the subject of individual choice. The intrigues in the name of political power and the betrayals which lead to death and defeat exemplify how what results from action is precisely the opposite of that intended. Thus the agent is placed both in the context of formal, public office and in the realm of historical indeterminacy.

These general truths elucidate neither the specific logic of pride nor its connection with a wider political world. Some insight is provided here by Hume in the Third Book of *A Treatise of Human Nature* where he discusses the nature of heroic virtue. By this Hume means the values of courage, boldness, intrepidity, ambition, love of glory, and magnanimity, all of which contain what he calls 'a strong mixture of self-esteem'. The historical exmple of this disposition which Hume discusses is Alexander the Great:

> Go, says Alexander the Great to his soldiers, when they refused to follow him to the Indies, go tell your countrymen, that you left Alexander completing the conquest of the world.[38]

This is explained by Hume in the form of a quotation from a contemporary:

> Alexander abandoned by his soldiers, among barbarians, not yet fully subdued, felt in himself such a dignity and right of empire, that he could not believe it possible that anyone could refuse to obey him. Whether in Europe or in Asia, among Greeks or Persians, all was indifferent to him: Wherever he found men, he fancied he had found subjects.[39]

There are clues here to the character of Coriolanus. Consider his reaction during the battle for Corioli when its conclusion is finely balanced. As the Roman soldiers are forced to retreat he says:

> All the contagion of the south light on you,
> You shames of Rome! you herd of – Boils and plagues
> Plaster you o'er, that you may be abhorred
> Further than seen, and one infect another
> Against the wind a mile! You souls of geese,
> That bear the shapes of men, how have you run
> From slaves that apes would beat! Pluto and hell!
> All hurt behind; backs red, and faces pale
> With flight and agu'd fear! Mend and charge home,
> Or, by the fires of heaven, I'll leave the foe
> And make my wars on you;[40]

This unshakeable confidence in both his principles and his military prowess enables Coriolanus to take Corioli almost single-handed. The qualities which give him this conviction – his courage and indifference to personal injury, his willingness to risk his life for the achievement of a public cause – are commonly thought to be reasons for praise or admiration. But it is a logical curiosity of the presence of pride that these values are negated and transformed into a dreadful parody of their original form. Pride itself introduces a degree of indeterminacy in the matching of action and evaluation. Hume, in an interesting passage, is aware of the political implications of this logical peculiarity.

> We may observe, that an excessive courage and magnanimity, especially when it displays itself under the frowns of fortune, contributes, in a great measure, to the character of a hero, and will render a person the admiration of posterity; and at the same time that it ruins his affairs, and leads him into dangers and difficulties, with which otherwise he would never have been acquainted.[41]

Hume asserts a connection between pride and political disaster, a claim which is intuitively appealing. Do the consequences of the decisions taken by Coriolanus just happen to turn out as they do or are they in some sense necessarily connected with his character? It is important to put the question like this because of the number of opportunities Coriolanus has for deciding differently. Here we may usefully contrast his position with that of Agamemnon portrayed by Aeschylus. Both are rulers doomed by their natures, but Agamemnon's decision on his return from Troy to walk on purple, so taking for himself the glory of conquest, results in immediate retribution. No space exists between his pride and his death. For Coriolanus the circumstances are different. His conduct during the speech to the people, his demeanour wearing the gown of humility, his decision to betray Rome and join forces with Aufidius, and finally his yielding to the pleas of his mother, Volumnia, all provide opportunities for self-awareness. Within these changing conditions of action and decision it is pride which maintains a permanent motif but its precise connection with its consequences – political strife, defeat, and death – remains elusive. Possible explanations of this connection refer to different dimensions of pride in its political aspect, as self-interest, class-rule, historical stratagem, and moral ignorance.

To say that the object of pride is self-interest is to emphasize the acquisitive element in human nature. It is to suggest that human motivation is ultimately egocentric and that human freedom can be measured in direct proportion to the capacity to satisfy wants. In his *Lectures on the History of Philosophy* Hegel describes self-assertion as:

> the working-day when man stands up independently, is master of himself and considers his own interests.[42]

It is important, therefore, both to identify material ambitions and to know how to satisfy them. Such knowledge consists in the skill of calculation. It is the art of knowing which means to employ so as most efficiently to achieve particular ends or the degree of exertion required to gain most reward. If the object of pride is self-interest then its political expression is the use of political power for personal advantage. A public role conceals private avarice. Here disaster or ruin results not from pride as such but from those inefficient, clumsy or unskilful tactics which are employed in its name.

Does this interpretation make sense of the conduct of Coriolanus? The motive for his military endeavour is clearly not material reward. When Cominius offers him a tenth share of the spoils of battle after the victory over the Volscians, Coriolanus refuses:

> I thank you general;
> But cannot make my heart consent to take
> A bribe to pay my sword: I do refuse it;
> And stand upon my common part with those
> That have beheld the doing.[43]

His sense of public duty is such that the very idea of rewarding a virtuous act with payment is a profanity upon his honour. Further, he thinks it is a vulgar mistake to conceive the state as merely a device for satisfying the particular wants of its members. In his scathing criticism of the tribunes he says:

> Your dishonour
> Mangles true judgement, and bereaves the state
> Of that integrity which should become it,
> Not having the power to do the good it would,
> For the ill which doth control it.[44]

His emphasis upon honour as opposed to prudence enables Coriolanus to entertain what Cominius calls 'odds beyond arithmetic'. His virtue is not for sale and his sense of his own nobility is not reducible to relative advantage. Coriolanus takes this to the point of self-sacrifice, a willingness to endure pain, suffering, and death for the sake of an ethical ideal. These are absolute obligations for him. There can be no negotiation with them and if they are compromised or conciliated then that is a reason for shame. It should be clear, therefore, that from the perspective of self-interest no light is thrown on why Coriolanus acts as he does. The application of its vocabulary to his conduct leads to absurdity. Self-interest presupposes the continued existence of the self. Coriolanus not only endangers it, harms it, and risks it, he ultimately destroys it. Political self-interest presupposes the continuation of a state through which to work its acquisitive psychology. Coriolanus not only risks it in defeat, he betrays it to its greatest enemy. His pride cannot be elucidated in terms of self-benefit, and his betrayal was not, as many acts of treason often are, motivated by greed.

Pride can be seen as a manifestation of the inequality of classes. The arrogance of Coriolanus becomes that of class superiority, his insolence an expression of class domination. On this view patrician and plebeian are divided by class interest. Famine makes the citizens aware of inequalities. They complain about the distribution of food and the rates of usury. When their tribunes incite them they are led to make increasingly serious challenges to patrician authority. Their demands play an important part in the banishment of Coriolanus and reach the point of near open rebellion. Here is the historical dimension of early Roman politics. It places emphasis on deep social conflict and on the existence of social identities which are independent of any individual characteristics. But in Marxist theory such antimonies are almost always exaggerated. There are important mutual dependencies between patrician and plebeian. The rulers realize that without the active support of the ruled warfare cannot be prosecuted successfully. Both accept the Volscians as a common enemy and a threat to Rome.

Unity within a class can be shown to be deceptive in other ways. It fails to explain the real political disagreement which exists between Menenius and Coriolanus. The two patricians argue how best to respond to the increasing demands of the People's Tribunes:

Coriolanus. 'What must I do?'
Menenius. 'Return to the tribunes.'

Coriolanus. 'Well, what then? What then?'
Menenius. 'Repent what you have spoke.'
Coriolanus. 'For them! I cannot do it to the Gods; must I then do it to them?'[45]

It is certainly true that Coriolanus reviles the plebeians in terms of open contempt, but what often goes unrecognized is that such sentiments are based on principles which actually lead to multiplying dangers for all members of the state. In his first speech Coriolanus says:

> What's the matter, you dissentious rogues,
> That, rubbing the poor itch of your opinion
> Make yourselves scabs?[46]

Such contempt is not simply wilful. It is based on a degree of pride which ultimately proves impossible for a republic to contain. The consequence is that, following his decision to betray Rome and join Aufidius, Coriolanus instils panic and indecision in patrician and plebeian alike. The reasons for this are identified as much by the citizens as they are by the aristocracy. During his questioning of Coriolanus in Act II the Third Citizen says:

> You have deserved nobly of your
> country, and you have not deserved nobly.[47]

Coriolanus is not seen here as simply a representative of class ascendance. This is to omit everything which makes him a constant exasperation to all factions in the state. The tribunes find that their attempts to manipulate him result in bewilderment. The political art cannot be reduced to intrigue and persuasion. One writer who notices this is Bertolt Brecht who, in his study of the first scene of the play, writes of Coriolanus:

> His switch from being the most Roman of the Romans to
> becoming their deadliest enemy is due precisely to the fact that he
> stays the same.[48]

Brecht is correct to emphasize that Coriolanus 'stays the same' but what he does not realize is that this wrecks the idea of Coriolanus as a class enemy. He is a traitor not to his class but to his country, and this arises because he is not a treacherous man at all. Class analysis, therefore, fails to take into account the full significance of moral character in politics and misunderstands the contrast between principle and prudence, value and policy.

Where pride is seen as historical stratagem it finds its object in political success: Coriolanus links pride with political disaster because he lacks the practical sense necessary to avoid it. He wears the garb of the lion but lacks the mind of the fox. The language here is that of Machiavelli, whose thought had become increasingly well known in England since the mid-sixteenth century. There are clear references to his ideas in the play and not merely to the obvious themes of duplicity and plotting. At a deeper level the Machiavellian concepts of Fortune and Virtue refer to the contingent and unpredictable movements of history and to the kind of political knowledge required to gain mastery of the times. Aufidius says:

> So our virtues
> Lie in the interpretation of the time;
> And power, unto itself most commendable,
> Hath not a tomb so evident as a chair
> To extol what it hath done.[49]

Later, Volumnia reflects on the problematic nature of action for individuals hamstrung by historical uncertainty:

> For myself son,
> I purpose not to wait on Fortune till
> These wars determine:[50]

The wise in politics are those most skilled in avoiding the perils of Fortune. Machiavelli provides a series of maxims for successful statecraft. Of these one of the most dramatic is the political necessity 'to learn how not to be good'. Political disaster may result as Hobbes says from vainglory, from a false estimate of our powers and capacities. Here the significant skills are clearsightedness and foreknowledge. For others it may come from having an unyielding commitment to moral principle. The statesman who refuses to be flexible and adapt principle to policy will necessarily fail. On this view what distinguishes Coriolanus from both Menenius and the tribunes is his refusal to compromise his honour for reasons of political advantage. Menenius is a diplomat, a political negotiator, a striker of bargains. He appreciates that in an imperfect world there is a need for conciliation. As he says of Coriolanus:

> All's well; and might have been much better, if
> He could have temporised.[51]

But here what is regarded as highly desirable by Menenius is impossible for Coriolanus. What for the Machiavellian statesman is a source of pride is for Coriolanus a reason for shame. It is this which makes him a political innocent. While possessed of the mature virtues of bravery and self-sacrifice, in politics he becomes childlike and unworldly. This means that he represents a deadly subversion of the political realm, but not simply because he is tactically inept. He is so dangerous because of his absolute refusal to see politics in terms of history and stratagem. Consider the advice Volumnia offers to her son in Act III. At issue here is the appeasement of the tribunes and the consequent political advantage to be gained. How can honour be compatible with policy? Volumnia adopts the full panoply of Machiavellian regalia:

> If it be honour in your wars to seem
> The same you are not, – which, for your best ends,
> You adopt your policy, – how is it less or worse,
> That it shall hold companionship in peace
> With honour, as in war, since that to both
> It stands in like request.[52]

Coriolanus must speak to the people, but not she says:

> by your own instruction,
> Nor by the matter which your heart prompts
> you,
> But with such words that are but rooted in
> Your tongue, though but bastards and syllables
> Of no allowance to your bosom's truth.[53]

Dissimulation loses its moral taint when employed in the service of ends seen to be politically worthy. For Coriolanus, however, this is not a moral imperative. He knows that it is false to his nature. He asks:

> Must I with my base tongue give to my noble heart
> A lie that it must bear?[54]

He decides to adopt what he calls the 'harlot's spirit', but his decision proves disastrous. He is incapable of disguise. His nobility leads to his banishment and his words:

> Despising,
> For you, the city, thus I turn my back:
> There is a world elsewhere[55]

It is not that Coriolanus is *unaware* of the value of the advantages to be gained by political pretence. It is rather that such pretence is impossible for him. There can be no doing deals with virtue. Nobility can never be matched with cunning. The sense of impossibility involved here does not arise because he does not know which stratagems to deploy so as to best protect the state against the ravages of Fortune. He is perfectly aware of the precepts which provide such advice. Impossibility arises because Coriolanus does not look at the political world in these terms at all.

Pride as moral ignorance asks precisely *why* Coriolanus sees certain actions as impossible. To begin we may stress that Coriolanus does not deceive anyone. When he enters the Forum in Act II wearing a gown of humility

> With a proud heart he wore
> His humble weeds.[56]

Coriolanus has no reason to pretend to a humility of which he considers himself unworthy. The objects of his pride – his courage, self-sacrifice, sense of honour – are precisely what we find admirable. Coriolanus may be distinguished from the person who feels proud of something he himself has not achieved or of characteristics he does not possess. Someone who gains an honour through cheating may end up feeling proud not only in front of others, but also in his own eyes. This requires a self-deception unnecessary to Coriolanus. He knows that his principles and achievements are genuine and yet his pride in these accomplishments proves disastrous both for himself and the city. How can this be so?

I want to examine a remark of Simone Weil in her *Lectures on Philosophy*. She says that:

Pride is, above all, an intellectual fault.[57]

To take pride in moral achievement is to have a mistaken under-standing of what that achievement is. It is to expropriate to oneself what is truly available to all. This preoccupation with self inevitably results in the devaluation of that which is normally highly prized. Thus, when Coriolanus is banished he betrays Rome not because his virtues are shown to be illusory but because his personal monopoly of them has been slighted. Furthermore, when his alliance with Aufidius threatens the very existence of Rome, Volumnia expresses her appeal for mercy in terms that she knows Coriolanus will under-stand. It is noble, she asks, for

> The mother, wife, and child to see
> The son, the husband, and the father tearing
> His country's bowels out?[58]

She exhorts him:

> . . . if thou conquer Rome, the benefit
> Which thou shall thereby reap is such a name
> Whose repetition will be dogg'd with curses;
> Whose chronicle thus writ: The man was noble,
> But with his last attempt he wip'd it out,
> Destroy'd his country, and his name remains
> To the ensuing age abhorr'd.[59]

Coriolanus relents, and in so doing sues for peace with Rome guaranteeing his death at the hands of Aufidius. The sustenance of his perfectibility results in disaster. Both tragedy and nobility require that Coriolanus knows this to be the case. He replies to his mother:

> You have won a happy victory to Rome:
> But, for your son, believe it, O! believe it,
> Most dangerously you have with him
> prevailed,
> If not most mortal to him.[60]

What he remains unaware of is the possibility of understanding his moral achievements with the veil of pride lifted. To emphasize this kind of ignorance is to stress precisely what it is about pride in virtue which distorts the understanding of our selves and their relation to a public world. This interpretation of Coriolanus elucidates pride as a source of moral blindness, but it leaves unclear the nature of its connection with political disaster. The consequences clearly do not just happen to turn out as they do. There is a necessity here which needs to be explained. I want to examine an idea which in theology has been traditionally regarded as an antidote to pride, namely, the idea of judgement.

How can pride be destructive of political judgement? The most general answer to this question is that pride impairs precisely the things on which judgement depends. Adam Smith in his *Theory of Moral Sentiments* emphasizes how pride distorts our capacity for making disinterested and impartial judgements. It is for this reason that the proud man is cut off from communal experience. Coriolanus constantly speaks with contempt about the weakness and self-interest of the common citizens. He says:

> *You common cry of curs! whose breath*
> I hate
> As reek o' the rotten fens, whose loves I prize
> *As reek o' the rotten fens, whose loves I prize*
> That do corrupt my air, I banish you;[61]

His self-estimation results in social isolation. There may be a similarity here between Coriolanus and Raskolnikov in Dostoevsky's *Crime and Punishment*. Raskolnikov speaks of the ordinary people with contempt. He calls them 'lice' and sometimes 'parasites'. He contrasts them with extraordinary individuals who are great because of their capacity for feats of vision and daring, which give them the right to break free from the moral obligations which bind other men. But the difference is that pride for Coriolanus has as its object not evil but good. There is, therefore, no room for moral development. For Raskolnikov reintegration with public virtue is possible. He can, and does, recognize that the murder he committed was a crime. For Coriolanus, on the other hand, there is no possibility of redemption. His sense of his own perfectibility precludes it. His exclusion, therefore, is complete. He dies defiantly. His character is unaltered:

> Cut me to pieces, Volsces; men and
> lads,
> Stain all your edges on me. Boy! False hound!
> If you have writ your annals true, 'tis there,
> That, like an eagle in a dove-cote, I
> Flutter'd your Volscians in Corioli:
> Alone I did it. Boy![62]

It is possible, therefore, to disentangle pride and nobility in Coriolanus. Pride removes the conditions of judgement by distorting the capacity for understanding ourselves and others. It diminishes our imagination and undermines agreement. When judgement is impaired political disaster is inevitable. It is in this sense that the character of Coriolanus represents a unique threat to the political world. Pride, in destroying judgement, removes the only ground of its rectification.

I have argued that morality is not simply severed from politics because of its refusal to countenance 'Dirty Hands'. This is not the full reason why Coriolanus represents so deadly a threat to political order. His nobility is openly contemptuous of the institutions and procedures of the republic, and this undermines the trust and mutual agreements on which such public rules depend. Judith Shklar writes of this form of betrayal:

> The public traitor is therefore a threat to the very existence of his society, and is so both because he leaves it to join its enemies, and because he denies its reality, its very definition as his place of origin. Whatever his personal character, in his public presence Coriolanus is a terrifying monster of dissociation. Nevertheless, he imposes mixed responses upon us, because he is far from being base, dishonest, or craven. He is not a treacherous man.[63]

She underestimates the interchange between personal character and public persona but is right to stress that nobility and courage are dispositions we admire. It is not uncompromising virtue which sets Coriolanus apart from the political life of the republic but his pride in his moral character and his scorn for those who seek to undermine it. For Coriolanus it pays to be good, not in the sense of providing external advantage or material reward, but in the sense of confirming his moral superiority.

But what of those whose absolute virtue is not mediated by pride? Such a disposition can have a fatal impact on politics which is not adequately captured by describing its integrity as pure and uncompromising. The idea of moral purity is a complex one – can it be understood as moral innocence? In what sense does it involve excessive virtue?

Chapter Four

ABSOLUTE VIRTUE AND POLITICS

Gwendolen: 'I am always smart! Am I not, Mr Worthing?'
Jack: 'You're quite perfect, Miss Fairfax.'
Gwendolen: 'Oh! I hope I am not that. It would leave no room
  for developments, and I intend to develop in many directions.'
                    (Oscar Wilde, *The Importance of Being Earnest*, I.i)

An *innocent threat* is someone who innocently is a causal agent in
a process such that he would be an aggressor had he chosen to
become such an agent. If someone picks up a third party and
throws him at you down at the bottom of a deep well, the third
party is innocent and a threat; had he chosen to launch himself at
you in that trajectory he would be an aggressor. Even though the
falling person would survive his fall onto you, may you use your ray
gun to disintegrate the falling body before it crushes and kills you?
                    (Robert Nozick, *Anarchy, State and Utopia*)

In his essay on Gandhi, Orwell considers the moral status of an
unyielding conception of moral belief. Is it the case that someone
who has a completely uncompromising view of morality may yet
exhibit moral corruption? Orwell's own judgement of Gandhi's moral
worth is equivocal. Gandhi's refusal to entertain exceptions to his
moral principles was a false morality, an ethic of extremes; contrasted
with the oscillations of politics it represents moral purity. This is
not, however, a condition which Orwell finds totally admirable:

The essence of being human is that one does not seek perfection,
that one is sometimes willing to commit sins for the sake of
loyalty, that one does not push asceticism to the point where it
makes friendly intercourse impossible . . . No doubt alcohol,

100

tobacco and so forth are things that a saint must avoid, but sainthood is also a thing that human beings must avoid.[1]

For Orwell, human imperfectibility cuts across political allegiances, but an absolute ethic not only makes political action impossible it does so at high human cost and with disregard for the historical and political circumstances which surround the actions it allows. Of course, Gandhi was not an innocent. His moral simplicity did not preclude a deep understanding of the policies of his political opponents, and he was aware that refusal to compromise involved great sacrifice not only for himself but also for others. Absolute ethics and political blindness do not always go hand in hand. Gandhi's understanding of a morally permissible politics did, however, pose a political threat which was a threat to all politics involving negotiation between ends and means. How can this be?

Robert Nozick asks us to consider the case of an innocent shield protecting an aggressor. The dilemma arises because the shield is innocent of any involvement and we are unwilling to accept a utilitarian solution which would involve sacrificing the innocent to destroy the enemy. The important feature of such complex cases is that the innocent is the agent of another's purposes. It is these which provide the threat and innocence is used in the attempt to make it more effective. It is not as if the danger arose directly from innocence, a danger missing, too, in the challenge to politics posed by Gandhi's moral sensibility. While his moral demeanour exhibited absolute faithfulness to moral principle he controlled political action in a volatile context in a manner which was neither simple nor crude. There is, in other words, in Gandhi's moral fabric a deep, residual political capacity. This marks him off from Pyle's fatal innocence in Greene's *The Quiet American*, and from the king's good intentions in *Henry VI* (3) where politics finds itself vulnerable to moral innocence in a way which is direct, open, and violent. There are complex differences between these cases but their common quality is that each exhibits a kind of perfectibility. It was this which Orwell resisted. What precisely is involved in this notion of goodness? We have to go beyond deontic ethical theories of obligation and rights to discuss absolute conceptions of morality. What form do such conceptions take? What kind of integrity do supererogatory virtue and saintliness exhibit?

Orwell finds difficulty with Gandhi's idea that if he were to make compromises with his moral beliefs he would be failing to live up to their demands. Orwell cannot simply approve the contrasting position in which someone holds the same beliefs but is prepared to allow a degree of moral trimming. Orwell's problem is two-fold. It is not clear that the second position would .express precisely the same moral beliefs as the first and it is equally unclear that he would then find it especially admirable. In what sense can an ethical consideration have an absolute value? I want to discuss this question in the light of two essays by R. F. Holland in his book *Against Empiricism*[2] because he attempts a defence of absolute ethics and offers a particular view of the connection between this and politics.

Holland takes issue with what he sees as the dominant tradition in moral philosophy which explains goodness in terms of judgements of relative value: an act, disposition, state of mind, or character is deemed good according to its fulfilment of function or satisfaction of purpose. Thus, any act which fulfils an all-embracing or comprehensive purpose has an absolute value because there is then no further purpose to which it is relative. In the history of philosophy there are many variants of what Holland calls 'the goal-seeking explanation of value'. It is found in relation to individual and social conduct, lists of moral aims and purposes, and in descriptions of the moral and political purposes of societies. This mode of explanation is common to a large number of standpoints in moral philosophy. Of these Holland writes:

> I reject the whole family. For the recognition of an absolute value
> . . . where one is struck by the egregious fineness of an action like
> the rescue of an innocent person who is harmed or wronged –
> acknowledgement of the goodness of such an action involves the
> awareness of a demand that can as readily obstruct as further any
> purpose howsoever elevated and irrespective of whether the
> purpose be conceived as private or communal.[3]

For Holland, far from it being the case that individual and social purposes explain values it is only from the standpoint of absolute value that such purposes can be morally assessed at all. Opposed to a goal-seeking argument, an absolute judgement of value involves the recognition of the purity of goodness – that an act is performed not for the sake of advantage or the avoidance of pain, or even out of duty. The value of such an act is intrinsic and does not allow evaluation or comparison. Understanding actions and judgements as having an absolute ethical significance means rejecting reductionist accounts of morality. It does not mean the discovery of morally right decisions, but rather the illumination of the standpoints from which decisions are made. Moral anthropology parades the purposes which it is claimed morality fulfils but it gives no account of the relation between them.

Moral judgements are absolute in three senses. First, they do not allow exceptions. A moral statement which is expressed in terms of rights can include morally permissible exemption clauses. It can include qualifications in the form of exceptions and mitigations. But a statement such as 'You ought to give special consideration to your parents' is unconditional or categoric. It is an absolute moral claim. Second, a moral judgement is absolute in the sense of not requiring an external explanation or justification of itself. We might contrast the statement 'This is a good chair' with 'This is a good act'. The former may be explained by reference to its fulfilment of function but the latter, say an act of kindness, does not require any justification outside itself. Equally, we can contrast 'You ought to take up swimming' with 'You ought to tell the truth'. An absolute conception of ethics implies that there is nothing further to be said in explanation of the second statement. Its imperative character is a part of its meaning so that we cannot ask for a further explanation without showing that we have not understood it. In this respect, Holland follows Plato in arguing that, as a model for ethics, geometry has far greater significance than considerations of need or advantage. If we ask why the base angles of an isosceles triangle must be equal then we have misunderstood what is being said because that is what an isosceles triangle means. But is an ethical misunderstanding of the same kind? Someone who questions a moral imperative may not misunderstand it but may prefer expediency to the considerations the moral imperative enjoins. They may require an account of the advantages morality offers or of the goals which it attempts to reach. This instrumental view of morality cannot be incorporated in the kind of absolute ethical vision we are considering. Morality is not justified by reference to something beyond itself. As Wittgenstein expresses it in the *Tractatus*:

> It is clear, however, that ethics has nothing to do with punishment and reward in the usual sense of the terms. So our question about the *consequences* of an action must be unimportant. At least those

103

consequences should not be events. For there must be something right about the question we posed. There must indeed be some kind of ethical reward and ethical punishment, but they must reside in the action itself.[4]

This is the third respect in which moral judgements are absolute. They are not subsidiary to any end or purpose. They are not derivable from such purposes and they do not constitute a higher purpose in themselves. Purposive judgements are hypothetical because they state that if a specific end is desired then these are the most efficient means to its achievement. On this view morality is an instrumental matter and the only important consideration is whether or not it is efficient in the fulfilment of its function. The language of purpose pictures the moral agent as existing outside his environment and his moral will as acting on it to bring about the changes he desires. Morality is seen as either more or less economic in bringing about desired ends. Moral judgements are absolute in the sense that they can never be subordinated to any other consideration or end. From the standpoint of absolute ethics the language of purpose is an impoverished vocabulary of morality.

Judgements of absolute value do not involve negotiation or reciprocity and they have nothing to do with advantage or the satisfaction of purposes. Holland writes:

> Consider the difference between rendering what is due when this is conceived in terms of equilibrium or compensation and on the other hand going on giving, forgiving, turning the other cheek . . . where repaying evil with good is the only kind of repayment there is; . . .[5]

Morality is construed as absolute when it is not reduced to some external consideration, when it is not understood legalistically as a kind of moral jurisprudence, and when we cease thinking of it in a utilitarian manner as a calculation of moral profit and loss. Holland further criticizes utilitarianism in relation to its production-line view of the connection between action and consequence. This does not adequately tackle the problem of whether consequences just happen to follow or whether they are internally related to the actions which precede them. To use Holland's example, it is not accidental that brutality brutalizes or that discouragement discourages. This enables him to chart internal relations between agent, action, and the world.

If a person is envious or malicious it does not just happen that evil consequences follow from this character or that the world is poisoned as a result. Absolute good and absolute evil work a transformation on the world which is not a contingent consequence of their nature. Here I stress what I take to be Holland's central point – that goodness is absolute by virtue of its emphasis on the idea of limit not simply in relation to what it is permissible to do and not to do, but in relation to the way it separates morality from other kinds of considerations.

One important implication is that moral goodness is prior to obligation. However, this leaves unclear the precise sense of its priority, the problem which arose from Orwell's ambiguous description of Gandhi – is the tie which binds him to his morality one of duty or one of inner regard? It is impossible to answer this question from outside the moral perspective involved, and it is important to consider why this must be the case. Theories of morality which are based on moderate egotism construe morality in terms of principle and benefit. It is to an agent's advantage to agree to rules which limit his actions and those of others. On this view, morality is a goal-based expression of those principles individuals require to pursue their goods, and, as such, it must be external to the content of those goods. This fails to explain how individuals may believe that morality has an absolute significance for them. Their goodness is not relative to desires or needs and does not depend on their satisfaction. Goodness in this sense is unqualified by considerations external to itself. One writer describes its appearance in the world:

> A concern with the absolute good manifests itself in a constant concern to relate to the world unconditionally and act accordingly; to do everything for the good of it, not because of what one can get out of it by way of satisfaction, social prestige, the admiration of others, and so forth. Such a concern essentially involves patience in the face of suffering the world may inflict and humility in the face of achievements which may come.[6]

Weston's description of the moral disposition of the person who wills the good absolutely implies that the moral value of an act resides, not in the goals it achieves or in the act itself, but in the manner of its performance. It is not what individuals do that is morally important but how they do it, how they perceive their conduct and relations with others. This has implications for our understanding of moral freedom which does not consist in the increasing satisfaction of an infinitely expanding range of desires. Individuals are not conceived as free simply because their choices are unconstrained. Freedom depends on the kinds of choices that are made and the way individuals conceive their relation to the world. Iris Murdoch describes the moral character which the individualist disposition expresses:

> He is rational and totally free in so far as, in the most ordinary law-court and commonsensical sense, his degree of self-awareness may vary. He is morally speaking monarch of all he surveys and totally responsible for his actions. Nothing transcends him. His moral language is a practical pointer, the instrument of his choices, the indication of his preferences.[7]

Freedom does not consist in widening the range of practical choice, which may be achieved in such a way as to make individuals less free. Moral individuals do not exist independently of their moral commitments and engagements in the world, and their freedom can be gained only by recognizing that the moral value of such commitments lies not in their beneficial consequences but in how they are borne and lived up to. This means that the source of moral value is not duty, which can be accommodated by meanness as well as generosity of spirit, but an inner love of the good. However, as Weston points out, the recognition of the absolute value of morality can only be expressed through human wants and needs. It does not consist in them, but expresses itself through them from its own standpoint. This is a feature of moral agency for all whose moral character falls short of sainthood.

What kind of moral character is presupposed by this account of absolute goodness? Both Holland and Weston emphasize the unconditional character of a life which is lived in this way, and they stress the difficulty of emancipating morality from the conditions and qualifications which are imposed on it by utilitarianism. It is essential that morality be indifferent to any gains or benefits, losses or disadvantages which may ensue when its demands are followed or when goodness is expressed in circumstances of personal danger or risk. The expression of absolute goodness can originate from a deep dissatisfaction with consequentialist accounts of morality. If morality is deemed valuable because of the benefits it brings then its value is without foundation. To persevere, the first requisites may be determination and moral courage. To be steadfast in the face of evil – and to resist the moral praise which such determination may elicit – involves a depth of moral understanding which is not open to all. However, absolute goodness may be displayed through struggle and effort and in spontaneity and complete naturalness. This latter, an unreflective expression of goodness, is equally unconcerned with the value its actions may have in the world but its effortlessness is a mask of moral innocence. For the morally innocent, virtue is absolute because they cannot believe that it can be any other way. They do not yet realize the complex temptations of the world and so they have not fought to reach a point where morality is intelligible and significant for them. They express a moral confidence in themselves and in others which they have yet to lose, and they do not need their goodness to be enforced by a rule-book of obligations. Orwell's problem may be solved by emphasizing that moral disposition precedes duty and that virtue is prior to obligation when considered from the standpoint of absolute goodness. This can be manifested in different kinds of moral character but we need to see more clearly how duty and goodness are related.

I shall not attempt a comprehensive account of the relation between a theory of right and a theory of virtue, but will be concerned rather with the connection between absolute, as opposed to relative, goodness and supererogation. In his recent book on supererogation David Heyd offers four conditions which must be satisfied if an act is to be defined as supererogatory.[8] First, it is neither obligatory nor forbidden for us to perform it. In other words, it is not like the obligation involved in keeping a promise and it is not like the duty of abstinence which corresponds to a negative right. Second, it is not wrong not to perform such an act and, while its non-performance does not justify blame, its performance does merit special praise. Third, it is a morally good act by virtue of its consequences and it has particular value because it goes beyond duty. Fourth, it is a voluntary act for the sake of another's good and so justifies additional admiration.

Both supererogatory and duty-based moral conduct exclude self-interest, but their divergence is not just one of degree. Someone who performs a supererogatory act does not simply do more than is required by duty; they express a particular kind of moral character. Supererogation is on a par with absolute goodness because both stress the altruistic intention of the agent. Consequences are not completely ignored but they are secondary to the spirit in which the action is performed. As Heyd points out, supererogation is conventionally associated with saintliness and moral heroism. The conduct associated with these moral characteristics involves overcoming considerations of personal interest and well-being, and a willingness to sacrifice basic goods for the sake of another. Generosity or beneficence are not virtues in the same way. They are virtues of giving more than is required, but this may be at small cost to the agent and will commonly involve no great degree of personal risk. In this respect supererogation and absolute goodness part company, because saints will not only give to those to whom they are not under any obligation, but give all they have. Similarly, in forgiveness, saints will repay evil with good, and they will volunteer to take suffering on their own shoulders not just because they wish to do more than their share but because it expresses their love for others. Supererogation and absolute goodness are not equivalent. Supererogatory acts are classified by contrast with those regarded as morally obligatory. They may be performed by those who understand morality as a system of rules of obligation which is generally to our mutual advantage. In other words, morality may be regarded as beneficial, except for supererogatory actions which are given special praise for that reason; but from this point of view absolute goodness would not regard supererogatory acts as exceptionally worthy. Such acts are commonly regarded as voluntary, open to individual choice in a way in which the acceptance of moral obligations is not. Heyd writes:

> The morality of supererogation is based on freedom and voluntariness in a more radical sense than that of freedom and voluntariness in the morality of duty. The decision to act beyond what is required is free not only from physical or legal compulsion, but also from informal pressure, the threat of moral sanctions, or inner feelings of guilt. It is purely optional.[9]

Supererogation is a break-out from moral egalitarianism, but this does not necessarily mean that it occupies a realm of spontaneous initiative or that this would be equivalent to moral freedom. Those who perform acts of great heroism often say that they really had no choice. Do saints choose their sanctity as if this was one among a number of moral alternatives available to them? What kind of human being is completely free from 'inner feelings of guilt'? Heyd's valuable account of supererogation is too dependent on Kantian conceptions of morality as rational freedom to express rival pictures of virtue. Supererogation is quite properly concerned with actions that go beyond the requirements of moral duty, but at least as far as political morality is concerned this does not mean that it escapes the dilemmas which often attend moral decisions. Supererogatory virtue may appear in the actions of an office-holder as a willingness to do more than the obligations their office requires, or a reluctance to make the moral compromises the office considers necessary. Both may be regarded as optional in the sense that they are not required by the duties of the office, and both may be based on the attempt to avoid guilt in the sense of personal blameworthiness. The disposition here may be one of saintliness or moral innocence and we need to enquire further into the differences between them.

The nature of moral saintliness has provoked considerable disagreement in recent moral philosophy.[10] Since Urmson's 1958 article there has been a strong tendency to discuss saintliness in terms of supererogation. While this is obviously not completely misleading, it does involve a neglect of the religious dimension which the concept quite clearly possesses. Sainthood may be understood as a gift from God, not only in the sense that it is not a disposition which may be chosen like an occupation but also because the actions of a saint take place in the context of religious beliefs regarding human evil and suffering and how they may be redeemed. Nevertheless, it should not be deduced from this that secular (or pseudo-) saintliness is morally less significant or that it is philosophically uninteresting for our purposes.

Urmson's discussion of saints and heroes involves an idea of supererogation of the kind just discussed. He argues that the traditional moral classification of action in terms of duties, permissions, and prohibitions ignores those who perform acts which go beyond duty, are not wrong and not merely permissible because they merit high moral praise. For Urmson, someone is a saint who performs actions beyond the limits of duty either by control of contrary inclinations or interests, or a hero if they perform the same kind of actions effortlessly or by controlling fear. According to Urmson the existence of supererogatory conduct means that the traditional classification of moral action must be revised, and it should be replaced by a two-fold distinction between a morality of minimum duty which can be required by all and a morality of aspiration which is highly admirable but not a matter of obligation.

Why does Urmson put forward this view? Part of his answer is a criticism of moral ideals:

> it is part of the ideal that a moral code should actually help to contribute to human well-being, and a moral code that would work only for angels (for whom it would in any case be unnecessary) would be a far from ideal moral code for human beings. There is, indeed, a place for ideals that are practically unworkable in human affairs, as there is a place for the blueprint of a machine that will never go into production; but it is not the place of such ideals to serve as a basic code of duties.[11]

Five substantial reasons are given in defence of this distinction. One, the absence of supererogatory virtue would mean an impoverishment of human life but the absence of a basic sense of moral duty would make it impossible. Two, supererogatory conduct is beyond the capacity of most human beings, so not to draw a distinction between such conduct and basic duties would be to construct a morality which it would be impossible to live up to, and if this is true it could not be understood as a matter of obligation. Three, which follows from two, it is impossible to universalize acts of supererogation in such a way that they generate manageable rules of moral duty. To employ Urmson's own example, while nursing lepers is an act of clear moral worth it cannot be universalized so it becomes a requirement of moral duty.

> it would be quite ridiculous for everyone, however circumstanced, to be expected to go off and nurse lepers. [And] . . . it would be absurd to try to formulate complicated rules to determine in just what circumstances such an action is a duty.[12]

Four, it is necessary to distinguish between duties which create legitimate expectations and demands and which justify blame in cases of non-compliance, and acts of high moral worth which may elicit hope and gratitude but not rightful expectation. Five, with minimum moral duties we act to some degree under constraint. They can be rightfully enforced. Supererogatory conduct cannot be so encouraged and, indeed, Urmson argues that it would be morally outrageous to expect that another person should act in a way that is saintly or heroic. For these reasons Urmson concludes:

No doubt from the agent's point of view it is imperative that he should endeavour to live up to the highest ideals of behaviour that he can think of . . . but it simply does not follow that . . . we should . . . demand ideal conduct from others in the way in which we must demand basic morality from them, or blame them equally for failures in all fields.[13]

Urmson is not alone amongst recent philosophers in his attempt to stress the limits of supererogation. Bernard Williams has gone further and argued that a world in which morality was universally respected by well-disposed moral agents would not be a desirable state of affairs,[14] and Susan Wolf has doubted whether it is morally desirable to be morally better than others.[15]

Wolf bases her argument on a particular conception of moral saintliness. She is generally more sceptical than Urmson, and she attempts a definition of moral sainthood which introduces the subject of the saintly disposition rather than the simple concentration on saintly acts. Wolf understands a moral saint as someone 'whose every action is as morally good as possible', 'who is as morally worthy as can be', and whose 'life [is] dominated by a commitment to improving the welfare of others or of society as a whole'.[16] She takes the view that Kantian and utilitarian versions of moral theory involve conceptions of moral saintliness which she calls the rational saint and the loving saint. She asks us to picture the moral life of a saint:

> a moral saint must have and cultivate those qualities which are apt to allow him to treat others as justly and kindly as possible. He will have the standard moral virtues to a nonstandard degree. He will be patient, considerate, even-tempered, hospitable, charitable in thought as well as deed. He will be very reluctant to make negative judgements of other people. He will be careful not to favour some people over others on the basis of properties they could not help but have.[17]

For Wolf, the distinctiveness of moral saints is one of degree. They pursue moral ends as others try to do and act in accordance with moral principle in ways which others aspire to, but their thoughts and actions are dominated by the need to act well. There is no qualitative moral difference because saints conceive their moral task as doing more for the relief of human suffering than others may choose to do. The saint is simply someone who spends more scarce resources than any other in doing good works. In this way saints have to sacrifice other activities and interests because they are distractions and obstacles to their charity. Saints gives more, and take more risks. Any weakness in the face of temptation diminishes their saintliness.

So Wolf agrees with Urmson that moral saints control contrary interests to virtue to a very great degree. The difference between saints and non-saints is a quantitative one, but even if we accept the Wolf picture of moral sainthood it does not include moral innocence because it places the emphasis on the restriction of interests of which the morally innocent would be unaware. Urmson particularly talks about the effortless control of inclination or fear in saints and heroes; while this may or may not be the case, not all effortless virtue is supererogatory. The morally innocent are carefree in their conduct because they are ignorant of the difficulties of acting well, but this does not make them saints. Moral saintliness and moral innocence have common conceptual characteristics without being logically equivalent. Wolf writes:

> I don't know whether there are any moral saints. But if there are, I am glad that neither I nor those about whom I care most are among them.[18]

The view that moral saintliness does not constitute a desirable model of individual or social well-being may be defended in a variety of ways. To criticize the idea of moral saintliness it is clearly not necessary to defend the view either that immorality *per se* is admirable or that immorality may sometimes contain moral attributes, such as courage. The traditional criticism of moral saintliness as a moral paradigm is that it would then be a universal moral requirement that everyone try to act as well as possible in each act they perform and that there is something morally deficient about those who do not. The standard solution to this unwelcome conclusion is to make supererogatory conduct optional and hence non-paradigmatic in relation to moral obligation. But, as Owen Flanagan points out, this means that

> it is something of a mystery how the thesis of the overridingness of the morally ideal falls so easily to our realistic attitudes about persons while the thesis of the overridingness of the morally required stands so imperiously over moral life.[19]

It is important to restrict the demands made by moral ideals, but the problem is to achieve this without diminishing the importance such judgements have in moral life or weakening the absolute significance of moral goodness.

Critics of moral saintliness concentrate on three areas: the connection between moral saintliness and interests, admirable immorality, and saintliness and the circumstances of justice. Doubts have been expressed by Susan Wolf, who argues that it is not simply that saints appear as too good but rather that they sacrifice excellences which are generally seen as praiseworthy. The moral saint, in other words, has no time, energy, or inclination to pursue good interests such as aesthetic or literary excellences. Saints are nothing other than their saintliness, except where, by coincidence, such interests are a vehicle for their virtue. Thus moral saintliness prevents the encouragement of excellences which we find praiseworthy in human life and which have a major part to play in our understanding of cultural ideals. Moral saintliness is an exclusive attribute. It dominates the lives of those who exhibit it to the exclusion of all else because it considers every situation and every activity from the standpoint of the moral good. The demands it makes are unconditional and it regards all other aspirations from art to zoology as potential obstructions to its satisfaction. In this way Wolf argues that moral saints are not admirable. We do not feel that we have failed or that we are deficient because we have not aspired to moral perfection in the performance of every action or the following of every occupation and interest. In exhausting life of everything other than its moral content the saint presents an ideal which is not fulfillable and which will condemn those who pass it by to a life of anxiety and guilt. So if it is good to pursue non-moral ideals and interests Wolf argues that this is incompatible with moral sainthood.

> if we think that it is as good, or even better for a person to strive
> for one of these ideals than it is for him or her to strive for and
> realise the ideal of the moral saint, we express a conviction that it
> is good not to be a moral saint.[20]

The second criticism concerns Slote's idea of admirable immorality[21] which would mean that there would be some circumstances in which moral saintliness was not good in the sense that it would be morally better not to possess it. Slote does not defend the strong thesis that immorality is admirable or the weak thesis that certain features of immoral conduct are thought to be admirable. His argument is that there are dispositions which are immoral and admirable. If this is true it establishes a sense in which it is not good to be a moral saint, and it involves the puzzling conclusion that a trait of character which we think of as ideal is a moral illusion. Slote's first move is to deny the claim that morality is over-riding if this means that there cannot be a moral justification for doing something which is morally wrong. There is conduct in which agents recognize that what they do is wrong but nevertheless feel morally justified and, further, that such a justification merits moral approval. Slote gives a number of familiar examples. The first is Gauguin's decision to leave his family to pursue his art in the South Pacific; the second concerns a father who believes it to be his moral duty to assist the police, but who misleads them regarding the whereabouts of his criminal son; the third is that of Churchill who showed a single-minded moral determination to defeat Nazi Germany to the point of authorizing the bombing of Dresden; and the fourth is a political leader who believes that torture for political purposes is wrong but who nevertheless employs it to prevent a terrorist group destroying innocent lives. Slote's general strategy in employing these examples is to show that they all exhibit admirable immorality because the act which is considered morally wrong is identical with the act which we find morally admirable. What we morally disapprove and what we morally admire are conceptually equivalent. Slote concludes that:

> if the fact of immorality is not always an overriding consideration for us and if we can think better of someone for acting without attention to right and wrong, is it so very surprising that we should sometimes see virtue in traits that actually run counter to morality?[22]

This means that the instances of moral experience which Slote gives lie beyond codification in terms of Kantian or utilitarian moral theories, but more important there is a significant sense in which moral saintliness is not an absolute or unconditionally desirable moral characteristic. However, the moral saint and the moral innocent would not contemplate the conduct which Slote argues may be admirable. We may not believe that this opens their actions to blame but it does imply that their goodness is precisely the obstacle to their behaving well.

It should be obvious that neither Wolf nor Slote denies the value of moral saintliness. Their arguments attempt to show its moral insufficiency, further developed in the third criticism which concerns the social benefit of saintliness. While it can be argued that super-erogation is a social value because of its optionality and its capacity to enhance mutual trust and altruism, it is nevertheless the case that it does not address the fundamental imperfections of a human society. Moral rules exist in the context of human fallibilities. They presuppose conflicts of interest over which they legislate and they express themselves in agreements between human beings who are occupied with their own concerns as much as the well-being of others. Rawls is following a long-established tradition of thought in moral philosophy when he writes in this respect:

> justice is the virtue of practices where there are competing interests and where persons feel entitled to press their rights on each other. In an association of saints agreeing on a common ideal, if such a community could exist, disputes about justice would not occur. Each would work selflessly for one end as determined by their common religion, and reference to this end (assuming it to be clearly defined) would settle every question of right. But a human society is characterised by the circumstances of justice.[23]

Rawls draws on Hume for his account of the circumstances of justice, which he says consist in relative equality, moderate scarcity, and moderate selfishness. Hume writes:

> Reverse, in any considerable circumstance, the condition of men; produce extreme abundance or extreme necessity; implant in the human breast perfect moderation and humanity, or perfect rapaciousness and malice – by rendering justice totally *useless*, you thereby totally destroy its essence and suspend its obligation upon mankind.[24]

Of course Hume argues that justice is an artificial virtue designed to protect mutual interest and to increase the general benefit. His account of the circumstances of justice includes intelligent self-interest but excludes complete altruism. Hume gives two reasons for this. In a world in which material possessions and resources are abundant, and in which virtue is effortless, there are no substantial problems for justice to settle. Additionally, benevolence is insufficient because it cannot alone evaluate competing claims and it is uncertain in establishing the constituency of its benefaction. In other words, the rights of those who do not receive benevolence, but who are in all significant respects in the same position as those who do, are unsatisfied and remain suspended in a moral limbo.

Hume's argument is aimed at those who believe that benevolence is sufficient for the construction of moral rules to govern conflicts of interest in the context of human imperfectibility, and later he comments that should society achieve a moral Golden Age then human virtue would be impossible. The attempt to make virtue effortless must end by making it obsolete. To remove forgiveness, praise, and mercy from the moral vocabulary is to convert those who use such language into machines. If this utopian way of life is moral bliss then it can only be the bliss experienced by those who have been trained to respond to commands. It is effortless for them because they have no conception of what it is to respond differently.

The same conclusion follows if we consider those who aspire to a community of saints. Rawls is mistaken if he thinks that selflessness necessarily settles every question of right. If this is something more than a definitional assertion then it has to explain the moral complexities unleashed in Iris Murdoch's *The Bell* in which the disinterested attempt to found an association based on faith discovers that innocent intentions and pure motives are not sufficient, and that experience and guile are required to respond to the personal and sexual rivalries which emerge.

In *The Pilgrim's Progress*, Bunyan writes:

> for just a little way before them, and that at the end of the clearest way too, was a pit, none knows how deep, full of nothing but mud, there made on purpose to destroy the pilgrims in.[25]

In their attempt to achieve moral and political perfectibility pilgrims discover a moral reality of which they were previously unaware.

Dystopian writings, like Nathaniel Hawthorne's *The Blithedale Romance*, are concerned with general projects for the transformation of society and they aim to show how such projects embody what Kierkegaard called 'the egocentric service of the good'. Hume is concerned with the derivation of rules of human justice and he argues that this is impossible on the assumption of complete benevolence. There is a deep illusion in the idea of effortless virtue, that human life could be changed in such a way as to make goodness guaranteed, that in a community of saints justice is not required.

Nevertheless, it might be argued that such criticisms go too far. In the context of human imperfection, of scarcity, suffering, and loss, saintliness expresses itself not without effort, but through strength of will, a moral determination not to weaken in the face of the work to be done. Such a disposition does not depend on a belief in the moral regeneration of society and it does not involve a diminution of the value of the rules of human justice. It asserts, however, that such rules are not sufficient. The accommodation of mutual and reciprocal interest they represent must be transcended by a courageous and self-denying virtue. There is, however, a sense of virtue which is, and cannot be other than, effortless. The morally innocent do not need determination to pursue the good. It is displayed naturally with a grace which is intrinsic, not acquired through experience, training, or self-awareness and control. We admire moral saints, but we do not blame ourselves for not feeling able to act as they do. We respond favourably to the innocent, but we do not grieve for them when their innocence is lost. Criticisms of unqualified goodness argue by contrast that such moral positions have to negotiate with non-moral excellences, with admirable immoralities, and with the circumstances of justice if their cost is to be reduced to a humanly manageable level.

Not all philosophers have been satisfied with Urmson's attempt to show how supererogation undermines the three-fold classification of moral action and requires a division between a morality of duty which applies to all and a morality of aspiration which is a matter of praise but does not create obligations. How can we admire the moral saint for doing more than we would do ourselves when we are not under any obligation to emulate him? To some extent this problem is created by critics' pictures of sainthood. Wolf, for example, tends to think of a saint as a moral entity which has to exhaust itself of non-moral excellence to try to alleviate the suffering and evil in the world. As it is not a good thing to ignore altogether the pursuit of non-moral excellences Wolf concludes that it is not good to be a saint. But is this a credible account of saintliness?

One critic of Wolf makes a number of important challenges.[26] First, saints may not be seen as offering infinite moral resources from their moral will so we might say they are just stronger than others or do more than them. Talk of will in this context encourages us to see the difference between saints and non-saints in exclusively quantitative terms. Rather we may wish to emphasize the saint as

117

actively embodying an unconditional goodness which originates from a divine source and is not subject to human constraint or limit. Second, saints do not have to make every action as good as possible. Their humility is a moral obstacle to their seeing moral worth in terms of the accumulation of credits. Third, while there is a tension between the pursuit of non-moral excellences such as art, sculpture, or music and a humanitarian concern we do not see it as a measurable disqualification from sainthood that a morally good person pursue such excellences to some degree. It may be true that a maximum devotion to morality of the kind shown by a saint is only possible in the context of a religious belief, but even without this as a major consideration Wolf has failed to establish the moral autonomy of sainthood. It is not the case, therefore, that we can describe the moral saint as possessing virtue in excess, as simply going beyond a due concern for others.[27] This exhibits the fallacy of thinking of saints in terms of the quantity and frequency of their good works, and it means that as the nature of sainthood has not been established the costs which it is supposed to involve have not been shown either. This may be brought out by challenging Urmson's claim that we can praise the saint without having to be one.

The residue of universalization in Urmson's moral thinking means he thinks it odd to consider a moral character as praiseworthy but not believe that we should emulate it. But what does emulating it involve? The moral ideals which we regard as praiseworthy do not represent a framework of duties, but they do describe a moral disposition which we ought to follow. One recent critic of Urmson puts the point in this way:

> To say, therefore, that someone is a saint or hero, and thereby to express a moral judgement, is to say that that person has succeeded in being what we all ought to be. He *is* realising the worthwhile through his actions. To say that someone is a saint or hero without believing we ought to be like him is not to express a moral judgement.[28]

This does not mean that we have to do exactly what a saint does in order morally to praise such a person's conduct. It does mean, however, that we attempt to live up to the same values. In this way the relation between judgement and action, between moral ideal and actuality, which Urmson's account severed, is reaffirmed. On this view saintliness is an ideal of a moral community. It is not conceptually distinct from the values which make up such a community but rather acts as their foundation. The saint as compared to those who admire and fail to aspire to his condition is simply more successful at doing more than unselfishness requires.

A. I. Melden claims that supererogation is not sufficient to explain what is morally distinctive about saintliness. It is, of course, true that what a saint does goes far beyond what most of us would feel capable of doing, but this only indicates how non-saints may not be required to follow the saint's example; it does not prove that the saint is not morally required to meet his high sense of obligation. This means that, while we may not blame the saint for not doing something of a supererogatory kind, it does not prevent the saint from blaming himself. The high moral demands saints make of themselves are neglected by labelling their conduct as supererogatory simply because it goes beyond the moral rules which we find generally beneficial. To abolish saints would then result only in impoverishment and not in brutalization. For Melden this is simply a special case of Hume's general asssertion that we value moral character because of its usefulness in promoting human well-being –

> special because saintly traits allegedly differ only in degree from the generous and benevolent traits of others – that we have the special regard that we have for saints because of their great service in promoting the happiness of mankind.[29]

This does not bring out the distinctive moral features of saintliness which set it apart from the kind of moral judgements we would normally make of our own conduct and of that of others. Melden describes this difference in the following way:

> Now what is striking about the conduct of a Francis of Assisi who cares for the sick and starving, or a Father Damien who sacrifices his own well-being in order to nurse and care for helpless victims of natural misfortune, is not merely the fact that they show unusual concern for helpless strangers in great need, but the fact that the love they display to these victims of great misfortune is of that special order that is commonly reserved by parents for their children.[30]

What is characteristic of moral saints is that they consider themselves to be under an obligation to care for and help any other human being who is in distress. In other words, the distinction between obligations to members of one's family and obligations to others has no significance for saints. This means that they *consider themselves* under a moral requirement to behave as they do, perhaps a conscious *imitatio Christi*, a requirement which expresses their conviction that their life bears a relation to others which is different in a significant moral way. It is not that we simply approve of such a character. Rather, when confronted by such unconditional virtue and acceptance of unrestricted obligation we turn to moral wonder. What distinguishes moral saints, therefore, is the intensity of their concern, the self-criticism which marks their failure, and their personal suffering when they can only helplessly observe the agonies of their fellow human beings.

The saint does not differ from others in a way which can be expressed in terms of moral degree which implies that we should be continuously reproaching ourselves for our comparative moral deficiency. Saints differ from others in kind because the special interests, in family, friends, and non-moral excellences, which we pursue are of no importance to them. This does not imply, as Wolf thinks, a measure of criticism. That would only follow if the difference was one of degree. For Melden saints are not like psychopaths or moral fanatics because unlike them they do have the moral virtues and understand what they involve, but like them they are a different sort of being – 'one to whose status, given the sorts of being we are, *we* cannot aspire'.[31]

We have considered views on the moral significance of saintliness. We have considered precisely what it is that distinguishes its morality from the moral rules which restrict interests and serve human life in the circumstances of justice. This discussion enables us to define more clearly what it is about morality that constitutes the obstacle in problematic political cases. As we saw, this was explained variously in terms of conscience, duty, and principle. Moral saints do not conform to any of these categories. Their conscience does not rest on the fulfilment of specific human obligations but on the satisfaction of an obligation to humanity. Their moral aspirations do not rest with the accomplishment of their duty but go far beyond it. Their absolute goodness resists codification in terms of principle and their humility prevents them from becoming zealous. Moral saints exist outside the limited taxonomy of morality employed in discussions of problems in political morality. It is not so easy, therefore, to describe their character as a moral obtuseness or a refusal to recognize the nuances of moral difficulty involved in such problems. It is true that morality may enter politics as blindness to the dilemmas which result, but moral saints are not blind. Equally, the moral choices which Slote discusses as admirable immoralities are not available to them. It is no accident that two of Slote's examples are 'Dirty Hands' cases in which the choice of immoral means is justified by beneficial ends. Some writers conclude from this that it is impossible to rule guiltlessly, and while the degree of guilt ought to be minimized it is undesirable that it should be removed completely. As we have seen, this argument rests on an attenuated view of moral goodness. It depends on individuals accepting moral compromise and recognizing that in politics there may be circumstances in which immorality is seen as admirable. However, these possibilities are not available to the moral saint. In politics we may do far less than is morally required because we seem to have no other choice. Moral saints blame themselves for not doing far more than is morally required. Their disposition places them outside the conventional way of thinking about moral considerations in politics, and this means that such considerations are of little help in explaining the problems which ensue. Exactly the same point holds with moral innocence. How are we to explain moral saintliness when it is tested by politics?

I would like to examine Holland's view of the relation between absolute goodness and politics as he expresses it in *Against Empiricism*. His arguments are interesting for our purposes because they involve an understanding of moral saintliness of the kind we have just discussed and point to the difficulties involved in attempting a non-consequentialist account of morality in politics. For Holland the language of politics, particularly in its large-scale, modern, bureaucratic sense, is the language of consequentialism.

There are two important respects in which politics exemplifies consequentialist ethics. First, it is Holland's view that in order to achieve anything in politics it is necessary to possess power. This is expressed as a capacity to effect change and it depends upon a consequentialist view of the human will as an agency for bringing about results. In this respect, politics and a utilitarian ethic are perfectly compatible. Second, politics is impossible without compromise, and morally the most significant thing with which compromise is sometimes thought necessary is evil. This is, of course, the morality of 'Dirty Hands'. It is tolerated as a feature of moral

121

thinking only on the basis of consequentialism, and while politics seems to provide an appropriate context for it this kind of calculative, instrumental thinking is not exclusive to it. Consequentialism, as Holland points out, allows the performance of evil. The 'Dirty Hands' problem simply gives this an added gloss by saying that in politics it is sometimes necessary to do evil to avoid greater evil or to achieve good.

Holland stresses that from a Platonic standpoint these moral propositions are puzzling, even contradictory. If evil means that I must not do it, this is not cancelled however great the advantage which results. Absolute goodness places evil-doing outside the range of permissible moral conduct, which means that some things, including some good things, have to be sacrificed. Holland writes:

> Absolute ethics is the ethics of foregoing, and politics belongs for over-determined reasons to the pursuits that have to be foregone.[32]

As Holland realizes, in the world as it is and not as it might be reconstructed the necessity for absolute ethics to forego politics creates dilemmas of an intractable kind. By refusing to compromise, absolute ethics seems to accept moral impotence while the consequentialist willingness to negotiate moral costs appears the essence of practicality. Holland considers Bernard Williams' famous example.[33] In a South American town a firing squad is about to shoot twenty Indians as a reprisal and a deterrence against acts of protest. A visitor, Jim, arrives and is offered a 'guest's privilege' of shooting one Indian with the guarantee that if he does the rest will go free, but that if he turns it down all twenty will be shot. There is no chance of altering the problem in any way, in which case what should the visitor do? For Holland and Williams the utilitarian answer is clear – the visitor should shoot the one Indian for the sake of the others. Utilitarianism is apparently indifferent to the process of selection. It does not matter that the one Indian is selected by lot, desert, or any other rational process as long as the others go free as a result. Equally, for Holland and Williams the utilitarian answer is not obvious. The initial difficulty is that utilitarianism ignores the perspective of the visitor, i.e. what sort of moral disposition he has or whether he has any worth the name at all. Holland writes:

> you cannot imagine a saint shooting that Indian. Nor is it imaginable that a saint would do nothing either; for the man I am

calling a saint would face the consequences and engage in the
suffering in a way that is different from the way an ordinary man
would, and his presence would not be without impact on the
outcome.[34]

The example has a simplicity which disguises its theoretical appeal.
The visitor's moral perspective is an essential, and not simply an
accidental, element in the way the predicament appears to him.
I shall return to the abstract nature of such moral and political
philosophy later where I argue by contrast that literary examples
provide us with a more concrete sense of such dilemmas and the
difficulties they involve because they offer a richer account not just of
the background but also of the characters and their moral dispositions.
For Holland, if the visitor in the example should turn out to be a
saint then that may bring about a dramatic change in the situation.
The captain in charge of the firing squad may respond differently
when argued with or addressed by a saint, but if not then, as
Holland imagines, the saint may

> manage somehow to take the place of the one Indian; or if he could
> not get himself shot instead of him, perhaps he would make sure
> that he was shot along with him or else as the first of the twenty.[35]

In this way Holland shows that it is not obvious, as utilitarianism
might suggest, that someone who refuses to shoot the Indian is
squeamish or morally self-indulgent. Equally, it is not obvious that
for such a person the integrity which prevents him from shooting the
Indian is a consequentialist value like any other, that not shooting is
a means to the maintenance of a valued moral end. For Holland, a
saint would not think about his personal integrity. Indeed, he may
not have a theoretical ethical position to fall back on. Here saintliness
and absolute ethics are at one. As Holland concludes:

> I brought in the idea of a saint because for all the difference
> between them there is this significant point of contact between the
> position of a saint and the position of an ordinary person who has
> absolute conceptions if he is true to them. Neither could shoot the
> Indian. The impossibility here is the impossibility of politics.[36]

For Holland, the tests which politics sets the moral saint are
illusory. However, Holland does not deny that such goodness may
make a political situation worse. Indeed, it is a part of his conception
of goodness that the increase in suffering which results is something

which has to be borne. But, as Holland implies, the refusal to shoot may arise from a number of ethical perspectives which, in more complicated cases, involve outcomes which are more difficult to trace. One such perspective is moral innocence, conceptually close to moral saintliness and absolute goodness, but which damages politics in altogether different ways. Further, Holland takes a firm consequentialist view of the nature of politics, its instrumental language suggesting that goodness is an obstacle to be overcome or traded with evil if political aims are to be achieved. But our political perspective changes radically if we construe politics not as consequentialist, but as an intrinsic feature of human experience. Politics is not a device for the maximization of wants, but the protection of a common human space and authentic aspiration. It is relatively simple to explain the importance of absolute conceptions of morality by contrast with a consequentialist politics in which everything is open to negotiation and moral bargaining. Morality by its absolute rejection of such trading threatens the outcomes which politics values. But does the same conclusion follow if we consider the rejection of virtue from the standpoint of non-consequentialist accounts of politics?

Chapter Five

THE DISPLACEMENT OF VIRTUE

> But in the world, absolute ethics by requiring withdrawal from politics creates a dilemma, and in general it creates dilemmas that otherwise might not be deemed to arise.
>
> (R. F. Holland, *Against Empiricism*)

> Saints and cynics alike too readily assume it agreed that birds, beasts, flowers and fast cars have nothing to do with the case or at any rate that they aren't good enough . . . only, as Solomon remarked, a dish of herbs is under certain circumstances better than much grander food, though those circumstances are of infinite subtlety.
>
> (John Wisdom, *Paradox and Discovery*)

What does it mean to propose the displacement of virtue? It may be a replaceable artifice, an invention which has outlived its usefulness which has to be renegotiated in terms of new moral agreements and contracts. In a different manner virtue may be a device for the satisfaction of wants and benefits. Its displacement may be suggested by those whose needs are urgent and who are impatient with the obstacles erected by the morality on which they once relied. They want a more efficient means and are prepared to make morality redundant if an alternative mechanism presents itself. If morality is an artifice or a tool of convenience there is no reason to believe it immune from the history of technological change. In a more sceptical mood, morality may be displaced by power, either as individual will or reason of state. Virtue is one of the masks worn by hypocrisy. It conceals the true motives of individual and political ascendancy which dominate human life. Morality may be given second place to history. Moral practices are relative to time and place. They are not

125

universal in value or obligatory force and they succumb to mortality in the same way as other human artifacts; the cathedrals of the spirit, too, fall to dust. The philosophers I consider in this chapter attack morality from within. They do not take a contractarian, utilitarian, or natural law standpoint from which to judge morality. All condemn the idea that virtue is a matter of artificial agreement or that it is something to be exchanged if a better offer should present itself. All agree that morality cannot be understood from a position which is external to itself. They represent, then, moralists contra morality.

Hegel, Nietzsche, and Arendt attack virtue from within morality. In different ways and to different degrees they both establish and respond to the crisis of modern thought. They display a powerful concern for human autonomy in the context of doubt and against a background of savage challenge to humanist assumptions regarding rationality, freedom, and morality. To some extent, of course, they are themselves responsible for the most serious of these assaults. Nietzsche is quite right to portray himself as an 'underground man'. But they have much in common. All reject the central assumption of positivism that science is the paradigm form of human knowing. Equally, they derive little logical nourishment from the empty propositions of abstract reason. The historical character of human existence is continually emphasized but offers no final resting place, merely a temporary protection against oblivion. Hegel's philosophy is architectonic, a metaphysical system which aspires to culmination and synthesis, but which contains, too, contingencies, rejections, and scepticisms. Hegel presses traditional speculation to its limit, and it may be that the incorporation of conventional philosophic rivalries is so comprehensive that post-Hegelianism cannot be other than sceptical. Hegel criticizes specific moral taxonomies which he claims are distortions of the moral consciousness and offer only an illusory ethics to the world. Hegel, Nietzsche, and Arendt offer a profound critique of absolute morality, presented so as to leave little room for escape from the impasse it creates. Moral existence is conceived in isolation from the consoling ideas of universality and rationality, but equally it is not a matter of subjective feeling. Morality bears a complex relation to thought. Arendt is preoccupied with the possibility that thinking does not guarantee the moral values which are a stay against the dark. In this dilemma the emblematic figure for her is Socrates. All three philosophers are obsessed with the tension between Christianity and virtue. Here, of course, the emblematic figure is Christ.

This triple devastation attacks the guiding assumptions of the Western moral consciousness. Absolute morality ceases to be the spinal cord of human existence. Virtue is displaced, not by considerations of need, benefit, or advantage which are strictly external to itself, but from within. Of course benevolence or compassion are single virtues and do not exhaust moral possibilities. Friendship may clash with or have priority over benevolence. Justice, promise-keeping, and rights all limit what can be done in the name of consideration or benevolent regard.[1] The philosophers we are considering recognize that moral aspirations can conflict, and they regard such conflict as tragic and not open to utilitarian solution. Hegel does emphasize the notion of a moral community as minimizing the incidence of such disagreement, but even with this important qualification his criticism of absolute morality is unyielding. Compassion becomes defective, not by reference to religion or to a transcendental universal morality, but because of what it is and the form it takes in the world. What is the status of moral aspiration if moral innocence is shown to be illusory? Political morality faces great difficulties if the criticism of absolute moral conceptions is valid. All three philosophers reject ethical nihilism and all bear a subtle and complex relation to Machiavelli. To chart these problematic philosophical engagements with the limits of virtue I shall begin with Hegel.

The dialectical interlocking of the components of Hegel's system means that no individual part can be understood as separate from any other, though how he characterizes such components is a matter for legitimate philosophical discussion. I wish to concentrate on Hegel's remarks on innocence, which have received little critical evaluation compared with his discussion of the 'beautiful soul'.[2] The political significance of his criticism of moral innocence has perhaps not been fully appreciated.[3]

Hegel's formative and mature thought stands in complex relation to both the Enlightenment and Romanticism. It aspires to the transcendence and incorporation of the idealist and empiricist traditions of philosophy in a form which is comprehensive and faithful to the radical autonomy of human agency. Neither idealism, with its stress on universal reason, nor empiricism, with its emphasis on the material conditions of existence, is capable of explaining the logically distinctive character of human awareness. Hegel's dominant aspiration is towards a philosophical standpoint which will provide such an explanation and which will act as the consummation of preceding philosophical world views. He writes in the *Lectures on the History of Philosophy*:

> Philosophy demands the unity and the intermingling of these two points of view; it unites the Sunday of life when man in humility renounces himself and the working-day when he stands up independently, is master of himself and considers his own interests.[4]

Against mechanistic conceptions of human nature Hegel understands human agency as self-conscious and self-developing. History is not a random sequence of isolated events. Human society is not a forum for the expression and control of atomistic will. Moral and political life does not provide an artificial vehicle for human desire. Each finds its necessary place in the development of human consciousness in which every stage finds itself fulfilled and logically displaced by its successor. History exhibits the progressive rationality and emancipation of the human spirit. Human life is not a function of nature but is self-aware and self-defining. This consciousness of self is expressed in the characteristic and diverse forms of human existence, in art, religion, science, history, a civic culture, a moral disposition, and philosophy.

For moral and political life two important considerations stand out in Hegel's thinking. First, the idea that human agency is expressive not of a bundle of desires which react to external stimuli but of an autonomous identity which is self-creating and which has a potential to realize itself in a world of its own making. Human expression as rational self-mastery excludes dependence on others, nature, history, or the state. But it cannot express itself alone. It requires a world to make itself manifest. Second, this is achieved by the notion of determinacy. Moral thinking is neither universal nor a matter of subjective feeling. Human agency determines the nature of its beliefs to itself and to others through self-consciousness and reflection. Determinacy specifies and clarifies moral thinking. The universal is given a form in the world. Without determinacy it would have no specific identity. This determination is shown in language, a shared communication in a common public world. Expression and determinacy indicate Hegel's concern with wholeness, with the idea that human existence must be articulated in a way which is unified rather than fragmentary, integrated rather than abstract, coherent rather than formal. This provides the background to Hegel's mature view of moral freedom, which is not automatically counterposed to nature, history, or the state, but incorporates them as necessary conditions of its own rational and complete expression.

For Hegel the divided condition of German cultural existence found philosophical expression in Kant, whose rigidly dualist metaphysics confirmed and did nothing to overcome a bifurcated sense of existence. The distinction between the noumenal and phenomenal worlds, between autonomy and heteronomy, between reason and passion, left human existence divided within itself and lacking full reconciliation. Kant's conclusions were an advance on traditional empiricism, but they left human autonomy unfulfilled. This difficulty is central in Hegel's criticism of Kant's moral philosophy. The criterion of universality as a formal ethical requirement is no test at all because it presupposes the ethical quality it attempts to justify. Kant assumes an unbridgeable gap between the integrity of the moral agent and the world in which he has to act. The moral agent is torn between duty and inclination, which, as Hegel points out, involves a dualistic account of moral identity and a self-contradictory view of the relation beween morality and the passions. On the one hand, it is committed to the obliteration of passion. On the other, without passion, morality would have nothing to be tempted by and nothing to overcome.

Hegel's deep dissatisfaction with Kantian thought was shared by Schiller. Both were concerned with the reformulation of a unity lost in the modern world, and both attacked Kant's view of the transition from what is to what ought to be. Here the ethos which dominates their thinking as both exemplar and unrecoverable ideal is Classical Greece, in particular fifth-century Athens. For them, the Athenian polis represented a cultural cohesion which they saw as an ideal aspiration. It was a model of social and artistic perfectibility for the modern world. In art, politics, and philosophy Athens was the first true manifestation of human creativity. Its culture was natural, spontaneous, innocent, a first flowering of a form of human existence which has subsequently atrophied and become sterile. To a great extent this was an idealized picture, but, as Schiller himself recognized, this unreflective unity could not last beyond the confines of the ancient Greek world. It contained its destruction within itself. Greek understanding ran ahead of experience and so required and inspired new artistic and social formations which challenged and displaced the old. Spontaneous unity could over time stultify and come to form an obstacle to progress.[5]

Schiller's solution to the problem of human diversity was to re-emphasize what he understood as the essential Classical Greek ideal – virtue as a natural and spontaneous delight. Schiller's notion of play incorporates the twin ideas of effortless goodness and virtue as beauty which distinguished human experience in form and in aspiration. But this synthesis did not confront the antagonism between the human and the natural worlds, but rather by-passed it in the hope that full human realization would be found in a perfect unity between knower and known, virtue and beauty, morality and aesthetics. Hegel was much influenced by both Schiller's diagnosis of the cultural malaise of the modern world and his prognosis, but, as Hegel recognized, it was primarily a programme of aesthetic re-education, and, as such, lacked a firm and comprehensive ontological foundation.

The philosophical reaffirmation of human unity is the most general description possible of Hegel's project. It involves charting human consciousness to reveal its logical stages, distinctions, and ultimate unity. It lays human history before us not as accidental or contingent but as constituting the development of human freedom. It portrays experience in its moral, social, economic, and political aspects as an organic unity, a process of fulfilment and completion. Vital here is his recognition that the overcoming of estrangement is a human achievement. Human activity is vulnerable in different ways to incompleteness. It may be threatened by false accounts of itself. What appears as an authentic moral ideal may turn out to be suspect and illusory. A moral stage of development thought to be permanent and complete in itself may be temporary and transitional. These are forms of error by which human consciousness may deceive itself and they constitute a spiritual disorder to whose nature we must now turn.

Self-consciousness and the development of mind form a conceptual starting-point for Hegel's discussion of moral innocence. It enables him to place it in the context of a dynamic ethic free from the static constraints of empiricism and moral psychologism. Innocence, therefore, is a stage in human development, one which is primitive and unformed. Hegel speaks of innocence involving an unbroken unity with nature. It possesses an unreflective perfection and vitality which is God-like in character. Perception is direct and immediate, offering a spontaneous harmony with nature and with others. It is a state which

> has not as yet passed over into division or dualism, which has not yet broken up into the dualism of good and evil, nor into the subordinate dualism represented by the multiplicity, intensity, and passion of human needs.[6]

This unity is not an illusion, but it is not sufficient for human self-consciousness. Its wholeness is unrelieved by difference and distinction. It has nothing to contemplate. Action is, therefore, impossible because innocence lacks a knowledge of good and evil and the development of human freedom is obstructed. Innocence is not simply at one with nature but is rather a capitulation to it.

> this innocence is not the true position of man; the morality which is free is not that of the child; it stands higher than the innocence just spoken of, it is self-conscious willing; and in this the true attitude is for the first time reached.[7]

For Hegel it is mere 'sickly philanthropy' to wish human beings back to such an innocent state. It retards the development of moral freedom, and its persistence translates childhood into childishness, simplicity to simple-mindedness. In his *Aesthetics* Hegel argues that the appropriate artistic vehicle for the expression of innocence is the idyll, an art form which he thinks exists only by ignoring all the deeper aspects of human moral existence.

> in this context to live 'innocently' only means to know of nothing except eating and drinking, and indeed of none but very simple foods and drinks, e.g., the milk of goats and sheep, and, at a pinch, cows; vegetables, roots, acorns, fruit, cheese made from milk; bread, I suppose, is really post-idyllic, but meat must be allowed earlier because shepherds and shepherdesses will not have wished to sacrifice their sheep whole to the gods. Their occupation consists in tending their beloved flock the whole live-long day with their faithful dog, providing their food and drink, and all the time nursing and cherishing, with as much sentimentality as possible, such feelings as do not disturb this

peaceful and contented life; i.e., in being pious and gentle in their own way, blowing on their shawms, scrannel-pipes, etc., singing in chorus, and especially in making love to one another with the greatest tenderness and innocence.[8]

This caustic passage expresses Hegel's contemptuous judgement of sentimental innocence as a moral outlook. It is not simply complacent. It is vacuous. Innocence is an indeterminate ideal, a condition which has not yet become a part of the world. It lacks the one-sidedness and separation which Hegel considers prerequisites for ethical development. He writes of innocence:

it is a state in which in its fullness and power of ethical life the monster of disunion still only slumbered, because for *our* examination only the aspect of its substantial unity exhibited itself, and therefore too individuality was present only in its universal guise in which, instead of asserting its determinacy, it disappears again without trace and without essential hindrance.[9]

Hegel half-recognizes the innate power of innocence which is later analysed by Kierkegaard,[10] and he hints at its moral dangers to the holder and to others. He describes a Golden Age:

Under such conditions on the one hand nature satisfied without trouble to meet every need that may stir within him, while on the other hand in his innocence he is content with what meadows, woods, flocks, a little garden and a hut can afford him by way of nourishment, housing and other amenities, because all the passions of ambition or avarice, impulses which appear contrary to the higher nobility of human nature, are still altogether quiescent.[11]

Why does Hegel consider such a life to be aimless, boring, and ultimately dissatisfying? It is restricted in a manner which robs action of any significance in the world. Innocence is a form of poverty for Hegel. It fails to recognize the moral necessity of work, interests, and needs as vehicles for the development of a deep range of moral expressions and judgements. Love is construed devoid of the threat of jealousy and ignorant of the shadow cast by passion. Generosity is understood in a world not limited by scarcity, and courage is not tempered by any serious risk.

These ethical limitations of innocence are further explored by

Hegel in his introduction to the *Lectures on the Philosophy of World History*. There he describes innocence as a pre-conscious state, one which exists prior to the consciousness of good and evil. It cannot, therefore, exist as an object of history because the innocent are not yet capable of reflective thought, and it is only in thought that historical practices can be apprehended. Hegel exaggerates when he describes total innocence as a condition of animality, but his implication is that it is not capable of full human recognition and action. Indeed, he gives this state a geographical location:

> in Africa as a whole, we encounter what has been called the *state of innocence*, in which man supposedly lives in unity with God and nature. For in this state, man is as yet unconscious of himself. The spirit should not remain permanently in such a state, however, but must abandon this primitive condition. The primitive state of nature is in fact a state of animality. Paradise was that zoological garden in which man lived in an animal condition of innocence – but this is not his true destiny.[12]

In this passage Hegel's implicit criticism of Schlegel has a wider philosophical bearing. True human identity requires the loss of innocence and a knowledge of good and evil. Human agency does not become authentic until it knows opposition, estrangement, and division, until it experiences the frustration of its will. Innocence construes the will as effortless and limitless. This means that it no longer has moral point. Innocence must be displaced if morality is to make sense at all. Responsibility and moral choice can only take place in an identity which has reached self-consciousness and which contains moral differentiation within itself.

When Hegel speaks of a true destiny he does not regard innocence as an original condition from which humanity has lapsed. Hegel reverses this traditional picture by redescribing the lapse as an opening of moral possibilities. In this way, innocence, the unity of the spirit with its determination, becomes a phenomenological aspiration only after the acknowledgement of the differentiation which marks its end. This makes it difficult for Hegel to appreciate the persistence of moral innocence as anything other than an ethical aberration in the development of full moral self-consciousness.

Hegel's understanding of the process by which moral self-awareness is reached enables him to identify moral anachronisms and stunted moral growth. Rosen develops this point further in his discussion of the pure conscience whose inadequacies Hegel charts in the *Phenomenology*, and strikingly illustrates the limits of innocence in the context of the actual world.

> Silence prior to the experience of Western history would be innocence or ignorance. Silence in the midst of cultivated enlightenment would be a surrender to nihilism. Silence after speech has been completed, or all possible interpretations have been offered, is potential wisdom.[13]

Hegel does not speak directly about the variety of ways in which innocence may be lost. This does not mean he thinks it a matter of moral indifference to a society how moral maturity and full self-understanding are reached. Equally, he does not explore in detail the political ramifications of innocence whose loss is delayed. Rather he relates this to a characteristic form taken by moral innocence – universal love. Here the representative figure is Jesus and Hegel's discussion anticipates his examination of the 'beautiful soul' in the *Phenomenology*.

In the *Phenomenology* Hegel describes the first appearance of Spirit in the world as 'innocent but hardly good'.[14] Hegel's criticism of conscience is based on his assertion that no private and subjective source of moral integrity can instigate public rules of conduct sufficient to form a moral community. As his criticism of Kant makes clear, this cannot be achieved by the location of moral imperatives in rationality alone. To what extent does Christian love provide an adequate basis for morality? Hegel's answer to this question is important for our purposes because such love is one of the guises worn by absolute virtue in the world.

Hegel understood the teaching of Jesus as a universal human love based not on a transcendent deity or on religious dogma but on a conscious appeal to a common human sentiment, and in his early theological essays he explains how a creed which was initially humanistic was transformed into a transcendental world view split from the community it attempted to reform. Jesus needed to speak in the religious language of the Jewish community if his revolutionary beliefs were to be understood at all. The consequent misunderstanding by his disciples led to his aphoristic remarks and exemplary conduct being converted into a doctrine, and incorporated into a Church separate from community and state. Whereas Jewish religion involved an authoritarian God separate from the community, Jesus attempted to unite religious faith with human existence. For Hegel this aspiration was close to his own concerns, the recovery of wholeness and the integrity of communal life. Nevertheless he considered Jesus' mission to have been a failure: Jesus never completely overcame the problem of addressing a community whose prevailing religious ethos ran against the ideas he wished to disseminate. To use the language of the community to spread his beliefs risked compromising them. To refuse to employ such language meant that his criticisms remained unintelligible to those who most needed to understand them. This criticism is not directed exclusively at Christian moral theology, but would apply to any revolutionary doctrine which used the vocabulary of the time to communicate its ideas.

Love is the central element in the teaching of Jesus but it cannot avoid conflict with a world in which evil exists. Taylor poses the question:

> Suppose I am attacked, and have to fight for my rights or let
> injustice be done. In either case I must transgress against the
> unity of life, by what I do or what I suffer.[15]

The resolution which Jesus arrived at was a willing sacrifice of rights and a determination to repay evil with good. For Hegel this retention of purity was possible only at the cost of withdrawal from the world. Is this why Hegel considers such love to be deficient? Withdrawal to a realm of private virtue was for Hegel the ultimate fate of love, and involved a further fragmentation between individual and communal life which Hegel became increasingly concerned to overcome. Love was the subjective expression of morality and demanded that the world accommodate itself to its singular will. As such it was bound to retreat from the world when it discovered that its moral requirements could not be met.

In one of his early essays Hegel reflected on the idea of a community based exclusively on integrity by considering the fate of the disciples after the Crucifixion. Here the weaknesses in love which he claimed to have detected in Christ are more clearly manifest. The isolated community becomes preoccupied with the security of its own virtue. It separates itself from the world and abolishes anything which tells against the common integrity. Love obliterates individuality; we are presented with a community bound together not by interest, fear, or rights, but only by love.

in love's task the community scorns any unification save the deepest, any spirit save the highest.[16]

All non-moral excellences which lie outside love, the various and manifold interests and activities of life, are regarded as inferior if love is placed at the summit of human experience. This is to render human life deficient by diminishing the practices into which human beings pour their energy and ingenuity. Thus a community based on love must restrict everything which threatens its existence. Hegel argues that

the contra-natural expansion of love's scope becomes entangled in a contradiction, in a false effort which would bound to become the father of the most appalling fanaticism, whether of an active or a passive life.[17]

So love as the exclusive principle of moral and social life must change into its opposite. Its flight from all determinate forms of life and activity must involve their eventual incorporation and destruction.

Later Hegel described love as 'the most tremendous contradiction',[18] incapable of sustaining the logical structure of an independent public world. As a matter of private feeling, love cannot account for the permanence and continuity of the public world of family, civil society, and state. Hegel considers that it is only by transition to Ethical Life, mediated through the institution of the family, that love can play a part in the formation of a substantial moral community. In this way, social practices and political institutions are understood as necessary to the unified development of consciousness. Such developments involve objective features, rules, and policies, which are logically separable from the subjective manifestation of love and which cannot be explained in its terms without instability and loss. Hegel's point here is that there is a fundamental conceptual difference between the private feeling of love and the public world of ethical life and political action. If these two worlds are not kept separate then the distances between individuals which political space involves are closed. All are judged by the exclusive standard of love, with heresies, fanaticism, and persecutions seen as natural consequences. Unlike moral innocence, which is not yet conscious either of itself or its place in the world, love is self-conscious in a way which is ambivalent even when directed towards its exclusive object. Hegel thinks that love particularizes its object in a way which is unstable and completely fails to account for the permanence of relationships outside its domain. Love polarizes the community into the assertion of itself and its opposite – hate. In terms of political action, then, love either instigates a withdrawal from the responsibilities of rule with the consequent disasters which result or it expresses its frustration in revenge.

> Intelligent, substantial beneficence is, however, in its richest and most important form the intelligent universal action of the State – an action compared with which the action of a single individual . . . is so insignificant that it is hardly worth talking about. The action of the State is, moreover, of so great a power that, if the action of the individual were to oppose it, and either were intended to be a downright, explicitly criminal act, or the individual out of love for someone else wanted to cheat the universal out of its right, and its share in the action, such an action would be altogether useless and inevitably frustrated.[19]

The maintenance of private virtue is possible only by withdrawing from the world. This paralyses action, separates the moral consciousness from the only source of its proper fulfilment, and leaves the agent divided against himself because he is no longer part of the world. It is the condition which Hegel described as 'the beautiful soul'.

In the *Phenomenology*, following his analysis of the terror experienced during the later stages of the French Revolution, Hegel critically dissects three forms of moral certitude all exhibited in Kantian moral thinking. Kant's opposition between morality and inclination is aimed at establishing the autonomy of ethics against heteronomous considerations. First, it establishes moral certainty by contrast with nature, but, as Hegel points out, this opposition is not accidental to morality but essential to it. Without inclination to struggle against, morality would have no point. Second, moral certainty is found in the distinction between duty and empirical will, but for Hegel this claim can only be formal. Its abstract principle of universalization is in principle satisfiable by anything. Thus, it cannot operate as a criterion of morality. Third, these weaknesses force Kant's notion of moral autonomy to separate from the world. Moral experience is, therefore, based on a division between what is and what ought to be. Kant's attempt to give ethics a certainty based on a separation from the world can only fail. The moral legislator allows Kant to draw illuminating contrasts with utilitarianism but offers the illusory morality of universalizability and a belief that morality can issue from rational individual choice alone. With these dualisms and negations before it the moral subject retreats into a realm of pure conscience. The gulf between moral intention and action in the world which was found to wreck Kantian morality is overcome by an act of pure will or moral intuition. There is no logical space between moral action and discursive interpretation. To allow this would be to re-open the gap which undermined formalist ethics. On this view, morality is a kind of inspiration; it is a pure virtue free from any further internal or external determination. But this can only be maintained by preserving its universality, which means that moral purity lives in constant fear of sacrificing its certainty to the world. For Hegel the Romantic notion of 'the beautiful soul' arose directly from the intrinsic weaknesses of Kant's separation of morality from nature. Duty can only manifest itself in particular actions but this contradicts its universality. The recognition of this creates 'the beautiful soul'. Rosen explains Hegel's point:

> When spirit recognises this, it inevitably retreats from a separate reality to itself as pure universality, or denies the reality of the particular while defining the Whole as an identity of beauty and goodness in the truth of self.[20]

The 'beautiful soul' functions to remove moral particularity. It has no determinacy. This means that its moral purity prevents its signification in the world. The result is that the 'beautiful soul' is incapable of action. This is the most important dimension of Hegel's criticism. The true element of 'the beautiful soul' is its embodiment of ideals, but it does this in a way which is purely universal. Morality has to be made articulate in the world and this is possible only by the exercise of judgement. Moral purity is a form of selfishness, not in the sense that it places its interests before those of others, but because it cannot act in the world at all without undermining its nature. It lives in constant dread of self-annihilation. But the 'beautiful soul' is in the end simply a highly sophisticated withdrawal from the world and one which Hegel considers to be virtually impossible to sustain. Human beings possess language, and speech is impossible without particularity in moral as in any other matters. Thus Hegel considers 'the beautiful soul' is a moral phantom:

> Its activity is a yearning which merely loses itself as consciousness becomes an object devoid of substance, and, rising above this loss,

and falling back on itself, finds itself only as a lost soul. In this transparent purity of its moments, an unhappy, so-called 'beautiful soul', its light dies away within it, and it vanishes like a shapeless vapour that dissolves into thin air.[21]

As Taylor points out,[22] the problem of moral purity is created by the fact that in a human context moral ideals require embodiment in action, institution, policy, and practice if they are to avoid a permanent state of non-existence. Hegel's reconciliation of the conflicting moral tendencies of universal and particular takes up the remainder of this section of the *Phenomenology* and in a strong sense provides a programme for Hegel's substantial moral and political philosophy.

The ethics of the heart for Hegel represent a profound source of moral disorder. This arises because their basis is nothing more than subjective feeling divorced from thought and therefore a form of vanity. Subjectivity is incapable of giving an account of morality. Thus, the moral sensitivity of the 'beautiful soul' is not a moral position at all but rather a psychic disturbance. As Hegel writes:

> if a good heart, a good intention, a subjective conviction are set forth as the sources from which conduct derives its worth, then there is no longer any hypocrisy or immorality at all; for whatever a man does, he can always justify by the reflection on it of good intentions and motives, and by the influence of that conviction it is good.[23]

The aspiration to a perfect, private virtue is unendurable and self-contradictory. Moral goodness is either confined to a personal cage or released to infect a community of saints, in which case it is no longer the exclusive possession of a single individual. The virtuous conscience comes into conflict with moral and civil law. The solution can be abdication from the world, a position taken by 'the beautiful soul'. Reconciliation is possible in a higher moral and political synthesis. The conflict between 'the beautiful soul', which above all else must maintain its moral purity, and the pure conscience, which attempts to act in the world, must be transcended.

In the *Phenomenology* this debate appears as a philosophical duel between moral hero and valet. Each accuses the other of hypocrisy on grounds of betrayal of the universal good, and, in the case of the moral hero, of being virtuous in name only. Hegel's adjustment of these conflicting moral understandings of the relation between virtue

139

and action outlines a higher conceptual platform on which both will appear. The moral hero accepts that he must act in the world if his morality is to be more than mere ideal. The valet recognizes that his willingness to act must acknowledge the guidance of morality if it is to be more than pragmatic adjudication. In this way Hegel seeks a more satisfactory way of explaining the relation between virtue and the world. His criticisms of the about-to-be morality of innocence, the limp self-enclosed preoccupations of love, and the refinements of 'the beautiful soul', all imply that moral individualism which looks on the good as its private domain requires transcendence.

> Virtue is not merely like the combatant, who, in the conflict, is only concerned with keeping his sword bright, but it has even started the fight in order to preserve the weapons. And not only can it not use its own weapons, it must also preserve intact those of the enemy and protect them against its own attack, for all are noble parts of the good, on behalf of which it went into battle.[24]

Moral goodness which is preoccupied with its own innocence cannot act morally in the world. It is morally impotent. In the struggle against evil Hegel's 'knight of virtue' participates only in a 'sham-fight':

> what he turns against the enemy and finds turned against himself, and what he runs the risk of wasting and damaging both in his own case as well as that of the enemy, is not to be the good itself; for he fights to preserve and accomplish that. What are risked in the fight are only the gifts and capacities which are not themselves at issue.[25]

Goodness is an object of individual pride only because it exists outside the world. It dare not risk its purity in action and it will be ignored by the historical and political processes it refuses to acknowledge.

Such ethical distortions require a transition to the idea of a moral community in which the individual will discover his autonomy and freedom. Hegel describes this process in terms of both the development of mind and the acquisition of its history. Moral choice takes place in a context which is collective and historical. In the course of critically building on the advances of Kant's republicanism and Rousseau's General Will, Hegel considered that morality as self-subsisting will required political transcendence in a number of important ways. First, following Aristotle, it was Hegel's view that what is most significant about human excellences, moral as well as non-moral, is that they cannot be pursued by individuals in isolation from one another. They require a public world for their expression, determination, and completion. Virtue, therefore, is not a private concern. To think this is already to estrange oneself from the moral community which is its only authentic source of life. Second, this public world must be comprehensively defined and expressed in terms of the state. It cannot allow completely autonomous associations within it if its authority is to be substantiated. Third, this public world is not a political artifice, a human invention. Political existence takes place, not in a moral vacuum, but in an historical context of shared discourse. In this way, Hegel claimed to provide a grounding for morality which avoids the excesses of subjective will expressed in terms of hedonism or absolute virtue. The move from individual to communal morality in Hegel has raised considerable difficulties, including the clash between the moral priorities of the individual and those of the community.

Hegel was clearly aware of the possibility of tragic conflict between moral duties, as his discussion of Sophocles' *Antigone* shows. But his response is coloured by a number of crucial intellectual considerations. Hegel's fierce criticism of all forms of moral individualism led him to search for a higher reconciliation of apparent moral conflict. The philosophical method of placing moral actions in social and civic contexts of increasing logical adequacy entailed the reduction of conflicts which would qualify as genuine dilemmas or clashes of right with right. Hegel's constant emphasis on history as both the process and condition of moral action leads him to give less weight to individual understanding and more to the historic role of individuals, their decisions and actions. His determined criticism of utilitarianism as the ethical arm of empiricism means that it is not open to him to reconcile such conflicts or resolve such dilemmas by reference to consequentialist considerations. These points come together in a notably complicated manner when we raise the problem of political morality. Does Hegel's criticism of the good will leave political morality in a state of unbearable tension with the structure of Hegel's civic vision?

Two crucial differences distance Hegel's thought from Machiavelli regarding the problem of political morality. First, Hegel considered that the realist who claimed to have found the key to human motivation in selfishness was as ignorant as the knight of virtue with his belief in universal good.

> The individuality of the 'way of the world' may well imagine that it acts only for *itself* or in its own interest. It is better than it thinks, for its action is at the same time an implicitly universal action. When it acts in its own interest, it simply does not know what it is doing; and when it avers that everyone acts in his own interest, it is merely asserting that no one knows what action is.[26]

History and sociality combine to make both the vision of the knight of virtue and that of the realist redundant. The Machiavellian politician, therefore, mistakenly identifies the world with his pessimistic vision of it. Whereas the virtuous man sees the political arena as better than it is, the realist sees it as worse. Second, in the *Philosophy of Right*, Hegel draws an explicit connection between what he terms the hypocrisy of the modern age and the doctrine that the end justifies the means. On this basis, any crime may be permitted, any gross immorality condoned, so long as it leads to a noble or morally worthy goal. Hegel considers this the form of hypocrisy appropriate to the modern world, a disease generated by an exclusive dependence on conscience as the source of moral inspiration and authority. Hypocrisy holds up evil as good and finds a reason in its own eyes for regarding the evil it does as good.

> Theft in order to do good to the poor, theft or flight from battle for the sake of fulfilling one's duty to care for one's life or one's family (a poor family perhaps into the bargain), murder out of hate or revenge (i.e. in order to satisfy one's sense of one's own rights or of right in general, or one's sense of another's wickedness, of wrong done by him to oneself or to others or to the world or the nation at large, by extirpating this wicked individual who is wickedness incarnate, and thereby contributing at least one's quota to the project of uprooting the bad) – all these actions are made well intentioned and therefore good by this method of taking account of the positive aspect of their content.[27]

Hegel's criticism of utilitarian instrumentality, of the idea of the state and civil association as merely technical devices for the satisfaction of wants, means that his account of political morality reaches beyond pragmatism. Instrumentality and technicality in relation to wants and needs both find expression in the complete human community in the form of Civil Society, but they have no place in the complex interface which exists between politics and morality. Hegel in his political writings expresses admiration for Machiavelli whose texts embody the historic necessities which surround the call for the liberation of Italy from foreign rule. But Hegel's ambition to explore the manifold unfolding of the Spirit as a form of thought means that it is impossible for him to be content with Machiavelli's ungrounded assertion of the separation of morality and politics. Hegel explains their distinctiveness in a way which attempts to show how one logically supplants the other without thereby abolishing it. This implies that Hegel sees the problem of political morality not as an ends/means difficulty but as a tragic moral dilemma. As such it is a necessary stage in the formation of objective Spirit. The conflict between the requirements of politics and the scruples of morality occurs at a stage when the harmony between individual and community is incomplete, but this is not accidental or purposeless. Such moral antagonism is necessary for the civic spirit to develop and fully understand itself. The moral conflict in *Antigone*, therefore, was for Hegel of much more importance for this development than a simple battle between conscience and *realpolitik*. Antigone represents authentic and binding human values. Her virtue is not merely that of the private and the subjective, 'the beautiful soul'. Equally, the character of Creon expresses a genuine political realm. Great stress is placed on the moral significance of this conflict in three main ways. First, Hegel emphasizes the tragic character of the disagreement. Neither protagonist can escape without loss. There is no simple consequentialist solution. Second, he tends to see the dilemma as arising from the conflicting tendencies within the city-state. It is, therefore, removed from the individual to the historical level of understanding; the conflict expresses the divisions within the polis at a particular stage of its development. Again, the conflict is not accidental or contingent to that development. It is an experience which must be undergone, with whatever pain and suffering attend it. These are not matters of individual choice. Morality is superseded by its historical conditions. Third, Antigone's guilt is not merely civil or legal. It is a necessary step in the development of the unity between morality and politics. For Hegel, Antigone in recognizing this reaches a sublime ethical plane. George Steiner writes:

The sacramental overtones in Hegel's idiom are unmistakeable. Antigone is set above Socrates, a formidable elevation if we bear in mind the literally talismanic status of Socrates as the wisest and purest of mortals throughout Idealist thought and Romantic iconography.[28]

As Steiner is aware,[29] this estimation of Antigone's moral importance displaces Jesus. Socrates to the end proclaimed his innocence of the crime with which he was charged. Jesus retreated from the world to protect his moral purity. Antigone in Hegel's judgement represents a profound ethical sacrifice, not only as individual symbol of universal moral awareness, but as embodiment of cultural transformation.

Hegel's analysis of moral innocence, love, and 'the beautiful soul' is of moral phenomena he considers half-formed. Love and the pursuit of moral purity are myopic perceptions of the moral; innocence is no perception at all. For Hegel these are perversions of morality rather than morality itself. They represent the formative stage of consciousness; innocence, which must destroy itself in its contact with the world or live on in a state of blissful ignorance, is youth understood on its own terms. Tragic moral dilemmas are understood, too, as manifesting moral ideals only half-known, virtue not yet fully grasped, awaiting completion by an additional dialectical shift or a further historical transformation. Philosophy and history in their most overwhelming presences dominate Hegel's conception of moral phenomena. They determine his understanding of ethical normality, of possible moral conflict, and of the nature of virtue in the world. This means that the tension essential to such features of experience is dissipated. Their existential significance is transposed to a broader intellectual and historic canvas. Thus, the dilemmas of political morality are diluted and the complex moral choices they involve are switched to a different logical plane. As Judith Shklar points out:

> Moreover, the adversary of Hegel's man of virtue is not a bigoted despot such as Philip II of Spain, but any Machiavellian politician willing to use whatever weapons are available to serve his ambitions. In the *Phenomenology* Hegel is concerned only with a Don Quixote who behaves, not like a feudal knight, but like a talkative pseudo-Plutarchian hero of the civil life.[30]

Hegel's estimation of Antigone is dependent on her being seen as bearing the guilt involved in acting in the world. She defends her moral beliefs and does not withdraw to an inner realm of safeguarded purity. While Antigone's moral problem is not one of ends and means her confrontation with Creon necessarily involves loss of innocence. If this is true then Antigone represents an enduring dilemma regarding the boundaries of morality and politics and not one which is just a significant stage in the historical development of a particular culture. Does Hegel give an adequate account of innocence and its political impact? Hegel's discussion of morality is found against the background of world history as the manifestation of freedom. However, his 'slaughter-bench' interpretation of the victims of the historical process requires some account of the relation between intention and outcome, of why it is that the victories of historical transformation are good and evil, civilized and barbaric alike. Hegel's own explanation in terms of the realization of freedom needed a supplementary but important reference to unwitting mechanisms like the 'Cunning of Reason' for it to work. It is possible to admit the existence of unintended outcomes but deny Hegel's attempt to explain them in terms of unconscious human foils. Hegel's explanation of how the most virtuous may endanger themselves and their world rests on his understanding of history, of the state, and of the development of human consciousness. If this fails we must revise our assessment of absolute virtue and its place in politics.

In Nietzsche's writings we find some of the most venomous attacks on innocence as a moral disposition. In *Daybreak* he speaks of the dangers of sexual innocence:

> The innocent will always be the victims because their ignorance prevents them from distinguishing between measure and excess and from keeping themselves in check in good time.[31]

For Nietzsche, innocence is described generally as a disposition which is blighted, corrupted, or ruined. He denies that the world has an essential ethical significance which it is the business of philosophy to discover and rejects the guiding assertions of Christian theology.

Nietzsche's philosophical explorations are an attempt to work out the implications of his nihilism. What kind of ethics, art, or philosophy would we have if we discarded our assumption that we inhabit a universe which is ordered, stable, rational, and permanent? The question represents a profound scepticism towards traditional metaphysics. There is no consolation to be gained from philosophical system-building. Theories of ethics are false attempts to imprison the world in a framework of illusory essences.

Realism in the Sophists, in Thucydides, and in Machiavelli is set by Nietzsche against what he calls 'the moralistic and idealistic swindle' put forward by Socrates. Nietzsche inverts the Socratic moral injunctions; his perception of the role played by 'the will to power' in Greek life protects him against seeing Greek culture as the realm of the 'beautiful soul' and of 'noble simplicity'. He turns down the dogmatic erection of theory above life and asserts instead the value of individual moral strenuousness in a hollow world. This individualism makes him reluctant to attach significance to associations as distinct logical entities. The problem of political morality is, therefore, for Nietzsche explicable only in realistic terms. His criticism of Christian ethics and his scornful rejection of Kantian moral formalism, 'the categorical imperative smells of cruelty'[32], leave him with the problem of elucidating the moral self in company with a sustained denial of the ethical value of selflessness, that is of describing moral innocence in the context of a belief in the inescapability of the will.

All forms of moral humanitarianism constitute decadence and elevate the slavish and the weak above those who are morally determined and strong. Nietzsche's emphasis is on the will as restless and striving and on practical intelligence as overcoming internal and external obstacles to achievement. Determination, endurance, and cunning are necessary characteristics of the admirable disposition. Nietzsche associates innocence with lack of power, with weakness, and with withdrawal. It is important to assert, however, that what is often taken to be moral scepticism is better understood as his attempt to release moral dispositions from their concealment beneath hypocrisy and social convention. More radically, his infamous claim that 'morality is a special case of immorality' may be read as neither scepticism nor a calculation of the costs of attempting to act well but as drawing our attention to the transformation of values such as pity in different types of moral character and circumstance. Nevertheless, it is undeniable that it is absolute morality which is the object of his critical attack and that this specifically includes innocence. The task of explaining this is not one for the faint-hearted:

the most distinctive feature of modern souls and modern books is not lying but their inveterate innocence in moralistic mendaciousness. To have to rediscover this 'innocence' everywhere – this constitutes perhaps the most disgusting job among all the precarious tasks a psychologist has to tackle today; it is part of *our* great danger – it is a path that may lead precisely *us* toward great nausea.[33]

Innocence is a state of continuous youth in which maturity is permanently delayed and illusion reigns. Nietzsche stresses the ignorance of innocence which prohibits self-awareness and hence self-mastery. If the innocent are ignorant of their weakness then they have nothing to struggle against or overcome. This ignorance creates moral havoc for the innocent and the world around them. They are unable to distinguish between measure and excess. They have unreal expectations of others and they believe that what they happen to be used to will continue irrespective of changing circumstances. Belief for the young is unconditional and lacks the nuances necessary for existence in a harsh world. Innocence alternates between extreme anger and extreme reverence. The standard description of innocence as naivety, however, surely does not capture its full moral force because innocence is both a stage of human existence common to all and the embodiment of moral purity.

Does Nietzsche have nothing to say about a lasting moral purity like saintliness? He explicitly states in *Ecce Homo* that he would 'prefer to be even a satyr to being a saint'.[34] For Nietzsche, saintliness is a problem of interpretation. It represents a conversion from evil to good which can only be explained by reducing both to a common origin. There might be a difficulty about saintliness if moral qualities were autonomous but they are not. They find their origin in the will in the same way as all drives to power. Nietzsche discusses saintliness as a neurosis, connecting it with sensuality and a determination to be too good for the world, 'the debauch' of sainthood. In *Beyond Good and Evil* admiration for saints is explicitly connected with the 'will to power'; when the saint is honoured it is because of his strength of self-denial and his capacity to dominate and resist his own nature.[35] This awakens not moral respect but fear. In the absence of God, sainthood is associated with severe penitential demands – solitude, fasting, and abstinence – which Nietzsche thinks can only be explained as neurosis. This savage reductionism leads him to explain sainthood as madness:

The recipes for becoming a medicine-man among the Indians, a saint among the Christians of the Middle Ages, an angekok among Greenlanders, a pajee among Brazilians are essentially the same: senseless fasting, perpetual sexual abstinence, going into the desert or ascending a mountain or a pillar, or 'sitting in an aged willow tree which looks upon a lake' and thinking of nothing at all except what might bring on an ecstasy and mental disorder.[36]

Successful sainthood is a matter of social and historical accident:

in that age in which Christianity proved most fruitful in saints and desert solitaries, and thought it was proving itself by this fruitfulness, there were in Jerusalem vast madhouses for abortive saints, for those who had surrendered to it their last grain of salt.[37]

When saintliness is severed from religious belief and when its moral qualities are regarded as epiphenomena Nietzsche explains it as a psychological abnormality. It is a curiosity, a disorder of expression which owes its origin to the universal impulse which controls all human dispositions.

For Nietzsche, innocence can also be expressed in compassion or pity. This is associated with his extensive diatribe against selflessness, against all those saintly dispositions which diminish self to attend to the sufferings of others. Selflessness distracts us from the value of self-assertion which Nietzsche argues is essential to the fulfilment of human creative potential and development. Like his attack on all forms of moral egalitarianism as decline and decadence this is not simple callousness or immoralism. It is perfectly compatible with a profound concern for human suffering and a stress on those values which Nietzsche considers neglected by moral humanitarianism. He argues that life is inconceivable without suffering. Pity exaggerates the significance of suffering and consequently promotes an attitude to life which is insufficiently affirmative. In this way, Nietzsche locates an active response to suffering in the values of endurance, mastery, nobility, and courage. What matters to him is not suffering itself but how we respond to it, how it is transcended and endured. It is this which he regards as a possible object of esteem. Self-pity in the individual or the community provokes Nietzsche's contempt because it distracts from the way suffering may be used for artistic or historical purposes and encourages a preoccupation with the weaknesses and inadequacies of the suffering self. In short, Nietzsche reserves his most damaging vituperation for precisely the kind of absolute morality we have considered, and which he terms ascetic morality. This is the kind of moral understanding most associated with pity, self-renunciation, and humility. It stresses the value of goodness for its own sake and not for advantage or the satisfaction of the contrivances of life. Such a morality,

> insofar as it condemns for its own sake, and not out of regard for the concerns, considerations, and contrivances of life, is a specific error with which one ought to have no pity – an idiosyncracy of degenerates which has caused immeasurable harm.[38]

Absolute morality is not opposed here by moral pragmatics. It is accused of elevating selflessness above all other values.

Nietzsche's aims are perhaps nowhere better explained than in the Preface to his *Genealogy of Morals*. The virtues traditionally associated with moral worth – goodness, self-sacrifice, compassion – are, he claims, actually obstacles to moral understanding, and in them he discerns the greatest threat to humanity. A full account of this transvaluation of value is impossible here, but if moral innocence can be shown as morally and politically catastrophic and not merely for consequentialist reasons what moral account can be given of this? Nietzsche asks:

> What if a symptom of regression were inherent in the 'good', likewise a danger, a seduction, a poison, a narcotic, through which the present was possibly living *at the expense of the future*? . . . So that precisely morality would be to blame if the *highest power and splendour* actually possible to the type man was never in fact attained? So that precisely morality was the danger of dangers?[39]

In *Human, All Too Human* he writes of the transformation required if the conventional hierarchy of moral sensibilities is to be overturned:

> bringing forth the wise, innocent (conscious of innocence) man as regularly as it now brings forth – *not his antithesis but necessary preliminary* – the unwise, unjust, guilt-conscious man.[40]

As has been claimed,[41] the notion of the 'wise innocent man' is difficult to articulate. Indeed, Nietzsche's concept of the will as the operating principle of self-assertion seems to reduce the manifestations of willing to the will itself. As a result it is hard to see how it can account for the variety of expressions taken by the will in the world, in its objectification. Why should this diversity – ruling, instructing, caring, serving, loving, etc. – all be reduced to the common factor of willing? Nietzsche's individualism implies a diminution of all associative human forms, which tend to be seen as either autocratic or unheroic and utilitarian. The stress on self-assertion means that he is prone to construe politics by comparison with aesthetics, as a practice to be moulded by forces outside itself. Nietzsche's moral scepticism involves a revolutionary claim to overthrow absolute morality. Either this means an attempt to rescue certain moral values such as nobility and courage from obfuscation and neglect stemming from the preoccupation with innocence and purity or it is an attempt to go outside morality altogether. If the former, Nietzsche is speaking to those who can understand. If the latter, his thought appears to be a conversation with himself. Nietzsche's self-picture was a philosopher of culture, but his conception of man as self-authenticating seems to distort the relation between a culture and individual awareness. With his rejection of transcendence the only possible account of the realm of human value is in terms of self-creation. His attempt to break down the categories of reason and to develop an unsystematic philosophy and his insistence on the necessity of a fresh start provide a significant context for Arendt's political philosophy. However, having revised the terms of philosophical debate Nietzsche cannot fully contribute to it. With Marx, it is Nietzsche whom Arendt describes as having overturned the traditional relationship between *vita contemplativa* and *vita activa*. The consequent equation of life and being with its location of meaning in the notion of the will must be reckoned with if the nature of the world is to be properly articulated and the problems of political morality adequately dissected.

A neo-Machiavellian approach to the relation between ethics and politics is taken by Max Weber, who asserts that politics is distinctive by its use of violence. The contrast is with the idea of absolute morality exemplified in the Sermon on the Mount, which issues in rules which are unconditional, unambiguous, and unqualified. For Weber these commandments make up an ethic of saintliness.

Political injunctions reverse the order of unconditional ethics. They tolerate and allow confiscation, taxation, strikes, the resistance of evil by evil, and untruthfulness ranging from deception to lying. These political strategies characteristically receive a consequentialist

justification which the absolute ethic cannot include. This leads
Weber to contrast an 'ethic of ultimate ends' with an 'ethic of
responsibility'.

However, the decisive vehicle of political action is violence, so the
'ethic of responsibility' in politics is required to make some calculation
of consequence, some balancing of gain against loss. But,

> If one makes any concessions at all to the principle that the end
> justifies the means, it is not possible to bring an ethic of ultimate
> ends and an ethic of responsibility under one roof.[42]

Weber does make it clear that means in politics are not to be
regarded as neutral devices, nor are those who advocate and employ
them free from the specific moral consequences of so doing. This
leads him to argue that political engagement involves the understanding of what he terms 'these ethical paradoxes' and he indicts
absolute ethics specifically on two counts. First, those who seek
moral perfection are excluded from politics because politics must
include violence amongst its means and a willingness to place the
demands of the city above the purity of the heart. Second, a preoccupation with moral self is damaging in politics because it lacks an
awareness of the consequences of its concern for others. Such considerations prompt Weber to praise not the saint but the hero.

This stark division reflects the antinomic character of Weber's
thought. Someone either decides to live a life of sainthood, in which
case they withdraw from the problems posed by the world, or they
actively pursue political ends, in which case they have to face up to
the inevitable moral compromises which ensue. But Weber's belief
that the problem of political morality is a choice between Christ and
Caesar is too simple and reveals a romantic conception of man as
isolated, individual chooser. Our conceptions of the political world
and of the place of the moral agent in it are more complex than
Weber can admit.

My specific point concerns the connection between moral aspirations
and the world. How are moral values affected by contact with a
public world? One answer is to see it as a test. Experience challenges
morality by searching it for vulnerability. The result can be the
discovery of weakness and a possible willingness to settle for less
than moral perfection, to accept moral compromise. However some
moral dispositions do not accept mere adequacy. One such is the
Hegelian 'beautiful soul', whose fictional representation we might

find in Myshkin, the princely idiot of Dostoevsky's novel, amalgam of Christ, Don Quixote, and saintly fool, whose moral sense is absolute, free from guile, candid, and endlessly compassionate of the imperfections, misfortunes, and sufferings of others. In the absence of universal moral reason and the certainties of religious faith Dostoevsky locates moral purity in the utterance of an idiot. The public world is the context of Myshkin's moral interrogation. As J. P. Stern comments:

> Meekness, to survive, must be armed. If the meekness and forgiveness Myshkin has to offer is to be armed with wisdom and strength, these qualities must be tested in contact and conflict with those who now encompass his horizon, who are now his world. This is how the testing is done.[43]

Moral innocence is faced with hypocrisy and evil, snobbery and betrayal, falsehood and deception. It is challenged by political corruption in the form of revolutionaries who do not believe their own ideology and aristocrats who do not disguise their self-interest. Myshkin meets the specific challenges with infinite moral patience and forgiveness. The more unjustified and vile the personal exploitation of him, the more willing he is to understand, to put himself in the place of the critic, to appreciate the other's point of view. But to base forgiveness on inexhaustible moral feeling proves to be insufficient. It fails to provide a specific logical location for forgiveness in the world or in the moral agent who wishes to act in that way. The actions and changes of heart which merit forgiveness, which make it understandable and give it a point, are brushed aside in a display of moral feeling mistakenly thought by Myshkin to be sufficient for any circumstance. His moral innocence is shown to be what it is and the reactions of others to him change from admiration to jealousy and bafflement. Universal compassion proves an impossibility, and in Myshkin it unleashes a chain of consequences over which he has less and less control and which are profoundly damaging for those who are touched by them. It is not accidental that absolute morality enters the public world in the guise of an idiot. It has been publicly tested and found wanting, even positively dangerous. The juxtaposition of innocence and experience has a tragic outcome which seems to establish the limits of moral perfectibility. There is a point of moral attainment, a limit to moral aspiration, which can be surpassed only at the cost of self-deception. This moral finitude would seem to set the limits of morality in relation to politics, and demand transcendence by religious faith. But Myshkin embodies Nietzsche's despised sentimentalism and presents us with choice on the edge of doubt. How can the boundaries of moral goodness be established in the absence of metaphysical consolation and theological support? For Arendt it is not contingent that Myshkin embodies the morality of innocence:

> No clearer symptom of this modern religious situation can be found than the fact that Dostoevski . . . portrayed pure faith in the character of Myshkin 'the idiot'.[44]

Arendt gives a rich and provocative account of moral goodness in the public world.

In *The Human Condition* Arendt insists that goodness must shun the world of human appearances:

> goodness that comes out of hiding and assumes a public role is no longer good, but corrupt in its own terms and will carry its corruption wherever it goes.[45]

This means that such goodness is culpable:

> Every effort to make goodness manifest in public ends with the appearance of crime and criminality on the political scene.[46]

Why does Arendt assert such a radical dichotomy between absolute morality and the public world of politics? Her arguments are rooted in Hegel and Nietzsche, and her criticism of Christ and Socrates as embodiments of distinct forms of goodness owe much to their views. Her rejection of the public appearance of goodness does not mean that she condones the expression of cruelty or evil in politics. Indeed she argues that evil is directly destructive of a common world. Arendt does not make the conventional distinction between morality and politics in terms derived from the language of *realpolitik*. Her relationship to Machiavelli is complicated and cannot be expressed as straightforward indebtedness as she stresses features of his thought which do not fit with the standard realist interpretation. She accepts that values such as love and goodness which may be appropriate in private life are inappropriate and dangerous when translated into politics, but she claims that this does not mean that politics is a morally inferior realm in which impure choices have to be made. In her reading of Machiavelli the criterion of political action is not power but glory, and this view expresses itself in her own writings as an attempt to reconstitute politics as a region of human aspiration and fulfilment. Arendt's notion of the autonomy of politics involves mutual engagement and shared understanding. It is a resolute defence of politics against its enemies whether these are bureaucratic instrumentalism or the moral good. It is not surprising that she is unsympathetic to the conventional view of political morality as utilitarian calculation, a balancing of evil against good, a moral accountancy. The act which is described as the lesser evil is soon seen as not evil at all, and the possibility that evil will be done only when it is necessary soon translates into the probability that it will be done when it is not.

> 'With a 100 victims we shall save a 1,000.' This sounds to me like the latest version of human sacrifices: pick seven virgins, sacrifice them to placate the wrath of the gods. Well, this is not my religious belief, and [it] most certainly is not the faith of Judaism. 3) Finally, the theory of the lesser evil. Result: good men do the worst.[47]

There is a strong element of paradox in Arendt's reflections on political morality. She rejects the view of politics which requires morality to give way to advantage, but not from the standpoint of absolute morality. She rejects absolute morality, but not from a willingness to entertain moral compromise for reasons of political necessity. This paradox takes us to the heart of Arendt's political philosophy. In her *Lectures on Kant's Political Philosophy* her criticisms of absolute morality have a political resonance:

> If you do not resist evil, the evildoers will do as they please. Though it is true that, by resisting evil, you are likely to be involved in evil, your care for the world takes precedence in politics over your care for your self – whether this self is your body or your soul. Machiavelli's 'I love my native city more than my soul' is only a variation of: I love the world and its future more than my life or my self.[48]

In politics, preoccupation with moral purity has to take second place to a concern for the world; to place your self before the world is a form of moral corruption. The moral contrast between self and world is not a utilitarian but an ontological one. For Arendt, public has a logical priority over private. It provides a world in which the individual discovers an existence, a network of relationships with others and with institutions. It is a location for an embodied life in a constitution which cannot be reduced to an aggregate of atomistic wills. Absolute morality is a preoccupation with moral self; as such it is antagonistic to worldliness and politics to which its presence is a source of danger. The manifestations of absolute morality for Arendt are love, goodness, conscience, compassion, and pity. All are forms of subjectivity which imperil politics. She finds the historical embodiment of absolute morality in the Socratic moral injunctions and in the maxims of Christianity. What is it about such expressions of value that requires their severance from politics?

In Arendt the contrast between love and politics could not be drawn more clearly. Love removes the distance between individuals which is created by politics and on which it depends. In a political community individuals are related, but independent, connected, but separate, bound by mutual respect and a common public world. This does not abolish difference but sustains it by recognizing the importance of indirect institutional and rule-governed mediations between individuals. Love in its striking immediacy and directness cannot be satisfied with anything less than its own completion and satisfaction. It is, therefore, an enemy of the public realm and if it succeeds in displacing it will create terror.

Similarly Arendt excludes conscience as a route for the entry of morality into politics. Conscience places the consolations of self before the requirements of a public world. On its own it is incapable of generating principles of justice and its self-regarding nature means that it is only its negative aspect which is morally admirable. Conscience may be asserted as resistance to oppression or evil in a manner that Arendt finds heroic, but it is open to abuse and, as she indicates in her writings on Eichmann, it is insufficient to prevent the perpetration of great evil.

Love and conscience can be seen as equivocal within the realm of ordinary moral relationships in addition to their incompatibility with politics. Absolute morality expressed as goodness is universally seen as admirable. Why should Arendt rigidly excluded it from politics? She sees such goodness in the life of Jesus, and in the character of Melville's Billy Budd. For Arendt, Christianity is other-worldly, a feature which derives from its moral eschatology and its practical moral teaching. Goodness cannot be expressed in public without transformation into something which is less than good. When good actions make a public appearance they cease to be performed for their own sake and become matters of public ownership and interpretation. Goodness cannot make itself public without the destruction both of itself and of politics. The reason is clear. Goodness is independent of speech, knowledge, and memory. It is not essential to goodness that its actions are spoken of, known, or remembered. However, these are qualities necessary to politics. Rapprochement is impossible without mutual destruction. Goodness cannot survive incorporation in the framework of politics. It is unpredictable and spontaneous, indifferent to the shared expectations of a common citizenship. Equally, politics cannot allow the emotional expression of goodness without being transformed into a private campaign against misery. Like Hegel, Arendt locates the terror in the aftermath of the French Revolution not in a hunger for power but in abstract compassion.

There are elaborate links between Arendt's rejection of goodness in politics and her moral diagnosis of the French Revolution. The feelings for the suffering of others do not simply provide an inadequate basis for a political community. Pity must instigate its opposite if its moral exclusivity is to be maintained. As the single, dominating motive for political engagement pity has to be unbounded. Everything is open to sacrifice in the name of the abolition of suffering. Moral limits are removed because pity always remains unsatisfied so long as suffering remains. It is the link between the moral sensitivity of 'the beautiful soul' and the extremism of coercive virtue. The limits and moral balances of republican virtue are entirely incompatible with a compassion which

> is directed solely, and with passionate intensity, toward suffering man himself; compassion speaks only to the extent that it has to reply directly to the sheer expressionist sound and gestures through which suffering becomes audible and visible in the world. As a rule, it is not compassion which sets out to change worldly conditions in order to ease human suffering, but if it does, it will shun the drawn-out wearisome processes of persuasion, negotiation and compromise, which are the processes of law and politics, and lend its voice to the suffering itself, which must claim for swift and direct action, that is, for action with the means of violence.[49]

As Arendt is aware, compassion and goodness are not identical but they share the characteristic of going beyond virtue and vice. Neither goodness nor badness have a place in the political world. Arendt is unusual amongst political philosophers in her recognition that innocence has a passive *and* an active sense; it can be harmed and suffer wrong, but it can also cause harm. How does she explain this? In a review published in 1946 she wrote:

The attempt of the Nazis to fabricate a wickedness beyond vice did nothing more than establish an innocence beyond virtue. Such innocence and such wickedness have no bearing on the reality where politics exists.[50]

Why is innocence incompatible with political life? Her answer is in terms not of its youth or its lack of realism and experience but of its unworldliness, a notion which is present in her remarkable reflections in *On Revolution* on Melville's *Billy Budd*. Billy is a paradigm of absolute goodness in an imperfect and often violent political world. His goodness is that of innocence, a state which Arendt, like Rousseau, considers is prior to virtue. Billy's moral character is unformed, unworldly, endowed with an unreflective goodness. She reads Melville as providing a sustained commentary on the state of nature theories of Romanticism, that man is good by nature and made corrupt by society. Melville's topic, then, is goodness outside virtue and evil outside vice. Budd's innocence is that of a foundling and Claggart's evil is that of a man whose origin is unknown. When Billy Budd is provoked by evil his response is to strike Claggart dead. It is immediate and direct. Billy's stammer means that it is not mediated by speech, the source of the political transcendence of good and evil. His act means the triumph of good, but it takes place in the world of political life where such absolute distinctions have no place. In this world his act is wrong, and it is this that creates the tragic dilemma for Captain Vere. Virtue must sustain human institutions and laws in imperfect association, built for men not for angels or devils, and this requires that the law take its course for the innocent as well as the guilty. What marks Billy Budd in Arendt's interpretation is his silent and infinite compassion, a feeling which is expressed in pity for Captain Vere when he sentences Billy to death. For Arendt, goodness abolishes the mediating institutions and practices of politics. The formal arrangements of politics are undermined. Political discourse is no longer between different individuals with differing concerns, wants, and interests, but is now between good and evil, a Manichean struggle between mutually exclusive opponents who will destroy all to achieve victory. Neither Billy Budd nor Claggart can sustain a political community. Only Captain Vere possesses the human capacity for virtue, to hang the embodiment of saintliness when it transgresses the laws and institutions of the imperfect human world. There is, therefore, a crucial connection between goodness and compassion. Arendt concludes her discussion of Melville with a series of assertions relating to guilt and innocence and their expression in politics.

> For goodness that is beyond virtue, and hence beyond temptation, ignorant of the argumentative reasoning by which man fends off temptations, and, by this very process, comes to know the ways of wickedness, is also incapable of learning the arts of persuading and arguing.[51]

For Arendt, the discovery of compassion by Rousseau received its political embodiment in Robespierre. It was he who 'carried the conflicts of the soul, Rousseau's *âme déchirée*, into politics, where they became murderous because they were insoluble.'[52] This discovery was itself a replacement of the ancient belief in original sin by the modern belief in original goodness. To give this political expression is to create a political economy of misery, so unleashing the dark possibility that violence is not only the prerogative of evil-doers.

These implications are drawn from Arendt's belief that absolute goodness is a form of solitude, not simply a disposition which withdraws from the world but one which cannot be expressed. Absolute badness is also beyond incorporation in the world. Claggart's evil is not merely perversion or sordid and sensual obsession. It is a direct challenge to the good and speaks to it on its own terms. Both obliterate the plurality on which political discourse depends. Neither is capable of conversation, of speaking in a public arena which is, on the model of the Athenian polis, expressive of freedom and citizenship alike. Motives are contrasted with words and deeds whose nature is bound up with appearance.

> motives behind such deeds and words are destroyed in their essence through appearance; when they appear they become 'mere appearances' behind which again other, ulterior motives may lurk, such as hypocrisy and deceit.[53]

Arendt's criticism of absolute goodness in politics does not rest on a straightforward distinction between conscience and political prudence, between goodness and a world in which men will have no choice but to act in a way which is less than good. Equally, she does not construe politics as purely a matter of administrative technique in which morally fundamental ends are suppressed. This means that the dilemmas of political morality appear for her in a paradoxical form. She refuses to understand politics as the area of utilitarian assessment and calculation and yet she resists the absolute morality on which such a refusal conventionally depends. This gives her conception of moral decision in politics a notably tragic quality.

Arendt's understanding of political morality is arguably the most idiosyncratic area of her thought. It exists against the background of her revaluation of politics as a realm of action in which the human aspiration for immortality can express itself. Politics is action in a public world and courage is needed to leave the comforts of the private life and assert and defend political judgements in public. She sees courage as the expression of human will. It is the opposite of prevarication and compromise. Decisiveness, determination, and a willingness to take moral and political risks are the hallmarks of courage in politics. In a public world it is an object of attention and observation in a way which is inconceivable in private. It is the logic of the public world which structures the moral values it can tolerate and admire. This leads Arendt to resolve the dilemmas of political morality through the persona of the political hero who, like the majestic figures of Machiavelli's *Discourses*, performs deeds of glory to preserve the republic against the onslaughts of temporality. The political hero has both courage and magnanimity and is contemptuous of 'beautiful souls' whose sensitivity, ignorance, and goodness makes them unaware of the realities of politics and of history. It should not be thought, however, that Arendt speaks about politics in an exclusively individual way. In her view, the distinctiveness of politics expresses itself only rarely in human lifetimes, but when it does it is within a public and communal frame of action. Thus she reserves her great admiration for the Athenian polis, for the Paris Commune, for the Soviets after the 1917 Russian Revolution, and for the 1956 Hungarian uprising. The value of such authentic political conduct is for her intrinsic, unrelated to outcome and desert. Courage is needed above all else to face the clear possibility of collective failure.

The emphasis on courage in a public world affects her understanding of the means/ends relationship, and Arendt gives this an
unconventional and dangerous twist. In *Men in Dark Times* she
writes:

> every good action for the sake of a bad end actually adds to the
> world a portion of goodness; every bad action for the sake of a
> good end actually adds to the world a portion of badness. In other
> words, whereas for doing and producing ends are totally
> dominant over means, just the opposite is true for acting: the
> means are always the decisive factor.[54]

Arendt rightly stresses that the conventional picture of ends being so
important that the choice of means is merely instrumental and
technical exists in thinking which is utilitarian and purposive. While
it is obviously true that bad ends are sometimes pursued courageously
it is equally true that this does not clinch the superiority of courage
as a moral value. Indeed, the significance of courage for Arendt
derives not from her revision of the ends/means relationship but
from the priority she gives to the public world.

Promise-keeping and forgiveness also play a part in Arendt's view
of political morality. Both are derived from the obligations necessary
to maintain a public world in which political action is possible. They
are values predicated of communities and their importance has to do
with maintaining stable human expectations and enabling shared
action to take place. This criticism of the private realm is at the
heart of her rejection of the Socratic moral absolute – it is better to
be harmed than to inflict harm. For Arendt this moral injunction is
concerned with private purity, with the avoidance of moral guilt and
remorse. There will always be circumstances in politics where self-
reproach is unavoidable and this requires not withdrawal to a private
life of solipsistic moral consolation but courage to face the moral
reality of a public world. Further, she believes that in the twentieth
century the modern evils of totalitarianism and genocide render the
Socratic position morally untenable. There are certain sufferings of
scale which cannot simply be endured.

Arendt does not approach political morality by way of the standard
contrast between a morality which is set by a framework of reciprocal
rights and obligations and an ethic which is supererogatory. She
attempts to derive courage, forgiveness, and truth-telling from the
character of politics as a public activity, often pursued in circumstances

of national danger in which the dilemmas of moral choice cannot be dispensed with by the methods of private consolation. The claim that there is a specific connection between politics and such values is intended to overcome the dualism which has traditionally beset discussions of the relation between politics and morality. Her reflections on truth-telling in politics resist the contrast between truth and opinion and concentrate instead on the idea of factual truth which, she says,

> is always related to others; it concerns events and circumstances in which many are involved, it is established by witnesses and depends upon testimony, it exists only to the extent that it is being spoken about even if it occurs in the domain of privacy. It is political by nature.[55]

The political dimension of factual truth may be discerned from what she calls its 'stubborn thereness', which provides a basic logical resistance to all persuasive attempts to manipulate truth – in the rewriting of history, the attempt to adjust reality to a desired image, and the wholesale distortion of truth in totalitarian rule.[56]

Nevertheless, Arendt recognizes that the limits placed on evil in politics by a residual core of truthfulness are fragile and insecure. To discover a form of thinking which resists claims to absolute truth and is not merely subjective, she turns to the notion of judgement, a logical intermediary between the *vita contemplativa* and the *vita activa*. In judgement she hopes to find a logically stable base for political action in the absence of absolute morality. Taking the broad framework of ideas for a theory of judgement from Kant she argues that judgement has a crucial but neglected political import. Like the notion of factual truth it has a singular connection with politics. It presupposes an 'enlarged mentality', a capacity disinterestedly to imagine oneself in the position of another; it emphasizes a common, public world in which judgements are intersubjective; and it stresses the central features of Kant's understanding of aesthetic judgement – disinterestedness, autonomy, and freedom. Judgement presupposes common standards of discrimination, and it is expressed not in the form of rules which are universally valid but as utterances which communicate with others to attract their assent and agreement. In this way, the notion of judgement incorporates the individual in a public world, and it runs counter to forces which encourage bifurcation and alienation. In Arendt's philosophy the idea of judgement is asked to bear a heavy conceptual weight. She employs it in aesthetics, in history, and as disinterested spectator. Overall, it is often unclear whether it is an exclusively political capacity or whether it is common to a variety of human dispositions and modes of thought. She tends to speak about judgement as a non-cognitive faculty, which means that she has little to say regarding the substantive conditions for the exercise of judgement. There are clear reasons for this. Her thought depends upon a strict dichotomy between knowledge and opinion. She is much concerned to stress the integrity of opinion and its expression as one voice amongst many in a public conversation. What she takes to be the formal conditions of judgement – publicity, universality, and community – exclude both the absolute morality of Christian moral theology and Socratic moral conscience. In one of her early writings on judgement she excludes from its exercise 'those who do not judge' and 'those who are not members of the public realm',[57] and she gives the acquisition of the capacity for judgement a dynamic and evolutionary sense:

> Judging is one, if not the most, important activity in which this sharing-the-world-with-others comes to pass.[58]

Those who are morally innocent do not yet appreciate the full responsibility of judgement in a public world and absolute goodness lies beyond the virtue appropriate to such a world. This is the burden of Arendt's remarks on the characters of Billy Budd and Captain Vere, and we are led to believe that Vere represents the only possible form of virtue in the world in his judgement that Billy must hang. This point is well put by one writer on Arendt's notion of judgement:

> To judge a genuinely human situation is to partake of the tragedy that is potential in circumstances where human responsibility is exercised and borne to its limit.[59]

These features are present in Vere's circumstances. He is morally aware of the nature of the dilemma which faces him and he bears his responsibility to the limit. But is this sufficient to provide a full account of the political morality involved in Melville's *Billy Budd*?

It might be argued that Arendt employs *Billy Budd* as an exemplification of her attack on absolute goodness and, in Vere, a confirmation of her understanding of the exercise of judgement in the context of human imperfection. Here literature is related to philosophy in the same way as example is to argument. Its role is to confirm the assertions already made in philosophy. But Arendt's philosophical lenses may show us less about Vere than they reveal and, indeed, in *On Revolution* her description of him is secondary to that of Billy and derives from her rejection of absolute goodness. This leaves many questions unasked. Is Vere's conduct admirable because his judgements take into account the demands of his office or because of the kind of man he is? What Billy did creates a moral problem for Vere which might not have existed for another officer with an equal concern to live up to the moral obligations of his office. Are we to assume that Arendt believes Vere's judgement to be more adequately grounded? We are talking of the problems of political morality which arise for office-holders. But if the exercise of judgement depends additionally on the moral character of the office-holder then the situation has a moral complexity which Arendt does not fully investigate.

Arendt's criticism of compassion and pity as embodiments of absolute morality may be taken to refer not to their genuine expression but to feelings which are corruptions of the original. What she rejects, however, is compassion, not its inauthentic copy, pity, not its hypocritical expression. Her problem is similar to the one raised by Myshkin, the idiot, in a letter:

> Can one love everyone, all men, all one's neighbours? I have often asked myself that question. Of course not, and, indeed, it would be unnatural. In abstract love of humanity one almost always only loves oneself.[60]

Arendt isolates love from the dispositions and values which surround its expression in individual human character. She neglects, therefore, the complex range of inter-relations which exist within such a conception of character – how pride may diminish the capacity for judgement or weakness be an obstacle to moral rule. But in terms of her contrast between absolute goodness and moral judgement we *can* appreciate what is lacking in moral innocence, the capacity to persuade, argue, and reason with others in a public world.

Arendt is very much aware of the devastation caused by the appearance of goodness in the public realm. Indeed, her reflections on the French Revolution are a sustained commentary on this possibility. But does this devastation follow necessarily or is it an accidental outcome? Arendt thinks of politics as a forum of collective human aspiration which is rarely satisfied, and by implication she regards much of what passes for politics in the modern world as administration. This means that when politics succeeds in finding a shape in the world, in the Hungarian uprising for example, its dignity is found in a heroism which pays little attention to consequence. But as much of the force of her rejection of absolute goodness derives from what she takes to be its fatal outcomes in politics we are entitled to enquire what kind of non-causal relation these have to one another.

Arendt's central aim in understanding a disposition or mode of activity is to elucidate its autonomy by bringing out its distinctive inner logic. Thus, the damage done to politics by absolute goodness will be found within its specific manifestations. The political devastation of compassion will only be found within compassion itself. The external character of Billy Budd can only be discovered in his innocence. This means that for Arendt when absolute goodness appears in public it will inevitably lead to catastrophe. However, inevitability does not fit easily with an awareness of the variety of forms taken by moral innocence in politics. This has been well-formulated by a sympathetic critic:

> Paradoxically, the method that was intended to enhance our appreciation of diversity and contingency in human affairs leads, in Arendt's hands, to reductionist oversimplification, essentialism and determinism.[61]

Of course, Arendt's conception of political philosophy runs counter to the dominant view of it as a theory of the rules of right. She stresses politics as an agency of public space within which human action discloses itself. Within this world it is the faculty of judgement which enables human beings to understand and act in the various situations which confront them. In 'The crisis in culture' Arendt argues,

> Culture and politics belong together because it is not knowledge and truth which is at stake, but rather judgement and decision, the judicious exchange of opinion about the sphere of public life and the common world, and the decision what manner of action is to be taken in it, as well as how it is to look henceforth, what kinds of things are to appear in it.[62]

The sharing of a common existence and the presence of a common faculty of judgement enable us to disclose truths about our political situation. Such an understanding will find its agency in story-telling which reveals truths about the human condition. It is the possession of judgement which enables us to distinguish between the profound and the superficial, as much in the stories offered by political philosophers as in those gleaned from actual political experience, in historical events, in political novels, and in works of art.

We have seen how Hegel, Nietzsche, and Arendt understand the notion of absolute goodness from within the terms set by their philosophical positions. For Hegel, innocence and goodness are related to the development of self-consciousness and rational freedom. Their bearing on politics is seen in terms of dialectic and history. Nietzsche's perception of absolute goodness exists in the context of his stress on the will as constant struggle against an alien environment which includes morality as one of its illusory consolations. Arendt's charges against compassion and pity share Nietzsche's counter-emphasis on courage, but they depend more on her elucidation of the public world and the criterion of judgement which is logically inescapable from it. These indebted but distinctive philosophical perspectives on moral innocence set certain problems. Hegel's understanding of the development of rational self-consciousness in history has difficulty in explaining contingency, inversion, and regression. Nietzsche's doctrine of the primacy of the will neglects substantial logical differences between distinct forms of disposition and utterance. Arendt's fierce attack on absolute conceptions of morality inhibits her achieving a rounded account of how judgement expresses itself in the moral dilemmas of politics where such absolute conceptions are involved; her account of Vere is radically incomplete and she interprets Billy Budd's innocence as simply the fictional embodiment of her philosophical rejection of absolute goodness. In different ways Aristotelian and Kantian conceptions of the nature of practical morality act as obstacles to understanding moral innocence in politics. Different philosophical accounts of morality seem to exclude moral innocence from their range. To bring out its paradoxical and manifold character in politics we may need to shake off the philosophical net. Literature presents us with the opportunity to analyse these complex dispositions. So we must consider how literature and philosophy bear upon one another. What weaknesses within moral and political philosophy might the use of literature remove? Is rapprochement between them possible in a way which recognizes their mutual autonomy and yet encourages the analysis of literary examples of moral innocence in political philosophy?

Chapter Six

POLITICAL PHILOSOPHY AND LITERATURE

As soon as philosophy gets into a novel, a work of literature, it ceases to be philosophy. It becomes something else; it becomes a plaything of the writer, and rightly so. The harder the writer works to present his ideas in abstract form, the less good his work of art is likely to become.

(Iris Murdoch, 'On natural novelists and unnatural philosophers')

A few months spent as a coolie building the Burma railway is worth more to one's moral thinking than the reading of a great many novels or even factual reports about under-developed countries.

(R. M. Hare, *Freedom and Reason*)

In Arendt's thought the link between morality and politics is found primarily in a public world which provides an area of disclosure for human action. The private is parasitic on the public, and can be a region of withdrawal, of escape from a domain in which action takes responsibility for itself. Arendt is led to exaggerate the moral significance of heroism as the pinnacle of public recognition and achievement in a common political life and to condemn those dispositions and activities which either cannot or will not sustain themselves in the context of public expression and scrutiny. But this exclusion renders her unaware of crucial moral distinctions within the private world which affect politics in ways she cannot explain. One recent commentator says:

If her criteria were consistently applied we would have to conclude that Mother Theresa, Albert Schweitzer, a woman who gave up a career to nurse her chronically sick mother and a politician who leaves public life to devote more time to his family are all living 'meaningless' and not fully human lives.[1]

In her understandable concern to halt the impoverishment of the public realm Arendt has neglected the importance of self-estimation and the various ways in which it tries to find expression in a public world. She therefore misses the power of the contrast between some self-regarding judgements and the world in which they are expressed. By concentrating on locating meaning in the public she has shifted the focus of attention away from the perspective of the private agent with the result that one side of the relation between self-estimation and the world is detached. We can avoid this and retain the logical importance she attaches to publicness by considering the ways in which words can change their meaning from terms of praise to terms of disparagement.

In *Studies in Words* C. S. Lewis discusses the meaning of the word 'simple' in a way which is directly applicable to the idea of moral innocence. Simplicity in its fundamental ethical sense is the opposite of duplicity. It is crucially connected with sincerity in that personal identity and its public appearance are identical. A person's professed and real motives are the same.

> Sincere people are guileless, and those who have no guile themselves are not quick to suspect it in others.[2]

But in a world where political skills are at a premium simplicity is dangerous, and so the degradation in the meaning of the word begins. From meaning unsuspicious it moves to 'gullible' and 'incredulous'. It declines further to mean stupid and ignorant, reaching its lowest point with 'mentally deficient'. From simplicity we have reached simpleton. This change of meaning raises two considerations vital to our understanding of innocence in politics. First, that moral disposition and public perception are no longer in harmony. As self-estimation, the moral fineness of simplicity is publicly perceived to be stupid and lacking in judgement. Second, moral simplicity will find itself lost in a duplicitous world in a manner which constitutes an expression of disorder, a breakdown of publicness, of measure, proportion, and restraint. Arendt misses the complex range of connections and disconnections between public perception and private self-estimation, between a corrupted world and an inner moral voice which is saintly, childlike, and innocent.

To recover these disturbed inter-relationships it is perfectly natural to wish to turn away from the confinements of theory towards the minute particularity of the concerns of literature. However, this has not been the response of mainstream political philosophy which has attempted to understand the complex interplay of moral and political values through the transformative lens of theory. Without a secure basis in systematic, comprehensive, and consistent theorizing moral and political beliefs are rendered subjective and contingent. In each of its dominant utilitarian and contractarian forms theory radically alters life by elevating one notion – utility or contract – as the single criterion of meaning. Utilitarianism transforms the character of moral conflict by reducing it to one common denominator. Contractarianism attempts to subvert the manifold complexity of moral and political values by offering a deliberately thin theory of moral agency. Rawls, for example, writes:

> we take moral persons to be characterised by two moral powers and by two corresponding highest-order interests in realising and exercising these powers. The first power is the capacity for an effective sense of justice, that is, the capacity to understand, to apply and to act from (and not merely in accordance with) the principles of justice. The second moral power is the capacity to form, to revise, and rationally to pursue a conception of the good.[3]

A mechanistic image of the relation between the agent and his world is powerfully implied in the language employed in this passage. Moral agency is construed as independent of the world and bending it to its will; the talk is in terms of capacities and powers, realizing and exercising. Of course, Rawls' restatement of contract theory forgoes substantive judgements regarding political goods in favour of a theory of political right. Individuals behind the veil of ignorance do not know their place in society, their social status, assets, abilities, strengths, intelligence, or character. They do not know their conception of the good, their rational plan of life, or their liability to optimism or pessimism. They do not know to which generation they belong or the particular circumstances of their own society – its economic or political situation, or the level of civilization it has been able to achieve. On the basis of this thin theory of the good Rawls claims it is possible to derive principles of justice without touching on the question of what constitutes substantive moral good and without getting trapped in arbitrary and contingent inequalities. It

168

is quite clear that to think about philosophical thinking regarding politics in this way is totally to exclude the claims of literature. There is no point of logical contact between Rawls' description of the original position and the openness and indeterminacy which characterizes literature. Rawls theorizes politics understood as a system of authoritative rules agreed by rational moral agents, an exercise which it is logically impossible to pursue without abstraction. Theorizing in Rawls has an explicitly Kantian character in the sense that it is concerned with the construction of moral and political rules which are both formal and rational. Contextual considerations of the kind found in literature are irrelevant and superfluous to political philosophy conceived in this way.

It has often been argued that theorizing does not exhaust the possibilities of philosophical method, and may even present an obstacle to philosophical understanding. For some there is an intrinsic absurdity in the idea of a theory built on a single criterion of morality which attempts to explain the manifold nature of moral and political life. Bradley writes in typical vein:

> If we wished to cross an unknown bog, and two men came to us, of whom the one said, 'Someone must know the way over this bog, for there must be a way, and you see there is no one here beside us two, and therefore one of us two must be able to guide you. And the other man does not know the way, as you can soon see; therefore I must' – should we answer, 'Lead on, I follow'? Philosophy would indeed be the easiest of studies, if we might arrive at truth by assuming that one of two accounts must be true, and prove the one by disproving the other; but in philosophy this is just what can not be done.[4]

The idea of philosophy as a theory distorts our understanding of the way we establish propositions to be true; it narrows our appreciation of the richness of moral and political experience, and it imposes an illusory structure of meaning on the world.

Iris Murdoch is one writer who has maintained an intractable hostility to theory and the ways of thinking with which it beguiles us. Theories in morality and politics consist of abstract categories which can deform concrete reality. Contingency and particularity are either distorted by theory or they escape its net. Murdoch's anti-Platonism concludes that a philosophical theory can be, in Wittgenstein's phrase, 'a *picture* that held us captive',[5] and expresses her belief that the extent to which language escapes from theory is also the extent to which it emancipates itself from constriction. Her concern with the reality of minute particulars is shared by T. E. Hulme:

> Something is always lost in generalisation. A railway leaves out all the gaps of dirt between. Generalisations are only means of getting about.[6]

Theory offers merely a network of abstractions which tyrannize the understanding by forcing it to conform to its presuppositions. Rawls is not unusual amongst philosophers in wanting to make capacity, choice, and action the basic elements in his theory of rational agency. But this encourages us to think of deliberation, choice, and action as bound by either the tight, logical inter-lacing of practical reason or the currency of psychological cause and effect. Such a picture excludes agency as expressive of moral character or disposition and it neglects what Murdoch calls individuals'

> total vision of life, as shown in their mode of speech or silence, their choice of words, their assessment of others, their conception of their own lives, and what they think attractive or praiseworthy, what they think funny: in short the configurations of their thought which show continually in their reactions and conversation.[7]

These incorporate 'the texture of a man's being' or 'the nature of his personal vision'.[8] Such expressions involve a profound shift in attention in moral and political philosophy away from formal contrasts between right and good, duty and inclination, towards an analysis of the specific dispositions which constitute human character. To understand political morality in this light is not to accept the simple focus of office and office-holder, but rather to stress the importance of particular moral and political visions of the world. The elementary contrast between private integrity and public good is set aside temporarily in favour of an account of human innocence or courage in situations of supreme political intensity. This allows us to see action and outcome as related morally but not simply consequentially. Human choices and decisions are understood against the backcloth of character and not simply in terms of a framework of imposed moral rules or by reference to a process of utilitarian calculation. This releases the temporality of human life from its suspension in theory and encourages us to see the relations between human beings and their world as a conversation which finds its understanding in the reflexivities of narration. The importance of narrative as a mode of explanatory discourse arises in different ways – in the context of idealist historiography; in the hermeneutic concern to understand human conduct from within and not by reference to predetermined theories of action external to the practice and assumed in advance to be applicable to it; and in the attempt to portray human understanding as a process of story-telling.

For W. B. Gallie narrative is essential if we are to reach a proper understanding of human conduct and, specifically, the relation beween accident and intention, luck and design, which marks the course of a human life. A story consists, for Gallie, in the interweaving of the unpredictable with the character of the agents who are involved in it. It does not deny contingency or attempt to remove the accidental in the manner of theoretical understanding but rather incorporates them into the narration in such a way that they are given meaning. Gallie writes:

> What is contingent, e.g. coincidental or unpredictable, is of course, *per se* unintelligible. But in relation to a man's life, or to a particular theme in a man's life, it can be understood as having contributed to a particular, acceptable and accepted, conclusion.[9]

Of course Gallie's interest lies in story-telling as a model for the historical reconstruction of sequential events and accidents alike, but others have wished to offer a more ambitious intepretation aimed at bringing philosophy and literature closer together and which brings out clearly the difficulties involved in such an enterprise.

A preoccupation with theories of the right and the good can impede our thinking about political morality. Arendt argues that the depth of the public world can be recovered only by investigating how a shared existence and a common faculty of judgement enable us to disclose truths about our political existence. The agency of this disclosure has been described as story-telling. The point of such stories is to reveal truth regarding the human condition. It is the possession of judgement which enables us to distinguish between the profound and the superficial, between the real and the fantastic, and this is as much at work in our response to the stories offered by political philosophers as it is to stories found in actual political experience, in historical events, in political novels, and in works of art. One defender of this view asserts:

> The ultimate measure of the truth of a given story is the depth of experience upon which it draws, and which it in turn communicates to us.[10]

So if a particular narrative fails it is not because some logical error has been made or an empirical mistake has been detected but because a deeper filling out of the story is required. This hermeneutic position bases its notion of truth on comprehension and coherence rather than deductive inference. It seems to offer an escape from the confining separation of philosophy and literature, and to allow that in political understanding we may draw upon accounts of politics which range from Thucydides to Hegel and Koestler. We are entitled to draw as much upon Camus' Algerian writings as on *The Rebel*. The ultimate test is the depth of political insight to be gained. Such a view has obvious attractions, but there are difficulties which must be made explicit before we go on to examine detailed literary treatments of moral innocence in political contexts.

The first problem is that modal neutrality with regard to the sources of political insight seems unaware of the dangers of using literature in philosophical discussion. There is no recognition of possible modal incompatibility between literature and philosophy which is brushed aside in the search for talismanic insight. Second, we are given no account of the distinction between the profound and the superficial. If, for example, it is claimed that Orwell's description of the proles in *Nineteen Eighty-Four* is superficial, then what kind of superficiality is this? To reply that this is established by contrast with, say, Marx's account of the class position of the proletariat would seem to commit a fairly obvious *ignoratio*. On the other hand, to say that any weaknesses in Orwell's description can only be understood from within the novel is to admit a categorical distinction between literary and philosophical concerns. Third, if we are encouraged to evaluate literature in terms of the depth of the political viewpoint it embodies this neglects the complexities of our responses to literary texts. It ignores the distinction between an author's moral and political vision and the aesthetic merits of his work, and it would, therefore, have difficulty in explaining Orwell's regard for Swift. In *Politics vs Literature*, Orwell writes:

> From what I have written it may seem that I am *against* Swift, and that my object is to refute him and even to belittle him. In a political and moral sense I am against him, so far as I understand

him. Yet curiously enough he is one of the writers I admire with least reserve, and *Gulliver's Travels*, in particular, is a book which it seems impossible for me to grow tired of.[11]

For these reasons, this understanding of the use of literature in political philosophy would seem somewhat inadequate. In contrast to Rawls' neo-Kantian moral theory which completely excludes literary treatments of politics this view is too all-inclusive and tries to by-pass unavoidable distinctions. It is, of course, misleading to describe the move from philosophy to literature as one from theory to minute particular. When Hulme attempts to liberate his thinking from the grip of abstract, scientific languages he simply assumes that the shift from logic to poetic image is fully emancipatory. It may for all Hulme knows be a change from one presuppositional tyranny to another. In other words, it is not clear what escaping from a mode of understanding or an image would involve. We must consider the parameters of danger between literature and philosophy.

To a large extent political philosophy has taken the general methods of philosophy as its guide and when these have proved beguiling then political philosophy has itself faltered. A dissatisfaction with rigid linguistic analysis has led philosophy to search for alternative sources of enlightenment. In recent years this has been most noticeably the case with moral philosophy, where it has been argued that it is its conventional methodology which constitutes the main obstacle to understanding moral and political life in its complex and manifold form. Similar arguments also apply to the methods of political philosophy. To some extent this has to do with a dissatisfaction with the construction of theories of morality and politics; and with the corresponding attempt to seek forms of understanding which better encompass the variety of political experience and which provide a more subtle recognition of the relation between thought and its object. There has, therefore, been an increasing use of literature, particularly the novel, in moral and political philosophy. Once the focus of attention shifts from moral theories to what Murdoch calls 'the texture of a man's being' it is unsurprising that this should be in portrayals of moral character in works of fiction. In many respects this has been of benefit to both literary criticism and philosophy, but it has weakened the distinction between philosophical and literary truth. Scruton, for example, argues that:

173

Philosophy explores the nature of things; not how they are but how they must be. Whether by conceptual analysis, by phenomenological examination, by dialectical speculation, or whatever, philosophy always aims at essence. Its means is argument, and its end is truth.[12]

Now it would be odd to suggest that works of literature, say novels, proceeded by argument. A philosophical argument concerning, say, the nature of the freedom of the will or the meaning of political obligation or the character of justice, commonly issues in conclusions of an abstract or general kind which can be stated and criticized. But we would clearly be misunderstanding what was going on in, for example, *Coriolanus*, *Sons and Lovers*, or *Under the Volcano*, if we said that they consisted of arguments which lead to conclusions. They are not statements of fact or matters of argument and they cannot be reduced to such statements without loss. They are concerned with the fictional, the non-existent, and the impossible. Unlike a philosophical thesis which can be translated, transposed, and re-expressed, a literary work is inseparable from the particular imaginative experience it creates. Literary truth derives its compelling power from within the text. Canons of falsification, verification, and analysis are inappropriate. This contrast between philosophy and literature is defended by Iris Murdoch who, in other respects, is critical of the dominant role played by theorizing in our thinking. To distrust theory in philosophy does not imply that the distinction between philosophy and literature should be collapsed. She writes:

> Philosophy aims to clarify: it is essential to philosophy that it should, in some sense, be clarification. Literature is, very often, mystification . . . Literature does many things, and philosophy does one thing.[13]

Whatever the value of this general distinction, the extensive deployment of literary examples in recent moral and political philosophy shows how much it has been ignored. But what kind of claim is involved when a literary example is a part of an argument in philosophy? For example, McDara in O'Flaherty's *The Assassin* asserts:

> That is the object of the revolutionary, to create a superior type of human being. Most revolutionary movements make the mistake of aiming at a change of government, seizing political power and

that sort of thing. That is not revolution. It is merely a transposition of the material wealth in a community.[14]

What hold does this have over us in the attempt to make sense of the idea of revolution? How could it be made a part of the argument, in the sense that Thucydides, Aristotle, Burke, and Marx present us with arguments regarding the nature of revolution?

To try to answer these questions it is necessary to distinguish the claim we are examining from two that have often been confused with it.[15] In the first place, there is the literary portrayal of philosophy, its manner of argument, and the impact of its ideas on non-philosophers and philosophers alike. Of a plethora of examples, there is the opening passage of E. M. Forster's *The Longest Journey*, which consists of the description of a philosophical argument regarding the existence of material objects and ends with the philosopher's disarming admission that his points are quibbles; or Lady Constance's exegesis of Lamarckianism in Disraeli's *Tancred*; or, again, Hardy's use of J. S. Mill's ideas in *On Liberty* in *Jude the Obscure*. This aspect of the relation between philosophy and literature is interesting but not directly relevant to the problem. The second claim is more relevant, and that is the view that some literary works embody philosophical theories. Here it is claimed that it is possible to distil from a novel, say, a set of philosophical propositions of a general kind. It would then make sense to say that literary works provide philosophical knowledge, and the gap between philosophy and literature would have been bridged. However, the attractions of this view are superficial because it depends on our having already accepted the philosophical colonization of literature, a state of affairs which it is perfectly possible to question. We might say that *Middlemarch* contains the proposition that past desires and present hopes govern our interpretation of experience, or that *Darkness at Noon* asserts that between absolute and teleological ethics there is irresolvable deadlock. It is, of course, open to defenders of this claim to argue that there are philosophical novels of a Sartrean kind in which the philosophy they contain is intrinsic to their nature, and that they are ignored only because we have accepted an over-sharp distinction between philosophy as argument and literature as imagination. However, it would be strange to assume that the meaning of such a novel was summed up in its philosophical paraphrase or that we could respond to aesthetic judgements *in the same way* as we evaluate philosophical claims.

Further, even if it was feasible to extract philosophical propositions from literature that would not give us a compelling reason to agree with them.

The sense in which political philosophy may meaningfully employ literature is distinct from both these claims. It is stronger than the view which merely delineates literary portrayals of philosophy, but not as strong as the view that we can derive philosophical conclusions from literary works. It is sensitive to the dangers of using literature in philosophy, but seeks to provide compelling reasons for doing so.

The deployment of literature in philosophical argument is some-times seen as a necessary counter to the prevalent tendency in both moral and political philosophy to use examples of a trivial, non-serious, and neutral kind. It is often argued that the use of serious examples would distract from the conceptual issues involved and generate too much emotional heat. I suppose Rawls' example of the man whose good in life consists in counting blades of grass is a representative instance of this.[16] The failure to confront serious examples seems both a reflection of philosophical weakness and a neglect of the considerations which give moral value its importance.

It has also been argued that seeing the part played by morality in politics is prevented by the philosophical assumptions brought to its examination. In other words, some philosophical theories of morality, by virtue of the narrowness or abstracted nature of their assumptions and the over-simplicity of their distinctions, obscure the very experience they aim to explain. It has been claimed that assumptions about the nature of rationality distort our understanding of the relation between moral value and reason and ignore the various limitations within which moral life is carried on.[17] An example of this narrowness would be Rawls' definition of a person 'as a human life lived according to a plan'.[18] In opposition to the formal thrust of moral theorizing it is claimed that here literature is of most value. It is not that the philosopher is concerned to extract some moral precept from the text, but rather that literature reminds us of the plurality of moral perspectives and the heterogeneity of values. In this way literature can enlarge the area of moral possibility and widen what is to count as moral experience. In 'Against dryness', Iris Murdoch refers to the way in which attenuated assumptions regarding human freedom and rationality can impair our understanding of the difficulty of moral existence and the struggle involved in acting well in private as well as public life.

We are not isolated free choosers, monarchs of all we survey, but
benighted creatures sunk in a reality whose nature we are
constantly and overwhelmingly tempted to deform by fantasy.[19]

Literature, she believes, can provide a challenge to illusory consolation
by warning us of the shallow view of the individual taken by liberalism.
It portrays a depth of character involving extremes of innocence and
evil which cannot be reached by the liberal emphasis on individual
choice and the priority of self. We can discern in literature resources
of discourse which arrest the superficiality of our moral and political
thinking. For Iris Murdoch:

In morals and politics we have stripped ourselves of concepts.
Literature, in curing its own ills, can give us a new vocabulary of
experience, and a truer picture of freedom.[20]

It is inevitable that this revision of the relation between literature
and philosophy should take with it a reassessment of philosophy. For
what is now made a matter of dispute is the validity of distinguishing
between philosophy and literature in terms of the universality of
the former and the particularity of the latter. Further, it is
suggested that not only can the craving for generality be an obstacle
to understanding in moral and political philosophy, but sensitivity
to singularity and detail are essential to it. It is not clear if
the challenge to this distinction is intended to eradicate all logical
difference between philosophy and literature or if the resultant radical
transformation of moral and political philosophy has been fully
appreciated.

The use of literary examples in philosophy has been further
defended by emphasizing how it 'can open our eyes to possibilities of
moral seriousness which are wider than those we happen to agree
with and wider than those prevalent in a society at any given time'.[21]
This introduces a distinction between the moral values held by the
literary critic or philosopher and the limits of possible moral values.
It is argued that imaginative literature strengthens our hold on this
distinction by alerting us to features of moral experience we may
have lost sight of, and which our own presuppositions may have led
us to ignore or diminish: it can identify restrictive and narrow
philosophical categories.

It might be objected that literary works cited in a philosophical
argument are not themselves intellectually neutral. They are not

pieces of evidence whose value can be assessed independent of their fictional character and the philosophical role they perform in the argument. If this is true then it must always be question-begging to deploy a literary work as a refutation of a rival philosophical account because it can never be devoid of philosophical assumptions of its own. The use of Koestler's *Darkness at Noon* in a debate concerning the nature and justification of collectivization is not like introducing an independent witness.

This raises a related problem. Those who employ literary works in the service of philosophy often speak as if the characters and situations they portray were real. This does neglect the logical differences between the real and the fictional; it makes no sense to ask if fictional characters could have behaved otherwise than they did. While we may experience an emotional response to a fictional death, say that of Winnie Verloc in Conrad's *The Secret Agent*, it is quite unlike our response to the death of a close friend.[22] However, literary works often emerge from real circumstances. *The Secret Agent*, for example, has some indebtedness to the actual Greenwich bomb outrage of 1894; though the meaning of a novel cannot be reduced to or derived from sets of historical circumstances. It may be argued further that imaginative literature can have an impact on our lives. Consider as examples J. S. Mill's response to reading Wordsworth as described in his *Autobiography*, or Henry Williamson's description in *The Pathway* of the impression made on him by reading Richard Jefferies' *The Story of My Heart*.[23] It would be strange to deny in these cases that something had been learned which could not have been acquired elsewhere.

Nevertheless, the objection to the philosophical use of literature can be more forcibly expressed. R. M. Hare, for example, writes:

> story books, though they may help to stimulate our imaginations, do not by themselves help us very much to separate what is really likely to happen from what is not, nor to assess the probable frequency of its occurrence.[24]

But are we to believe that in moral and political life prediction is more important than hope? Surely a good novel does tell us what it is like to hope for something when its outcome is unlikely, a reality which is established within the novel by contrast with fantasy and not statistical expectation.

The strengths and weaknesses of using literature in philosophical argument are found in consideration of the problems of political morality. The use of literary examples may indicate the abstract nature of some accounts of the relation between moral belief and political obligation. It may enable us to see that describing the relation between the individual and the state exclusively in terms of moral principle and political expediency is too simple; it is impossible to generalize from this to cases whose logic is categorically different. The value of literature here is precisely in its expression of the complexity of the relations between moral and political beliefs, and its capacity to portray motivation, character and action, historical circumstance, and commitment to policy.

Literature does not provide evidence for philosophy in the same sense that empirical data provide evidence for, say, biology. Our response to literature is not like having something proved to us. It is more akin to being shown something which we did not previously see or understand. Goya's *Etchings of War* and Homer's *Iliad* have a claim over us which is inimical to philosophical re-translation, and yet political philosophy cannot do without such works. To attempt to do so is to be indifferent to the distinct insight they provide. Political philosophy becomes self-absorbed and loses sight of the limits of its own kind of understanding. This intellectual narrowness can appear as preoccupation with theory, expressed in the belief that if politics does not conform to the conditions laid down by theory then it must be either inexplicable or reduced to a form which theory can explain. But political philosophy does not have to take the form of a theory in order to be systematic. As Renford Bambrough has pointed out,[25] philosophy and literature reveal a 'unity of method' which can easily be neglected:

> In conversational conflict between the obvious and the obvious, and therefore in literary and moral and philosophical conflict too, it is necessary for both sides to state the obvious; for each to re-affirm what the other knows but denies or forgets because it seems to conflict with what is also obvious and is nearer to the front of his mind . . . And reminders are usually of minute particulars, of forgotten instances to which some hasty generality is vulnerable.[26]

Understanding the relations between morality and politics means overcoming conflict between theories which have become ossified. This is to draw attention to the concrete and the contingent areas of our experience which theories in their adversary relation to each other are prone to ignore.

Our interest is with the literary portrayal of innocence in politics and with the importance this has for political philosophy. A reading of Henry James' *The Golden Bowl* enables us to see the world from the perspective of the morally innocent and to appreciate the kind of blindness this involves. One philosophical commentary on this work[27] stresses Maggie Verver's innocence and moral simplicity and identifies as its public consequences an unawareness of sexuality and a failure to appreciate moral values and moral persons as having an objective, independent existence. This failure of recognition means that it is also impossible for the morally innocent to be aware of moral conflict and of moral cost. Martha Nussbaum writes perceptively of Maggie:

> Knowledge of a good, that is to say a value, in the world requires, we see, knowledge of evil, that is to say of the possibility of conflict, disorder, the contingent necessity of breaking or harming. Without eating this fruit she is just a child, ignorant of the value of the good as well.[28]

This establishes that the loss of moral innocence and the ensuing recognition that a commitment to moral value may require that something of great moral importance be sacrificed can be given a non-consequential sense. The world of the innocent, secure in its expectation that morality is stable and reliable, is left behind and is replaced by a realm of moral uncertainty and fragility. Moral values and moral costs are so interlocked that perfectibility is impossible. *The Golden Bowl* pursues this theme in relation to the moral development of private individuals. In *The Princess Casamassima* James makes the same point on a less personal and more political canvas. Here the moral focus is Hyacinth Robinson who, like Stevie in Conrad's *The Secret Agent*, is pure, trusting, and vulnerable to the selfishness and evil in the world. Hyacinth kills himself in despair when he realizes the true nature of political commitment. Stevie is killed while unwittingly carrying a bomb on a pointless anarchist mission.

James in *The Princess Casamassima* and Conrad in *The Secret Agent* are both concerned with the loss of innocence, with how it may be corrupted and exploited by others, and with how innocence recoils when it first sees evil in the world. It is natural that moral innocence be portrayed here as being acted upon rather than itself acting in the world. It is, of course, possible that moral innocence is incapable of action. Its ignorance of the objectivity of values and persons, of anything evil existing in the world, might seem to disqualify it. But action in politics is characteristically, although not universally, mediated by the demands of office and by the awareness that public decisions affect the lives of large numbers of people unknown to the office-holder or corporate body which makes the decision.

Indeed, if the full force of the moral dilemmas surrounding innocence is to be brought out then a rich political understanding is essential. Such an understanding is present in the three texts I have chosen to examine in the following chapters. All are concerned with moral innocence as an active force in the world. They stress the variety of forms innocence takes in morality and politics and they examine its potential for danger from the standpoints of those most threatened by it. Moral disposition in all three works is placed in the context of severe political disruption and strain, of civil war, of war arising out of revolution, and of insurrection in the face of foreign involvement. Each lays out different moral presuppositions regarding the character of ruling and each examines the complex interplay between office and office-holder. When moral innocence appears in the character of ruler or in the policies of intervening state the large-scale moral consequences lie heavy, for both the involved and the uninvolved alike. The innocence found in these works is not simply moral. It involves an ignorance of politics which is rooted in moral candour and simplicity, though it is not a straightforward reluctance to lie for political necessity. Innocence is counter-posed to evil, but goodness is not the only form taken by morality in the world. A realistic, stubborn sense of virtue stands as much opposed to goodness as extreme evil. These texts are preoccupied with the incomplete relation between intention and outcome, of how it is that purity of heart can destroy those closest to it and how unblemished policies can lay a nation in ruins. But the consequences of such innocence do not only concern those touched by it; the morally innocent, too, must suffer the moral hazards of their candour. The conjunction of goodness and death has a tragic character in these works which expresses in an extreme and limiting form the political loss of innocence. Here the contrast between theory and literature is most apparent.

Finally, it is from Rousseau's writings that we can derive one statement of the political theory of compassion. In his thought, innocence, pity, and politics are brought together in an obscure and fatal conjunction. As Arendt remarks:

> If Rousseau had introduced compassion into political theory, it was Robespierre who brought it onto the market-place with the vehemence of his great revolutionary oratory.[29]

Compassion is the crucial link in Rousseau between a state of natural, unfrustrated innocence and the politics of the General Will. It stresses an absolute contrast between the selfishness of particular interests in the world and the selflessness of pity, the capacity to understand the suffering of others which Rousseau takes to be the distinguishing sentiment of natural man. The intolerable tension between natural innocence and the corruptions of existing society is such that individuals either lose their natural simplicity and honesty or they adopt various masks to preserve their integrity but which serve merely to brutalize their nature by hypocrisy and dishonesty. The alternative is to reconcile the individual and society by their re-education according to their nature, which Rousseau attempts in *Emile*, and the restructuring of society according to the principles of political right, which he attempts in *The Social Contract*. The programme to educate people consistent with their nature is little more than a crude, manipulative behaviouralism. Loss of innocence is controlled by the requirements of Rousseau's dualism between the purity of the natural condition and the corruption of society. The innocent are puppets whose actions are controlled by the puppet-master, the actor dramatist of a new society. In Book Four of *Emile*, Rousseau gives an example of how to control the acquisition of knowledge, of how to direct the awareness of passion. He tells the story of a father who is attempting to restrain his son's growing consciousness of sexual temptation. At the point when the son seems to be beyond his control,

> he decided to take him to a hospital, and, without telling him what to expect, he introduced him into a room where a number of wretched creatures were expiating, under terrible treatment, the vices which had brought them into this plight.[30]

The experience has the desired effect, and the young man confesses:

> 'I have been a man', he said to me, 'I have had my weaknesses, but even to the present day the sight of a harlot inspires me with horror'.[31]

On which Rousseau comments coolly that it is essential to choose practical examples to ensure that they have the necessary effect on character and conduct.

Innocence here is not lost by contingent, accidental contact with the world. It is suspended in the political theory of compassion, artificially transformed by theoretical device, and when attached to a revolutionary sensibility creates moral and political havoc. Rousseau attempts the unnatural retention of innocence in the questionable morality of pity. In politics, selflessness requires the abolition of limit. The political expression of pity requires that nothing obstruct the alleviation of suffering. Is there a necessary connection here? Innocence has these particular ramifications only because it is transfixed by the dualistic extremes of self and selflessness which dominate Rousseau's political thinking. Released from Rousseau's inflexible contrast between nature and society, innocence may be perceived in a variety of literary treatments which bring out the diverse nature of its connection with the political world.

Chapter Seven

POLITICS AND INNOCENT INTENT

It is now customary to play down the violence of the Wars of the Roses and to present them as dynastic skirmishes fatal, perhaps, to the old aristocracy but generally of small concern to the common people and without much effect on the economic routines of the kingdom. Statistically, this may be arguable; imaginatively, the Battle of Towton itself commands one's belated witness. In the accounts of contemporary chroniclers it was a holocaust.

(Geoffrey Hill, *Funeral Music, An Essay*)

This is what is most unforgivable in you: you have the power, and you do not want to rule.

(Nietzsche, *Thus Spoke Zarathustra*)

The appearance of moral innocence in politics involves a strong element of paradox. Like the honourable man who finds himself dependent on those he likes to think are his moral inferiors, the morally innocent, persons of sweet disposition and pure intent, discover that in politics their compassion is self-defeating. We find a graphic illustration of this in A. L. Rowse, *All Souls and Appeasement*. After emphasizing the moral nature of the appeaser's motives, Rowse comments:

The total upshot of their efforts was to aid Nazi-Germany to achieve a position of brutal ascendancy, a threat to everybody else's security or even existence, which only a war could end. This had the very result of letting the Russians into the centre of Europe which the appeasers – so far as they had any clear idea of policy – wished to prevent.[1]

This contradiction between intention and outcome is crucial to understanding Henry VI. His rule is altruistic and mild, a model of kingly restraint. He says of his subjects:

> I have not stopp'd mine ears to their demands,
> Nor posted off their suits with slow delays;
> My pity hath been balm to heal their wounds,
> My mildness hath allay'd their swelling griefs,
> My mercy dried their waterflowing tears;
> I have not been desirous of their wealth;
> Nor much oppressed them with great subsidies,
> Nor forward of revenge, though they much err'd.[2]

The consequence of this saintly rule is a kingdom in ruins, suffering for its citizens and the replacement of legitimate rule by tyranny. The explanation of the rise and fall of states which most preoccupies Shakespeare is offered by Machiavelli. Those too weak to master Fortune are swept aside by the flood of events. However, although there are many references to Fortune and fate as the mainsprings of historical change, the play contains other passages where Shakespeare's meaning is not that of Machiavelli. In Act IV, Edward says:

> Though Fortune's malice overthrow my state,
> My mind exceeds the compass of her wheel.[3]

Machiavelli's account of the connection between intention and consequence is cyclical and its determinism understates the human capacity to reflect on the historical process.

We have noted already that Hegel and Arendt are dissatisfied with Machiavelli's view that good intentions fail in politics simply because they neglect the realities of power. In a passage from his early theological writings, Hegel writes in a way which is strikingly applicable to the character of Henry VI:

> In love's task the community scorns any unification save the deepest, any spirit save the highest.[4]

Henry's character disowns the moral imperatives of dynastic politics and it leads to disaster for his rule and for the community his office requires him to protect. Arendt explores this further by raising the question of culpability. She insists that goodness shun the world of human appearances. Henry's ignorance of the political world – its mediating character and the formalities and distances it makes possible – arises from absolute moral scruple. For Arendt, such moral innocence in the harsh arena of politics is culpable. But this does not derive simply from Henry's obvious unwillingness to dirty his hands. We can imagine someone who wishes to keep their hands clean in politics and yet is not lost in a duplicitous world. It is Henry's moral innocence that marks the nature of the disharmony between moral disposition and political rule. Against the background of the immorality it does nothing to prevent, Henry's moral guile-lessness is unsuited to the recognition of political evil. The outcome of his saintliness is the abolition of trust, the lynch-pin of the relation between morality and politics; the destruction of moral agreement, with the stability and certainties it implies; and the consequent multiplication of political crime. Henry's innocence has to be placed in the context of the world if it is to have a full, logical purchase. Warwick, the embodiment of political experience, says in Act V:

> These eyes, that now are dimm'd with death's
> black veil,
> Have been as piercing as the mid-day sun;
> To search the secret treasons of the world.[5]

Such treacheries have an external existence and in their context Henry's innocence is fatal both to himself and to the community he is supposed to rule. How can this be? To answer this question I will examine innocence of intent in the context of the treacheries of the world.

The most general moral theme of Shakespeare's first great historical tetralogy is the political theory of order.[6] As E. M. W. Tillyard has shown,[7] the history plays embody the Elizabethan world-picture, and they are preoccupied with the dangers of political disorder. Shakespeare, in effect, dramatizes the historical thesis of the chronicles of Hall and Holinshed and so shows one specific way in which the Elizabethan mind connected the idea of didactic history with the political theory of order. Thus, *Henry VI* (1) lays emphasis on the hierarchical relationship between subject, king, and Deity, a central feature of the theory of the Divine Right of Kings, and an idea which had dominated thinking about political obligation for generations prior to Shakespeare's age. The play stresses the need for political obedience and for government to conform to God's will. These ideas are clearly found in a speech by Talbot in a scene which perfectly exemplifies the kind of politics which ought to exist in an orderly kingdom. Talbot says:

> My gracious prince, and honourable peers,
> Hearing of your arrival in this realm,
> I have awhile given truce unto my wars,
> To do my duty to my sovereign:
> In sign whereof, this arm – that hath reclaim'd
> To your obedience fifty fortresses,
> Twelve cities, and seven walled towns of strength,
> Beside five hundred prisoners of esteem –
> Lets fall his sword before your highness' feet,
> And with submissive loyalty of heart,
> Ascribes the glory of his conquest got,
> First to my God, and next unto your Grace.[8]

The idea of order in this speech stands as a reference point by which to judge the moral and political decline which follows. Order and disorder are linked in an historical thesis which attempts to explain the effect of disobedience and the transgression of proportion and degree. On this view, the loss of England's French possessions and the suffering of the civil wars are seen as the inevitable consequences of the usurpation of the throne by Henry IV. This violation of the legitimate order demanded retribution, and it is the reign of Henry VI which provides it in the form of the king's weakness, the ambition of Margaret of Anjou, and the disunity of the English nobility. Thus, the defeat and murder of Henry VI were a divine retribution for the deposition and murder of Richard II. The killing and oath-breaking continued in the illegitimate rule of Edward IV, and culminated in the tyranny of Richard III, the embodiment of evil whose physical deformities symbolize both the moral corruption of his nature and the political disorder of the state over which he ruled.

This broad theme of cosmic order, historically traceable, is a necessary reference point in the first history plays. Order implies, too, a fear of its disintegration. The Elizabethans, like the ancient Athenians before them, had a justifiable terror of civil strife. When a community breaks apart common moral value and political expectation are cut adrift. There is no basis for trust, legitimacy has no agreed source, murder becomes the method for the resolution of rival dynastic claims, force is the ultimate arbiter of human affairs, and revenge the primary form of political commitment. In this barbarous world a father kills his son and a son kills his father. It is an experience with which the modern world is more than familiar. The American Civil War, the civil war in Russia after the 1917 revolution, the Spanish Civil War, contemporary Lebanon, provide us with the exemplars of stasis for our age. Morality has dissolved, innocence is dangerous, reason is impotent. What, then, governs the occurrence of events? This is the narrow focus on 'the secret treasons of the world', and it brings us to the most precise explanation of Henry's innocence.

We may approach this by contrasting the responses of Henry and Warwick to their disordered country. The reaction of the king is grief. Warwick, on the other hand, offers an indictment of those responsible for the corruption of the deepest political values. After his realization that he had been manipulated by King Edward he says:

> Alas! how should you govern any kingdom,
> That know not how to use ambassadors,
> Nor how to be contented with one wife,
> Nor how to use your brothers brotherly,
> Nor how to study for the people's welfare,
> Nor how to shroud yourself from enemies?[9]

The values implied in Warwick's speech are moral in character, but for most of the protagonists they are merely obstacles to the achievement of power and control over others. In a world in which anger, pride, and ambition flourish we find a Machiavellian emphasis on policy before principle, on end justifying means. Northumberland says:

> It is war's prize to take all vantages.[10]

This emphasis on political realism is found in many passages. It is Henry alone, of course, who stands against it, and is rebuked for doing so. Henry's insistence to his son in Act II, 'learn this lesson, draw thy sword in right',[11] finds its antithesis in Gloucester's nihilistic refusal to allow his craving for power to be restrained by any ethical considerations. In the famous speech in Act III, Gloucester signifies his capacity to 'smile, and murder while I smile',[12] and shows his determination to 'set the murd'rous Machiavel to school'.[13]

It is a mistake, however, to assume that Machiavelli's political maxims are capable of bearing the whole burden of the moral and political action of the play. As murders and atrocities multiply, as revenge requires greater acts of cruelty and inhumanity, we are taken far beyond the political advice given by Machiavelli, even in a work of such notable political realism as *The Prince*. Gloucester, 'the devil's butcher', as Queen Margaret calls him in Act V, embodies the swiftness of this moral decline. In civil war when moral values are displaced by political morality we do not have long to wait before they vanish altogether.

What, then, are the main elements of the political chaos which results? To begin with there is a total absence of agreement regarding the nature of legitimate succession. Sovereignty is, therefore, placed in doubt and we see the emergence of the first cracks in a stable political order. The contention between York and Lancaster expresses itself in continual and inconclusive appeals to the past. The arguments involve lengthy historical appeals, to lines of blood, pedigree, dynastic claims, and family connection. The deposition of Richard II, the greatness of John of Gaunt, the reign of Henry IV, the conquest of France under Henry V, the coronation of Henry VI at 9 months old, the loss of France, and the restoration to Richard Plantagenet of the title of Duke of York; all these testimonies are invoked to support rival claims. But in the absence of a settled and agreed language of political succession their invocation is futile. This is most apparent in the parley between the rival parties in Act II. It is not surprising that here argument collapses into abuse. As the Prince puts the problem precisely:

> If that be right which Warwick says
> is right,
> There is no wrong, but everything is right.[14]

As Warwick himself realizes in a later scene, in a world devoid of common meaning pedigree and falsehood go together. Further, the human cost of abstract disputation is high. When the parley has failed Edward says:

> These words will cost ten thousand lives this day.[15]

These dissensions make succession a matter of political ambition, a direct result of which is the destruction of family bonds. This finds its most dramatic expression in Henry's unnatural decision to disinherit his son. But we see this also in the development of the House of York. Here a family originally united by ambition turns in upon itself, and its sons become rivals for the throne. It is worth noticing here that relations between and within families become increasingly unrestrained. As this process quickens, political crimes multiply. They take three major forms – revenge, murder, and perjury.

First, each successive crime produces a call for its revenge. Clifford is obsessed by the death of his father, Warwick is betrayed, the killings of Rutland, York, and Clifford are all inspired by revenge. The moral descent involved here is seen most clearly in the exchange between Gloucester and Clifford in Act II:

> 'Twas you that killed young Rutland,
> was it not?'
> 'Ay, and old York, and yet not satisfied.'[16]

We see the terrible symmetrical logic of revenge in the events at York. There Clifford is taunted by York's sons, and his head is placed on the gates where he had placed York's. Warwick says:

> From off the gates of York fetch down
> the head,
> Your father's head, which Clifford placed there;
> Instead whereof let this supply the room:
> Measure for measure must be answered.[17]

The 'must' in 'must be answered' embodies the logical requirements of revenge. What this means is precisely explained by Hegel in his *Philosophy of Right*:

> Revenge, because it is a positive action of a particular will,
> becomes a new transgression; as thus contradictory in character,
> it falls into an infinite progression and descends from one
> generation to another ad infinitum.[18]

Second, the form taken by revenge is not a simple killing for political advantage, a political assassination. The murders are of a noticeably cruel and inhuman kind. The child killing, of course, is motivated by dynastic advantage, but it is performed so as to produce greatest agony for those closest to the victims. Clifford murders York's son, Rutland, who is 12 years old and still in the charge of a tutor. When York is captured by Queen Margaret, Clifford, and Northumberland, she will not allow Clifford to kill him immediately. In a famous scene, she makes York stand upon a molehill, gives him a napkin stained in the blood of his son, Rutland, to wipe away his tears, and then crowns him with a paper crown. In words of cruel degradation she shows her victim nothing but contempt:

> . . . where is your darling Rutland?
> Look, York: I stained this napkin with the blood
> That valiant Clifford with his rapier's point
> Made issue from the bosom of the boy;
> And if thine eyes can water for his death
> I give thee this to dry thy cheeks withal.[19]

When in her turn Margaret suffers the murder of her son she curses the murderers, so perpetuating the cycle of killing:

> But if you ever chance to have a child,
> Look in his youth to have him so cut off
> As, deathsmen, you have rid this sweet young Prince![20]

If murder is the most palpable expression of decline then the third element, perjury, breaks the moral spine of a political community. All such communities depend in various ways upon conditions of trust. The nature of these conditions is one of the major problems of political philosophy. What Shakespeare portrays in Henry VI is their gradual disintegration. It is a society in which trust no longer holds, in which promises are broken to facilitate revenge, ambition, or the needs of the moment. Edward persuades his father, York, to go back on his agreement with Henry, and he breaks faith with Warwick for immediate personal advantage. It is, of course, Gloucester who casts most doubt on the obligatory nature of promise-keeping. In Act I he says:

> An oath is of no moment, being not
> took
> Before a true and lawful magistrate
> That hath authority over him that swears:[21]

This passage raises the crucial problems of political obligation. If an oath is dependent on authority, and authority is disputed, then promise-keeping has no solid foundation. If this is the case, Gloucester's argument would proceed, then oaths may be broken with moral impunity. The only sanction is failure. The political relationship here is between authority and obedience, and in the Chase scene in Act III Henry is brought face to face with the consequences of his

deposition in precisely this area. When the Second Keeper describes
him as

> . . . the king King Edward hath depos'd;
> And we his subjects, sworn in all allegiance,
> Will apprehend you as his enemy.[22]

the disguised Henry is forced to realize the connection between
authority and sworn obedience. Edward is now King. Henry is
precisely described as 'the quondam king', and the oaths taken in
his reign no longer have obligatory power. Henry's failure here is
culpable, and what this scene shows is the close connection between
promise-keeping, obligation, and civil order.

The general dissolution of moral restraint and the turbulent politics
which result mean that for the protagonists in the drama events soon
go beyond their control. All experience unpredictable changes of
luck. Some are ignorant of events which have a crucial bearing on
their plans and policies. In this respect, the idea which most dominates
the play is Machiavelli's notion of Fortune, that rather mysterious
element which governs the throws of the historical dice. This political
uncertainty does not only take place within the boundaries of the
state. As with many instances of civil war, adjacent states are sucked
into the chaos – with contemporary Lebanon it is Syria and Israel,
and, more broadly, America and Russia. In Henry's time it was
France, and in Act III we find Margaret at the French court asking:

> . . . how can tyrants safely govern home,
> Unless abroad they purchase great alliance?[23]

Security at home and foreign policy are intimately connected. Thus,
we find Montgomery emphasizing to Edward why he should not
marry Lady Grey:

> . . . to have joined with France in such alliance
> Would more have strengthened this our commonwealth
> 'Gainst foreign storms, than any home-bred
> marriage.[24]

The broad sweep of political events makes pressing demands on the
policies and decisions of the characters they involve. Here grasp of
political imperatives is crucial. This provides the key to the relation
between Henry's innocence and the world I have described.

We first see this problem when Henry himself raises it in the first

Act. Warwick has accused him of losing control of France, and Henry defends himself by pointing out that as a child he was innocent of such matters and so cannot be blamed. He says:

> The Lord Protector lost it, and not I:
> When I was crown'd I was but nine months old.[25]

It is Richard, of course, who sees the political irony of this remark. He replies:

> You are old enough now, and yet,
> methinks, you lose.[26]

Henry, in other words, has reached an age and a position in the world where innocence of character is a culpable weakness.

We see this more clearly on the two main occasions of collision between Henry's character and his world. Both have disastrous consequences. First, he unnaturally gives up the succession to York. The events which follow this have the same logic which governs the consequences of a mistake in a chess game. He alienates his own supporters, he is forced to go back on a publicly made promise to York, and, in so doing, he releases the forces which lead directly to a brutal civil war. Warwick describes this course of events with great precision:

> . . . The proud insulting queen,
> With Clifford and the haught Northumberland,
> And of their feather many more proud birds,
> Have wrought the easy-melting king like wax.
> He swore consent to your succession,
> His oath enrolled in the parliament;
> And now to London all the crew are gone,
> To frustrate both his oath and what beside
> May make against the house of Lancaster.[27]

As this speech makes clear, Warwick is fully aware that Henry's weakness is the pivotal connection between the dissolution of civil order and the outbreak of civil war. As the pace of events increases so does Henry's ineffectiveness. He allows himself to be silenced whenever he tries to intervene. His protest against the barbarism of placing York's head above the city gates is too easily brushed aside. Henry the moralist has become Henry the sermonizer so guaranteeing his political isolation. The second notable expression of political weakness is his abdication of government to Warwick and Clarence. This naive decision leads to Richard's tyranny and to Henry's own murder, the supreme outrage against the political order and the divine order on which it rested.

Most commentators interpret Henry's character as a vehicle for the concept of order. They tend to follow Tillyard here in emphasizing the medieval idea of order and Machiavelli's disruptive and unpredictable notion of Fortune. Cairncross, for example, writes:

> In spite of his own weakness, and the breaches of faith he has been led into, he [Henry] is a standing protest against the horrors of the civil war.[28]

This interpretation is unpersuasive. The phrase 'in spite of' does no logical work, and it leaves us with an over-generous picture of Henry as an unlucky moral protestor. We are given no account of the paradoxical nature of Henry's moral innocence – that decisions taken in complete purity of mind lead to outcomes which deny their intentions. Furthermore, if Cairncross's interpretation were true, we would be at a loss to understand Henry's response to the suffering which has resulted from his character and actions. Why should he feel grief and pity for his subjects enduring a civil war if his moral innocence was not culpable? Why should he attempt to escape from politics if he saw no connection between holding fast to moral principle and political failure?

These questions first become important for Henry during the brutal battle at Towton. He realizes that the acts of cruelty he sees around him have some connection with the nature of his kingship. With this realization the security of his world is unavoidably broken. His first response is to create a world of artificial order, a haven of pastoral peace, to counteract the 'care, mistrust, and treason', as he puts it, of the realities of politics. When he commends the shepherd's life against the burdens of politics in the famous speech in Act II we know that Shakespeare's purpose is ironic. Henry indulges in these reflections while sitting on York's molehill. Fantasy is replaced by grief with the entry of a son who has killed his father, and a father who has killed his son. The only sentiment Henry offers them is consolation. In a dreadful parody of political responsibility he mimics their bereavement. In a series of lamentations, all the more ghastly because they are genuine, Henry bemoans his subjects' fate. We realize at once that the fake currency of political innocence is pity.

When his subjects require assertion, policy, and decision Henry offers moral self-reflection. It means, of course, political paralysis, and Clifford among Henry's friends and Richard among his enemies both realize it. Before Towton, Clifford warns Henry that 'too much lenity and harmful pity must be laid aside', and after the battle he rebukes him, asking:

> . . . what doth cherish weeds, but gentle air?
> And what makes robbers bold but too much lenity?

Later,

> . . . the foe is merciless, and will not pity;
> For at their hands I have deserved no pity.[29]

By the Chase scene in Act III Henry's preoccupation with his own goodness has reached the point of complete public impotence. Even his virtue is unavailable. He responds to one of the keepers:

> My crown is in my heart, not on
> my head;[30]

This disposition guarantees his exclusion from politics. It is patronizing and insulting to his subjects and it means that his abdication comes as no surprise. Henry's innocence first expressed itself by creating the political chaos which led to civil war. His subsequent responses were nostalgia, grief, pity, and private moral consolation. Abdication is his attempt at complete withdrawal from the public world. He says to Warwick in Act IV:

> . . . that I may conquer Fortune's spite
> By living low, where Fortune cannot hurt me,
> And that the people of this blessed land
> May not be punished with my thwarting stars,
> Warwick, although my head still wear the
> crown,
> I here resign my government to thee,
> For thou art fortunate in all thy deeds.[31]

Later to Warwick and Clarence he explains his reasons:

> That no dissension hinder government:
> I make you both protectors of this land,
> While I myself will lead a private life,

195

And in devotion spend my latter days,
To sin's rebuke and my Creator's praise.[32]

Innocence still blights these final pronouncements. It ensures that outcomes contradict intentions. First, it is not Fortune which is responsible for Henry's public failure but his own character. This means that he deceives himself by thinking that he 'may conquer Fortune's spite, by living low'. This is impossible for him. Second, his attempt to both abdicate government and retain the crown confirms his political ignorance and his fate. He is left with the worst of both worlds. Withdrawal from politics is not open to him. An important aspect of his innocence is his belief that he can easily divest himself of public office. His attempt to escape politics for reasons of moral scruple leaves him naked in the face of Gloucester's predatory assaults. Henry's assassination is the ultimate reward for his innocence.

The disjunction between intention and outcome may be further brought out by noticing the contrast between Henry and Clifford. In Act II, Clifford's speech before his death is almost a political autobiography – a reflection on his political aims and an indictment of Henry for causing civil war. Clifford's deepest political motives are the desire for an ordered state, love of Lancaster, and revenge for the crimes of York. His policies and actions are consistent with these aims. He knows the risks and is prepared to run them. His death in the Battle of Towton is a perfectly logical outcome. He has fought and lost.

Clifford's life is not paradoxical. He has made no secret of his aims. The means he employs to achieve them are consistent and risky. He will not deal with his political opponents and he is prepared to dirty his hands to destroy them. Henry, too, is motivated by the ideals of peace and love of country. But Henry is a peace-loving man. His belief in political virtue leads him to trust his enemies. Unlike Clifford, Henry is willing to deal with his opponents. He is not prepared to use any means to destroy them. It is this innocent sense of the moral limits on politics which guarantees the defeat of his ideals and not the swords and pikes of York. Henry is, of course, a political figure. He is the legitimate monarch and the structure of rights and duties which make up his office requires political knowledge and skill if he is to rule effectively. Henry's ignorance of the mediacies of politics, its conciliations, confrontations, and duplicities, of when to trust and when not to, places him half in and half out of the political world. He has neither the purity of a saint nor the energetic and evil sagacity of Gloucester. His idealism creates political havoc and ensures victory for his enemies.

Henry's moral character is complex. He is both compassionate and weak. We may better appreciate the political impact of goodness by divorcing it from weakness, by contrasting Henry's innocence with that of Billy Budd in Melville's short novel. Both Budd and Henry represent goodness confronted by evil in the forms of Claggart and Gloucester. But whereas Budd in the rage of pure innocence murders Claggart, eliminating evil at its origin, Henry attempts to compromise with it, tries to strike deals with evil. Budd, unlike Henry, is completely outside the political. His goodness is innocent both before and after his encounter with Claggart. It is this which creates the dilemma for Captain Vere who must decide Budd's fate. Compassion plays a significant part in both texts. Budd shows it for Vere who sentences him to death. Henry feels it for the victims of civil war. In both their compassion resists, as Arendt puts it, '. . . the drawn-out wearisome processes of persuasion, negotiation, and compromise, which are the processes of law and politics'.[33]

A willingness to engage in such processes requires moral realism. It embodies the imperfect courage of Clifford and Warwick, the acceptance of the responsibility of judgement by Vere, and the worldly experience of Vigot in *The Quiet American*. In Budd, innocence as moral purity destroys evil by violence. In Henry's character, innocence appears as weakness and vacillation. Budd's goodness means that no other medium of expression is open to him. The political world is closed. Henry, however, is a part of that world, but his innocence disqualifies him. Thus, in the speech he makes before his death in Act V he realizes at last the nature of Gloucester's tyranny and his own incapacity to eliminate it:

> Ay, and for much more slaughter
> after this.
> O, God forgive my sins, and pardon thee![34]

In *Henry VI* innocence straddles the boundaries of politics. In *Billy Budd* it appears as outside the political. What transformative impact on politics does this involve?

Chapter Eight

MORAL PURITY AND POLITICS

Happy are they who know not the taste of evil.

(Sophocles, Antigone)

Why is there this cruel haste to corrupt innocence, to make a victim of a young creature whom we ought to protect, one who is dragged by this first false step into a gulf of misery from which only death can release her? Brutality, vanity, folly, error, and nothing more.

(Rousseau, Emile)

In the character of Henry VI moral innocence is an obstacle to effective kingship. It prevents him from carrying out the duties of monarchic rule and it encourages him to attempt withdrawal from the world to seek solace in private security and contentment. To friends and enemies alike Henry appears as weak and incapable of fulfilling the political expectations of office. But Billy Budd in Melville's short novel[1] holds no formal position, save that of sailor. He is ignorant of the world and politically uninvolved. He represents no party, ideology, or interest, and, yet, for those who have to decide his fate he poses a profound moral dilemma. Henry as king is 'the beautiful soul' adrift in politics. Billy Budd holds no office, and yet his story offers a powerful insight into the political condition. How can this be? How can natural goodness qualify politics?

Melville's deceptively simple tale is, of course, a late work, written in 1890, one year before Melville's death, and not published until 1924. *Billy Budd* intertwines political with theological themes in a manner which is enlightening for moral and political philosophy. The conflict between goodness and evil is antinomic and irreducible, and it takes place in the context of a state at war. The basic political fear of stasis, of unrest and insurrection within and the imported influence of revolutionary ideas from without, is an essential element in the tragedy. The contrast between natural goodness and conventional imperfections heightens the moral dilemmas of modernism, and there is a strong sense in which *Billy Budd* provides a fictional commentary on Rousseau's attempt to reconstitute innocence in the mature world of politics. These difficult and complex themes, vital to political morality, involve inescapable areas of moral ambiguity and uncertainty for those who are neither naturally good nor pathologically evil. Vere embodies the virtues fit for the world, and it is Vere who has to face the moral dilemma which results. However, his is a virtue appropriate to politics and this means unavoidably that politics has to bear the burden of the clash between goodness and evil. Billy's innocent morality takes in his life the emblematic force of natural goodness and in his death the redemptive power of spirituality. Neither nature nor lost innocence is sufficient to support a political realm. It is to Vere that we should look for such a foundation, but Vere's dying words take the form of Billy's name. What is the nature of this indebtedness? What dependency on natural goodness does politics exhibit?

To ask such questions is to run ahead. The novel is set in 1797 on board a British naval vessel, HMS *Indomitable*, during the French Revolutionary Wars, and in a year which saw the navy mutinies at Spithead and the Nore. Billy Budd is an impressed seaman from a merchantship, the *Rights-of-Man*, who is a foundling. He has a moral and physical beauty and his only blemish is a stammer – worn, as Auden expresses it poetically in *Herman Melville*, 'like a decoration'.[2] His captain is 'Starry' Vere, a cultured and direct man who is an excellent seaman and a good officer. The master-at-arms is Claggart, unpopular with the crew, a mysterious character whose evil emerges gradually with the unfolding of events. Claggart's attitude to Billy seems equivocal. To Billy it is incredible that he should bear him ill-will, as the old hand, Dansker, warns him. But after a number of attempts to incriminate and provoke Billy, Claggart reports him to Vere as the main instigator of discontent and revolt among the crew.

Alone with his accuser in front of the captain, Billy's stammer prevents him from responding to Claggart's false charges in speech, and in the rage of affronted innocence he strikes him a violent blow which kills him. Billy has killed the master-at-arms of one of His Majesty's ships on active service. Vere knows the facts of the case –

that Claggart lied and that Billy's stammer prevented him from defending himself in speech. A drumhead court is summoned, but the agonizing decision is Vere's. He decides as captain what the sentence must be, and it is that Billy should hang. Prior to the execution Billy shouts a blessing to Vere, and when he hangs there is no physical frenzy, no violent twisting of a body in pain. It is almost as if Billy had died before the noose was put around his neck. Later, Vere, dying of wounds received in action, says Billy's name, but not in remorse.

The bald facts of the story conceal a moral and political parable. Billy Budd, the innocent foretopman of the story, is variously described as Noble Savage, child-man, an amalgam of feminine beauty and bullish strength, a peace-maker, well-liked by the crew who mostly have no suspicion of his true moral nature. His persona is explained in terms of Greek ideals of beauty and he is compared to Apollo, Hercules, and Alexander. He is a young Adam before the Fall. Billy is a foundling, illiterate but with the natural capacity of song. His only physical imperfection is his stammer which disqualifies him from the world of speech, and his unself-consciousness expresses itself in the spontaneous reactions of laughter and sadness. Like his complexion, his happiness is pure and untroubled by concealed motives. Indeed, he is incapable of satire or irony, and unaware of the double meanings in utterance upon which such sophisticated modes of discourse depend. Further, as Melville puts it, Billy is 'essentially such a novice in the complexities of factitious life'[3] that his lack of conceit prevents him from harm in the knowing world of a naval ship on active service. Billy's natural virtue has returned Christ-like to the corrupt world of cities, commerce, and war. His moral personality is that of an upright barbarian, and, as Melville puts it,

> The character marked by such qualities has to an unvitiated taste an untampered-with flavor like that of berries, while the man thoroughly civilised, even in a fair specimen of the breed, has to the same moral palate a questionable smack as of a compounded wine.[4]

The crucial qualification to the civilized man, 'even in a fair specimen of the breed', serves to indicate Billy's unique moral character. It is morally *sui generis*, serene and incapable of envy or malice. Billy's innocence is that of a child-man and his unawareness of vice makes him ignorant of its presence in others. Melville writes:

> But in Billy Budd intelligence, such as it was, had advanced while yet his simple-mindedness remained for the most part unaffected. . . . he had none of that intuitive knowledge of the bad which in natures not good or incompletely so foreruns experience . . .[5]

Billy lacks an habitual distrustfulness of the intentions of others, which means, of course, that he is unprepared for Claggart's evil. He thinks Claggart to be well-disposed towards him, if 'rather queer at times', and he is incapable of recognizing that a pleasant word is not what it seems. He has never heard of 'the too fair-spoken man'. Billy is ignorant of the proximity of the malign, 'innocence was his blinder', as Melville writes. After Claggart's false accusation Billy's innocence remains. He is neither apprehensive nor distrustful when Vere calls him to his cabin to respond to Claggart's charges, and his rage and striking Claggart dead are natural responses of inarticulate innocence against evil and unjustified assault. His last cry, 'God bless Captain Vere!' is an expression of a blind trust in Vere's virtue which indicates the redemptive power of natural goodness and the moral limits within which Vere has to act.

Billy's innocent goodness finds its antithesis in Claggart who is evil incarnate. As with Billy Budd's former life, we are ignorant, too, of Claggart's past which remains a mystery, a matter only for unsubstantiated rumour. As master-at-arms, Claggart is deferential to his superior officers, but he has a 'peculiar, ferreting genius' for duplicity and manipulation. His wickedness stands apart from Billy, and at first he tries to tempt him through underlings until his hatred seeks satisfaction in the final, false charge of sedition. What is the nature of Claggart's evil? Why does it choose goodness as its object?

It is precisely Billy's goodness which forms the object of Claggart's hate. Apart from Vere, only Claggart realizes the true nature of Billy's moral sense and it is a knowledge which forces him to persecute Billy, to test his goodness, to experiment with it. In his moral ugliness Claggart perceives Billy's character as a constant source of reproof, an ideal standard which he can never meet, and which he can only hate and attempt to remove. It is important to note that Claggart has no material reason to hate Billy, at least in terms of interest or advantage. There is no external gain for his hatred to achieve. The kind of evil Claggart represents is described by Melville in this way:

> Though the man's even temper and discreet bearing would seem to intimate a mind peculiarly subject to the law of reason, not the less in heart he would seem to riot in complete exemption from that law, having apparently little to do with reason further than to employ it as an ambidexter implement for effecting the irrational.[6]

Claggart's 'conscience being but the lawyer to his will', we are presented with evil willed for no external purpose, embroidered by the appearance of rationality, which tortures itself in the presence of a goodness it knows it can never equal. As Benn argues persuasively, a man like Claggart envies the good

> with resentment and hate for them and the things they love and value just because he knows that there is no possibility that he could be like them, think like them, feel like them, or care like them. Precisely because the good that he sees cannot motivate him, he hates it for its very inaccessibility.[7]

We do not grasp the full nature of Claggart's evil until we realize that, *contra* Kant and Socrates, it is willed for its own sake as the destruction of good. It is for this reason that, when faced with Claggart's lie and his fate, Vere exclaims that 'It is the divine judgement on Ananias!'

While goodness and evil find expression in Billy Budd and Claggart, their antagonism exhibits a curious logical symmetry. Neither innocent goodness nor malignity can be explained in terms of some external purpose or moral law. Both have to be understood on their own terms, as expressing the attitudes and values appropriate to their natures. In *Billy Budd* goodness and evil are not in conflict over an external advantage, interest, or prize, and their disagreement cannot be resolved by reference to a common framework of rationality. Billy's innocence is pre-rational, and Claggart's evil is in his heart, not captured by the abstract structure of moral principle and precept.

It is Vere who is faced with the actual resolution of this dilemma, and it is presented as a highly political choice even though its first appearance is clearly moral. The captain of HMS *Indomitable* is a mature, aristocratic figure, a man of prudent, Aristotelian virtue. His character is direct and intellectual. Vere's reading displays his moral nature, a dislike of cant and hypocrisy, of impractical idealism.

He opposes revolutionary and innovative political ideas not from the self-interest of privilege but 'because they seemed to him insusceptible of embodiment in lasting institutions, but at war with the peace of the world and the true welfare of mankind'.[8] Vere is a humanist, his qualities are honesty and directness, his realism that of Montaigne. His moral personality, then, is far from simple. As captain he has responsibility for a ship at war and for the prosecution of the policy that ship represents. He has, of course, the Naval Code, but he is equally aware that abstract rules do not capture the full moral significance of his choice. Billy's innocence and Claggart's evil are not matters to which he is indifferent, but he realizes that the judgement he arrives at must be disinterested. Further, the context of his choice involves political considerations – a state at war, the influence of revolutionary ideas, the maintenance of military discipline in the light of recent insurrection and mutiny. Vere is described as morally unswerving, not distracted by extraneous considerations, his honesty, as Melville describes it, 'never heeds when it crosses a frontier'. How does innocence force Vere into a situation of moral paradox?

It might be argued that Vere's position embodies the classic dilemmas of political morality, that the conflict he must resolve is between private conscience and military duty. But as the following crucial passage makes clear this interpretation is too simple and will not do:

> In the jugglery of circumstances preceding and attending the event on board the *Indomitable*, and in the light of that martial code whereby it was formally to be judged, innocence and guilt personified in Claggart and Budd in effect changed places. In a legal view the apparent victim of the tragedy was he who had sought to victimise a man blame-less; and the indisputable deed of the latter, navally regarded, constituted the most heinous of military crimes. Yet more. The essential right and wrong involved in the matter, the clearer that might be, so much the worse for the responsibility of a loyal sea commander, inasmuch as he was not authorised to determine the matter on that primitive basis.[9]

Vere's moral categories are not simply those of private conscience and public duty. To show why this is so I shall examine three philosophical readings of *Billy Budd*.

Peter Winch's philosophical attention is drawn to *Billy Budd* through a consideration of the problem of moral judgement.[10] How is the moral agent related to the moral judgements he makes? One view, which winch wishes to support and clarify, is that the individual bears a unique relation to his moral judgements. An opposing position, which he associates with Henry Sidgwick, is that it is the situation in which an action is performed which determines its rightness or wrongness, and the agent's moral understanding is relevant only to the extent that it affects the situation. Winch wishes to contest Sidgwick's claim that it is possible to move from actions which it is right for one individual to perform to actions which it is right for others to perform in similar circumstances. Quite clearly if the moral standpoint from which such judgements are made can be shown to be logically crucial then Sidgwick's position will not hold up. It is important to note that Winch does not wish to deny the place of consistency and rationality in moral concerns. Indeed, he accepts Sidgwick's implication that if someone were to make contesting spectator judgements in situations which were identical in all morally relevant respects we would find it difficult to regard them as saying anything intelligible at all. Winch emphasizes that agent and spectator judgements are logically different, and that universalizability, if it means that to judge rightly is to judge the same, involves too strong a claim.

How does Winch see the dilemma of Captain Vere in this philosophical context? He stresses Melville's remark that in a situation of active war service, in which there was a well-grounded fear of mutiny, a naval commander requires 'two qualities not readily interfusable – prudence and rigor'. He accepts that we might initially wish to describe Vere's dilemma as a conflict between morality and his duty to uphold military law, but that this neglects the sense in which Vere considers the demands of military service as something to which he has a moral commitment. Of course, not everyone in Vere's position would decide in the same way, and to understand why this is so Winch turns to a close examination of the speech made by Vere to the summary court martial to which he has already given evidence as the sole witness to the event. Winch stresses that there Vere brings out the moral character of the dilemma which faces the court. Vere distinguishes the moral obligation to administer military law from the moral inclination to compassion and clemency. He contrasts the moral force of the Naval Code with private moral conscience.

Winch quotes Vere's way of putting the tragic dilemma to the court:

> 'Now can we adjudge to summary and shameful death a fellow creature, innocent before God, and whom we feel to be so? Does that state it aright? You sign sad assent. Well, I too feel that, the full force of that'.[11]

The conflict Vere is faced with is between two moral considerations, not between a moral consideration, say that of administering the rules impartially, and a simple, personal inclination to be lenient however understandable and praiseworthy. Winch argues that both moral 'oughts' are universalizable in Sidgwick's sense, but his main concern is with Sidgwick's thesis in relation to the moral decision which Vere makes to uphold the law. His first point is that the dilemma cannot be removed by universalizing the two imperatives. Indeed, it is because they are each in principle universalizable that the dilemma has its tragic quality. Equally, Vere's decision does not mean that he simply accepts one and rejects the other, or that he regards the law as erasing the moral claims Billy has on him. This is clear, Winch thinks, from Vere's behaviour after the trial, and from his scrutinizing the moral requirements of law in the light of private conscience. For Winch, the 'ought' which grounds Vere's decision lies within his character, and not exclusively in terms of public authority or private conscience even though this is the form the dilemma takes for him. He quotes Vere's question:

> 'But tell me whether or not, occupying the position we do, private conscience should not yield to that imperial one formulated in the code under which alone we officially proceed?'[12]

As Winch points out, the 'should' in this passage is unintelligible if we identify it with private conscience or public duty. Winch asks if Vere's moral judgement commits him to the logical corollary of Sidgwick's thesis, that anyone in the same position ought to act in the same way. Winch argues that it would have been morally impossible for him (Winch) to have made Vere's moral decision, and, further, this does not mean he must believe that Vere acted wrongly. In admitting this Winch is certainly loosening the moral hold of universalization on our moral imagination, but he does not consider that he is thereby committed to a kind of Protagorean subjectivism.

205

this certainly does not mean that, if A believes that X is the right thing or him to do, then X is *made* the right thing for A to do by the mere fact that he thinks it is. It was clearly important to Vere that he did the right thing and he did not think that whatever he thought would be the right thing would in fact be so.[13]

The process of moral choice here is more like finding out what is the right thing to do than applying a set of moral propositions to a particular situation. A view of moral decision which likens it to self-discovery must have some way of distinguishing between better and worse judgements. Here Winch offers three considerations. First, Vere's judgement takes place in a genuinely moral context. This might not always be so. Another captain might be completely indifferent to Billy's innocence and Claggart's evil. He may reach the same decision as Vere, but on the basis of an automatic or mechanical application of the rules. Second, that where someone decides with the appearance of moral concern, our understanding of right and wrong is so different that we are unwilling to accept his decision as it stands. This is clearly not applicable to Vere's case. Third, a moral decision is accompanied by features of conduct or subsequent behaviour which suggest insincerity or hypocrisy. In this respect, the problematic utterance is Vere's recitation of Billy's name on his death bed. His lack of remorse is intelligible only in the context of the moral ideas which he explores in the course of arriving at his decision. These are essential to understanding how moral situations and difficulties appear differently to different agents. And this, for Winch, restricts the claims of universalizability.

> the situation at the courtmartial clearly struck Vere very differently from the way it struck the senior officer of marines, who was for acquitting Billy. But what did this difference consist in? Surely in the fact that, faced with two conflicting sets of considerations, the one man was disposed to give precedence to the one, and acquit, the other to give precedence to the other, and convict. If such dispositions as this have to be taken into account in applying the notion of 'exactly the same circumstances', surely the last vestige of logical force is removed from the universalizability thesis.[14]

It is not my concern here to assess Winch's criticism of Sidgwick, but I would like to consider several possible lacunae in his reading of *Billy Budd*, and I raise these in the realization that his interpretation is not intended to be a comprehensive treatment of that work. My general argument is that Winch gives insufficient attention to Billy's innocence. Indeed, for him Vere's dilemma could equally well have arisen from someone committing the same offence but in different extenuating circumstances. This point may be illustrated in a number of overlapping ways. In his directions to the court martial Vere consistently emphasizes that it is with the action and its consequences that they have to be concerned. Even if they could gauge the mystery of Claggart's motives or Billy's state of mind they would be superfluous to their concern. Vere says:

> Quite aside from any conceivable motive actuating the master-at-arms, and irrespective of the provocation to the blow, a martial court must needs in the present case confine its attention to the blow's consequence, which consequence justly is to be deemed not otherwise than as the striker's deed.[15]

Later, Vere repeats:

> The prisoner's deed – with that alone we have to do.[16]

When he explains why states of mind should be put aside Vere does so in terms of the public character of their enterprise. His moral commitment is to a public office which alone sanctions their military activity. This does not depend on private judgement or on their happening to approve the war undertaken by the state on whose behalf they serve.

> War looks but to the frontage, the appearance. And the Mutiny Act, War's child, takes after the father. Budd's intent or non-intent is nothing to the purpose.[17]

But this does not mean simply that Billy's mental state takes second place to military discipline and that Vere is reluctantly disregarding considerations such as acting under duress or great provocation. This is to take an over-legalistic view of Vere's moral difficulty and it misses the decisive part played by Billy's innocence. Billy is guilty of the act, but innocent not merely of intention but of Claggart's evil attempt to corrupt him. It is Billy's purity which constitutes the moral problem, not simply the innocence which may be called on in mitigation. When Vere requires the court justly to identify consequence with deed, Billy is serenely and angelically unaware of the dangers that such a reference has for him.

This utterance, the full significance of which it was not at all likely that Billy took in, nevertheless caused him to turn a wistful interrogative look toward the speaker, a look in its dumb expressiveness not unlike that which a dog of generous breed might turn upon his master, seeking in his face some elucidation of a previous gesture ambiguous to the canine intelligence.[18]

In his military service Vere must have experienced many such moral conflicts where guilt or innocence before a military tribunal hastily convened was difficult to prove and where the justice of the decision reached was less than perfect. Why should he respond uniquely to Billy Budd? Winch's exegesis leaves the answer unclear.

An explanation is to be found in the way Vere argues that it is precisely Billy's natural goodness which must be put aside.

It is Nature. But do these buttons that we wear attest that our allegiance is to Nature? No, to the King. Though the ocean, which is inviolate Nature primeval, though this be the element where we move and have our being as sailors, yet as the King's officers lies our duty in a sphere correspondingly natural?[19]

Billy's innocence is a natural goodness, unself-conscious and ineffable. This places it outside incorporation in legal judgement, beyond instantiation in a political community. But Billy's goodness expresses compassion, a natural fellow-feeling which cannot be easily sacrificed. A state of natural innocence, of paradigm goodness before the Fall, has an essential hold over our moral imagination. This explains why Vere's decision remains in his memory and why he repeats Billy's name without remorse on his deathbed. Vere has placed paradise aside without any sense of wrong-doing.

In Winch's view it is essential to realize that Vere's dilemma is a genuinely moral one. It is a conflict between two moral imperatives, not merely between a moral imperative and an inclination or a consideration of political advantage, which means that it excludes explanation in terms of means and ends. Vere does not merely sacrifice a man whom he knows to be innocent to discourage others from seditious and mutinous enterprise. This is not what troubles him. It is true that consequentialist considerations play a part in his rejecting the sailing master's suggestion that the court should convict and yet mitigate the sentence –

No, to the people the foretopman's deed, however it be worded in the announcement, will be plain homicide committed in a flagrant act of mutiny. What penalty for that should follow, they know. But it does not follow. *Why?* They will ruminate. You know what sailors are. Will they not revert to the recent outbreak at the Nore? Ay. They know the well-founded alarm – the panic it struck throughout England. Your clement sentence they would account pusillanimous. They would think that we flinch, that we are afraid of them – afraid of practicing a lawful rigor singularly demanded at this juncture, lest it should provoke new troubles. What shame to us such a conjecture on their part, and how deadly to discipline.[20]

but this does not mean that Vere's morality is one of calculation. First, Billy is guilty of the act of killing Claggart, a superior officer, in time of war. Second, what troubles Vere is the problem not of weighing immoral means against moral ends but of attaching priority to one of two equally powerful moral demands on his imagination – innocence falsely corrupted by the world and the moral imperatives of his enterprise however imperfect they are in practice. Third, Vere's reference to the moral demands of office is not explicable solely in military terms. A key part of Vere's rejection of private conscience is that responsibility to office involves a judgement regarding public reaction to decisions. Acquittal and mitigation imply that Billy's natural goodness has a place in the public realm which will not be misunderstood. Vere's refusal to take this course, to allow that Billy's moral innocence can sustain a public appearance, entails the sacrifice of innocence, and it is this which disturbs him at the end.

The second reading of *Billy Budd* is Hannah Arendt's who writes in *On Violence*,

The point is that under certain circumstances violence – acting without argument or speech and without counting the consequences – is the only way to set the scales of justice right again. (Billy Budd, striking dead the man who bore false witness against him, is the classical example.)[21]

She describes Billy's rage as a 'natural *human* emotion'; whilst its anti-political character is beyond dispute, to remove such expression from a human moral capacity is to 'dehumanize or emasculate'.

This introduces a certain ambivalence not found in her criticism of absolute goodness in *On Revolution* where she was more concerned to stress the complete incompatibility between inarticulate moral purity as a naturally good state and the possibility of politics. In her earlier work, *Billy Budd* is seen as a sustained fictional commentary on the excesses of the French Revolution. It teaches us 'that absolute goodness is hardly any less dangerous than absolute evil', that it does not reside in selflessness, and 'that it is beyond virtue, even the virtue of Captain Vere'. Billy is natural man returned to inhabit an imperfect world. Like Claggart, his origin is unknown. Evil and goodness clash in disinherited forms, in wills which are not dependent on history or origin. Arendt comments in a way which brings out the contrast between Billy and the moral innocence of Henry VI:

> The greatness of this part of the story lies in that goodness, because it is part of 'nature', does not act meekly but asserts itself forcefully and, indeed, violently so that we are convinced: only the violent act with which Billy Budd strikes dead the man who bore false witness against him is adequate, it eliminates nature's 'depravity'.[22]

The problem as Arendt sees it, is that the good individual in the act of eradicating evil in the form of Claggart has become a wrong-doer. It is only with the introduction of virtue in the shape of Captain Vere that the conflict becomes a tragic moral dilemma. Virtue is weaker than goodness, but it must supersede it if human institutions and practices are to prevail. Vere's decision does nothing to identify Claggart's corruption and it ignores his criminality in his bearing false witness against Billy. What it achieves is the punishment of innocence, and Arendt regards Vere's stand as an achievement because it alone retrieves the priority of politics. Absolute goodness can only express itself in violence and this places it beyond enclosure in the political realm. Arendt writes:

> Laws and all 'lasting institutions' break down not only under the onslaught of elemental evil but under the impact of absolute innocence as well. The law, moving between crime and virtue, cannot recognise what is beyond it, and while it has no punishment to mete out to elemental evil, it cannot but punish elemental goodness even if the virtuous man, Captain Vere, recognises that only the violence of this goodness is adequate to the depraved power of evil.[23]

When Billy shouts 'And good-bye to you too, old Rights-of-Man' on his departure from the merchantman, his meaning is unintentionally ironic. No absolute framework of values, of rights, duties, or obligations, can subsume the political.

For Arendt, compassion and pity are the values which dominate the story. Billy expresses compassion for Vere who sentences him to death. Billy's natural gaiety, his stammer, his physical expressiveness are consonant with a goodness which Arendt thinks signifies its presence in countenance rather than speech. Such goodness can only take account of people in their singularity. It cannot go beyond the suffering experienced by one person and if it attempts to do so it is transformed into its opposite. Billy's speechlessness and his compassion are at one in their incapacity to ground political communication. But when compassion appears in politics Arendt argues that its shape must be violent. As goodness confronts what it takes to be evil with direct and unequivocal action it is showing its intrinsic inability to acquire the political arts of persuasion, justification, and judgement. Billy's moral innocence makes it impossible for him to answer Claggart's charges. It is Arendt's conclusion that moral innocence as assertive, absolute goodness is deeply subversive of politics.

This interpretation has the great merit of bringing out the political character of *Billy Budd*, by stressing the complex political circumstances against which the action is set and by showing how it is that neither absolute goodness nor absolute evil can sustain a polis. More positively, Arendt clearly regards Vere's decision as epitomizing political judgement. It alone embodies the virtue appropriate to human practices and institutions and it is willing to sacrifice goodness if that is the only way of maintaining them. We are shown, too, how the characteristic values of goodness, compassion, and pity may be extrapolated to reveal the ways they threaten politics. Nevertheless, Arendt's admiration for Vere does not fully explain why his decision is to be read as a political judgement. What gives it this character?

The third reading of *Billy Budd* is Thomas J. Scorza's who asserts, with Arendt, that it 'is an emphatically political novel'.[24] His general theme is that Melville's story shows how political virtue can be undermined by modern science, technology, and Enlightenment philosophy, and his critical aim is to overcome the disagreement between those who portray Billy as sacrificial victim and those who see Vere as embodiment of duty. Billy, he argues, is to be understood by reference to the paradigm of the 'Handsome Sailor', the archetype of natural physical and moral superiority, of goodness which is pre-scientific and hence independent of articulation in knowledge or intellect. Billy is, of course, physically beautiful and strong. He has an instinctive, natural intelligence and lacks an understanding which is self-reflective. However, Billy has no political capacity – his stammer makes his being pre-political in nature. He has not yet learned a political language. He is, as Scorza puts it, 'fresh from Rousseau's state of nature'. Billy is modern man unmasked, with the corrupt veneer of civilization stripped away to reveal the natural innocence and goodness beneath.

Against the 'Handsome Sailor' and its manifestation in Billy Budd, the narrator in the tale counterposes the 'Great Sailor', its historical embodiment, Lord Nelson, and its fictional presentation in the person of Captain Vere. Political virtue takes place against the background of the French Revolutionary Wars, the political complexities of the period, and the military turbulence of a nation at arms. The moral heroism of the 'Great Sailor' gains its logical purchase from its taking place in this context, but there is an important consideration which Scorza adds to the standard reading. Advances in the technology of warfare make courage and gallantry otiose. They weaken our admiration for bravery for the simple reason that modern inventions seem to dispel its necessity. This point is extended by the narrator in his argument that self-sacrifice is disparaged by modern thinking about war. He refers to 'martial utilitarians' who see Nelson's heroism as 'foolhardiness and vanity', to 'the Benthamites of war' who emphasize calculation and advantage. However, as Melville's narrator points out,

> the *might-have-been* is but boggy ground to build on. And,
> certainly in foresight as to the larger issue of an encounter, and
> anxious preparations for it – buoying the deadly way and mapping
> it out, as at Copenhagen – few commanders have been so
> painstakingly circumspect as this same reckless declarer of his
> person in fight.[25]

The utilitarian emphasis on self-preservation does not capture the nature of the 'Great Sailor's' ideals. His military prowess enables him to defend the community's aims and values. His honour prevents him from seeing this as an exclusively personal matter or his victory as a personal achievement. Melville's narrator writes, in a passage which could equally well describe Machiavelli's stress on political glory or the Classical ideal of public virtue,

> Personal prudence, even when dictated by quite other than selfish considerations, surely is no special virtue in a military man; while an excessive love of glory, impassioning a less burning impulse, the honest sense of duty, is the first.[26]

For Scorza, Vere is a modern expression of the Aristotelian idea of magnanimity. He is a distinguished sailor and aware of his obligations and responsibilities to his crew. He is not tolerant of ill-discipline, but his command is not brutal or excessively zealous, and he maintains the necessary civilities of a common life by example and a conscientious regard to the duties of his office. He wins loyalty by nobility and regard, not despotism or privilege. But unlike the 'Great Sailor', Vere is an intellectual, bookish to the point of pedantry, and his reading is not of technical or naval literature, but of those like Montaigne who 'philosophize upon realities'. This regard for prudential wisdom is essential to magnanimity, and it arises from the recognition that in practical life natural heroism and spontaneous virtue are not sufficient. As Scorza puts it, 'in action, truth gives way to prudence', and, in this sense, cannot attach itself to abstract moral and political doctrine or novelty.

These themes come together in the form of Vere's dilemma after Billy has struck Claggart dead. Scorza stresses how Vere's practical reason, his sense of prudence, is not capable of preventing the outcome. He relies on legal procedure and neglects Billy's incapacity to answer the charges against him. It is Vere who chooses to confront Billy with his accuser, and it is Vere who fails to anticipate the instinctive fury of Billy's reaction. Vere's prudential wisdom is ignorant of the possibility of the irrational manifestation of goodness. It fails to prevent the conflict, and for Scorza this indicates that 'tragedy remains endemic to political life, at least where wisdom aspires to rule but cannot in fact rule'. But Vere's prudentiality is not the only disposition whose limitations are revealed. Billy's natural innocence lacks the moderating influence of speech and as the embodiment of Rousseau's Noble Savage he is

> forced into a state of war because he has no recourse to speech of conventional procedure. Thus, if the case of Captain Vere shows

that practical reason is not a sufficient condition for peace, the case of Billy Budd shows that speech is a necessary condition for dealing with evil.[27]

Scorza, therefore, reads Melville as transcending both Burke and Rousseau in their responses to the Enlightenment. Practical reason and prudential wisdom are no guarantees of moral rectitude, and the natural innocent is outside the rules of a political community. Scorza's emphasis is that of Nietzsche. The conflict between Billy and Claggart, their mutual destructiveness, is not merely between good and evil. It is between life and knowledge, existence and philosophy.

It is possible to pull together these three readings of *Billy Budd* to highlight the unconventional understanding of political morality it contains. In the novel the relationship between morality and politics is not simply between private conscience and political necessity in which well-intentioned individuals may on occasion have to act less than well. This simple view misses the precise transformation which happens when a moral value like compassion is extrapolated into politics. But this transformation is neither accidental nor exceptional. It is not as if the simple view was generally true, a standard position in relation to which such moral complexities are to be regarded as aberrations. When Billy's innocence appears as guilt, and Claggart's guilt as innocence, we have an insight into what the political world can and cannot sustain. This shift in meaning is not peripheral to the problem of political morality. It is central to it. It cannot be explored in terms of interest or advantage because the conflict between good and evil cannot be translated into this vocabulary. In conventional language, Claggart has nothing to gain from hating Billy. Indeed, his malice is a dreadful parody of goodness in the sense that in his hatred it might be said that Claggart risked all. Equally, it is a misrepresentation to describe Billy's innocence as an interest which needs protection. The absence of advantage or interest means that the problem of political morality is not expressible in terms of ends and means, of the calculation of consequence, or of the balance of one gain against another. The conflict between good and evil is not open to further reduction, and yet it is not an abstract dispute. In fact it takes an altogether familiar human shape in a highly political context of great urgency, and this comprehends the nature of political morality in a way ignored by the conventional view.

These considerations affect our understanding of the dilemma which faces Vere. What Melville calls 'the jugglery of circumstances' has affected the meaning of the actions which Vere is called by his office to judge. This meaning is no longer simple but multiple, and it cannot be unravelled by reference to the original context or disposition or by drawing on some common standard of interest, because no such currency is available. But further, as Winch convincingly shows, what Vere thinks he ought to do can be rendered intelligible not by reference solely to private conscience or the demands of a military code, but rather by discovering why Vere arrives at the decision he does. To think of the problems of political morality from the outside, as conventional theories mostly do, is to think about them on the model of spectator judgements, and this means a failure to see political morality from the standpoint of the agent which is crucial in understanding Vere. This does not imply either that his office and the duties associated with it are unimportant or that we are prohibited from including consequences in our interpretation of Vere's moral thinking. Quite the contrary is true because Vere does take the demands of his office seriously and that means a moral responsibility to consider the likely consequences of his decision which is a public act. The perspective of the agent has switched the way the office/office-holder relation is normally understood, but it has not obliterated the requirements of office altogether.

However, it is true that Vere's dilemma arises from Billy's predicament. While it is Vere's moral temper which explains the problem to him it is posed by Billy's innocence and his goodness and the response it stimulates in Claggart – an envy of a nature 'that . . . had in its simplicity never willed malice or experienced the reactionary bite of that serpent'.[28] Claggart's hatred takes the form of 'cynic disdain, disdain of innocence – to be nothing more than innocent! . . . he despaired of it'.[29] It is the clash between innocent goodness and evil which creates Vere's dilemma, and this means that his decision must be imperfect. There is no possibility of a choice adequate to the issues involved. To put the dilemma of political morality in this way is to realize the tragic and incomplete nature of political action, the limits of the political and its strengths. It shows how in the conflict between absolute goodness and evil it is in the autonomy of politics that an unsatisfactory resolution is to be found.

Political action bears the burden of releasing us from the affliction of innocence, and it makes this manifest in judgements like that of Vere. This is the true dimension of political morality.

Vere's capacity for political judgement, for a virtue which can be sustained in human institutions and practices, a justice which is capable of common appearance and understanding, is, for Arendt, a source of profound attachment. What are its conditions? Why in *Billy Budd* is it ultimately insufficient? Vere's decision is not made for reasons of personal advantage or to secure his position of authority. It is not that of a captain who simply reads off the rule-book auto-matically or solely assesses consequences in a spirit of mechanistic, utilitarian calculation. He is aware that Billy's goodness is not negotiable in that way. His decision is disinterested in the strong sense that it embodies his attempt to come to an impartial under-standing of the requirements which his office imposes on him in this particular case and in these particular circumstances. He places moral feeling aside, and his honesty warns against the illusions of moral compromise – that it is possible to pass the sentence and not exact the necessary and expected punishment. Vere's directness forbids him the craven deceptions of an easy sympathy, but his spirit here is not one of an unyielding devotion to duty and to rule. If this were so, the fact that he finds the decision difficult and is morally troubled by it would be simply inexplicable. He attempts tacitly to put himself in the position of his crew, of the sailors' response to the decision of the court martial. None of these considerations alone would be enough to explain why Vere decides as he does, but together they constitute conditions of political judgement which, to a very great extent, his decision meets. But it is important to stress that this does not mean the avoidance of tragedy. In fact it means quite the opposite because the individual stages of Vere's practical decision-making are each essential in sealing Billy's fate. A captain who did not have the moral wit to become involved, and who simply tossed a coin, or who arrived at his decision as a result of a bribe or for reasons of personal advancement not only could not be described as having made a political judgement, but also may have averted the tragedy. Are we to say, then, that Vere's moral sense and his determination to reach a considered judgement are responsible for Billy's death?

Of course, it does not follow that political and moral judgements guarantee the right outcomes. There may be considerations extraneous even to the most perfectly considered judgement which render it unsound. On the other side, a judgement may be weakened by prejudice or predisposition. However, it is not clear that either of these possibilities fits Vere's case. No external circumstances are introduced between his decision and Billy's execution. Vere makes determined efforts to put personal feelings aside. Some may argue that we need look no further than Vere's judgement itself. There is no logical gap between judgement and outcome. Vere has already taken Billy's goodness and his innocence into account. No common enterprise can tolerate unmediated goodness. Vere's office requires that he upholds the rules of an imperfect human practice, and, as Billy's spontaneous reaction to Claggart shows, no such practice could include it and survive.

At the centre of Billy's innocence is his ignorance of evil; his belief that others are as much incapable of wishing harm to him as he clearly is to them. While it is obviously true that Vere's is not the only moral decision which can be arrived at in his circumstances, it would not be possible for a moral innocent to judge what was happening or to face up to the dilemma. In *Henry VI* such innocent compassion expressed itself as inaction and weakness. In *Billy Budd* innocence does not turn the other cheek and appears to the world not as meekness but as strength. Henry's innocence is religiosity, vacuous and dangerous to politics. Billy's goodness is founded on natural resource, unafraid of facing up to the world and asserting its will in it. *Billy Budd* charts the course of such unrestrained assertion and we have seen its consequences for politics. But Billy is a victim. His execution is the reward for his innocence. The pattern of political morality changes if we examine a case which combines Henry's limitless compassion with Billy's assertive and confident will. Here moral innocence appears as certainty and commitment, an intense determination to ensure that compassion is the foremost of its political principles. This is moral innocence active in the political world. It is policy completely sure of its moral perfectibility. To see how a liberal state, certain in the purity of its motives, convinced of its pity for the suffering and inadequate existence of others, and determined in its power and capacity to remove them, can ensnare itself in its moral innocence to the point where we are inclined to speak of the victims of goodness, we must turn to Greene's *The Quiet American*.

Chapter Nine

INNOCENT IDEALISM

The generation of rationalist politics is by political inexperience
out of political opportunity.

(Michael Oakeshott, *Rationalism in Politics*)

[T]hose who . . . give a false account to themselves of their own
experience, so deform that experience that it loses its highest
qualities and actually becomes something not altogether unlike
what they falsely think it.

(R. G. Collingwood, *Speculum Mentis*)

Greene's *The Quiet American*, written over a period of three years from
1952, is poised between his serious works and his 'entertainments'.
It reflects on moral and political themes in the conduct of individuals
and states and bears directly on the nature of religious faith. These
themes are interwoven with the problem of commitment, with the
moral frame of mind necessary decisively to see through a political
action. Once more we are to change the perspective on political
morality and see it from the standpoints of two agents, one who is
innocently certain of his beliefs, the other who is experienced and
knowing but unable to fix upon a determined commitment in the
world. Innocence here does not make its appearance in politics as
weakness and indecision. It does not attempt withdrawal from the
world, but publicly asserts itself in the full confidence of the truth of
its political beliefs and values. In *The Quiet American* it is experience
which hides and tries to protect itself from further pain and suffering.

Commitment and religious belief are connected by doubt. The
immediate practical concern is with what it means to experience
moral predicament, devoid of religious sustenance or resource, placed
in a political context of supreme intensity. In Greene's novel, this

context is French involvement in Indo-China and the increasing American participation in that war. *The Quiet American* looks back to past colonial uncertainties and forward to Vietnam with its moral contradictions, atrocities, and entanglements. It stands, therefore, in an intriguing relationship to Conrad's *Heart of Darkness*, for both works explore how a moral hollowness can penetrate a civilization and how a liberal state can deceive itself about its intentions in foreign involvement. The themes of innocence and political commitment raise the complex question of moral and political intentionality. It is not an accident that Greene chose quotations from A. H. Clough and Lord Byron with which to preface the book, and the latter raises the paradoxical relation between private motive and public action in a particularly acute way.

> This is the patent age of new inventions
> For killing bodies, and for saving souls,
> All propagated with the best intentions.[1]

The problems of political morality are not treated only from the standpoint of the individual. The political context is framed by the policies and actions of states, and the mutual incomprehension of an involvement in an alien culture is the consequence of governmental authorization. Pyle, albeit in an unspecified and mysterious way, is an agent of public policies. He is the innocent representative of an innocent state. As Nietzsche saw, the conjunction is not accidental:

> Consider the practice of every prince, church, sect, party, corporation: is the innocent person not always employed as the sweetest bait in really dangerous and infamous cases? – as Odysseus employed the innocent Neoptolemus to trick the sick old hermit and monster of Lemnos out of his bow and arrows.[2]

But in Indo-China the deployment of innocence is not a form of deviousness. It is both unself-conscious and certain and its political expression veers drastically between bravery and stupidity. In politics, where not everything is as it appears, tragedy and comedy are the constant companions of innocence.

The first-person narrator of Greene's novel is a cynical, world-weary English journalist named Fowler. He claims to be aloof from the turbulent political complexities of the world around him, and he considers himself uncommitted and uninvolved. Professional, journalistic objectivity is employed as a screen to mask a deeper absence of personal commitment.

> 'You can rule me out,' I said. 'I'm not involved. Not involved,' I repeated. It had been an article of my creed. The human condition being what it was, let them fight, let them love, let them murder, I would not be involved. My fellow journalists called themselves correspondents; I preferred the title of reporter. I wrote what I saw: I took no action – even an opinion is a kind of action.[3]

Fowler's main concern is to avoid moral commitment. Later, he will realize that this is impossible and he will discover moral and political involvement and the variety of motives it reveals.

Into this quietistic, detached, opium-smoking existence, shared with a passively regarded Indo-Chinese girl, Phuong, comes Pyle, an innocent Harvard graduate, supposedly on an Economic Aid Mission to Indo-China, who confronts political disintegration with a naive faith in American democracy sustained by reading such works as York Harding, *The Advance of Red China*, *The Challenge to Democracy*, and *The Role of the West*. In the face of the complexities of internal unrest and foreign intervention Pyle offers a sincere belief in the principles of liberal democracy. Unlike Fowler, Pyle is certain, engaged, and innocent. He believes in liberal values sincerely and abstractly. There is no question of his being insincere and his innocence resides in his seeing life as clay to be remoulded by his principles. As a man of principle, Pyle believes that compassion has a place in politics. As a man of principle, he is unaware of the consequences of that belief. Morally Pyle is a man too innocent for a corrupt world. Fowler believes he can stand aside and report on life as a spectator. This is as innocent as Pyle's belief that decisive and principled actions performed by those of goodwill and pure in heart will determine the course of political life.

Such fundamental antagonisms provide the basis for Pyle's effect on Fowler's life and the meaning that effect has for him. Pyle disrupts his complacency. He saves his life during an ambush; he attempts to take Phuong away from him with protestations of love and a promise of marriage; and his crucial involvement in a series of bomb explosions in the centre of Saigon leads Fowler, as an expression of disgust at Pyle's invincible and naive faith in the American democratic ideal, to commit himself by decisively contributing to the arrangements for Pyle's assassination.

From York Harding Pyle had obtained the idea of a Third Force to oppose the spread of Communism, locally led and, as a representation of National Democracy, avoiding colonial associations. However, Pyle puts this ideology into practice with an innocent unawareness of its implications. He chooses a corrupt and tyrannical tribal chieftain as the embodiment of indigenous democracy, and, as the local representative of a clandestine, governmental organization, Pyle is involved in the Diolacton affair, an attempt to discredit the Communists by blaming them for bomb explosions which Pyle has organized in civilian areas of Saigon. It might be argued that Pyle's actions fall under the classical ends/means description of political morality. The end is the defeat of Communism, and if the means of achieving this involve suffering and loss of life then, as Pyle remarks, they are simply casualties of war who have, anyway, died in a good cause. But this account ignores the moral disposition of the agent. In concentrating exclusively on external action and consequence it leaves out the moral difference beween someone who employs such measures in a spirit of utilitarian calculation and another whose innocent goodness prevents him from realizing what he has done. As Narrator, Fowler asks:

> How many dead colonels justify a child's or a trishaw driver's death when you are building a national democratic front?[4]

A utilitarian may attempt an answer to such a question, but Pyle's innocence protects him from asking it. Conventional statements of the 'Dirty Hands' dilemma fail to recognize this kind of difficulty. Pyle is not a man who enters politics in the anticipation that he may have to act in ways which are often blameworthy. Equally, he is not morally indifferent, prepared to use any means so long as they achieve the end. His political schemes derive from his moral obtuseness which is an expression of his innocence. Fowler reflects after the explosion:

> 'What's the good? he'll always be innocent, you can't blame the innocent, they are always guiltless. All you can do is control them or eliminate them. Innocence is a kind of insanity.'[5]

It is quite obvious that Greene's 'Quiet American' is ironically intended to highlight the raucous confidence of American liberal attitudes and post-war foreign policies. Here we see a liberal state venturing into increasingly complex interiors, where moral and political bafflement is commonplace, and where, as with Kurtz in *Heart of Darkness*, increasingly desperate acts become unavoidable. In this context, a technical vocabulary of military involvement screens the moral issues at stake. The lethal enthusiasm of an American moral crusade is identified through Fowler's caustic and uncommitted observations. Of many exchanges with Pyle we have:

'Is that how you make love in America – figures of income and a blood-count?'[6]

He asks scornfully:

Is confidence based on a rate of exchange? We used to speak of sterling qualities. Have we got to talk now about a dollar love? . . . A dollar love had good intentions, a clear conscience, and to Hell with everybody.[7]

American culture is associated in Pyle with a firm belief in good health.

'Like a sandwich? They're really awfully good. A new sandwich-mixture called Vit-Health. My mother sent it from the States.'[8]

Pyle's preoccupation with his physical well-being belies the state of his soul and that of the society which produced him. Americans abroad are treated in exactly the same way. They are portrayed as instantly identifiable and special. After the bombs have exploded, Pyle's concern is all too obvious; Fowler comments:

'There mustn't be any American casualties, must there?'[9]

The Americans are described as privileged Harvard graduates in morality, both untouched by and divorced from the world they claim to rescue but fail to understand.

But this is neither low-level political polemic nor Old World snobbishness. Anti-Americanism is mediated through Fowler. It is through his disposition and experience that criticism of American attitudes and conduct is directed and maintained. His possessiveness of Phuong, his fear of losing her, his jealousy of Pyle focus such criticisms. They do not have an independent existence as they might in the form of a slogan or pamphlet.

I began – almost unconsciously – to run down everything that was American. My conversation was full of the poverty of American literature, the scandals of American politics, the beastliness of American children. It was as though she were being taken away from me by a nation rather than by a man. Nothing that America could do was right. I became a bore on the subject of America, even with my French friends who were ready enough to share my antipathies. It was as if I had been betrayed, but one is not betrayed by an enemy.[10]

This is not an argument for which we could sensibly demand evidence or reasoned justification. It exists within Fowler's experience of what might cause him to suffer. The signal which implicates him in Pyle's death – the act of reading the poem – connects his moral and political beliefs with the possibility of commitment and so endows them with a meaning that they would not have otherwise possessed. This is separable from mere anti-Americanism as slogan or rhetoric. Fowler's opposition to American intervention is clear throughout the book, but it is not sufficient to generate commitment until he becomes aware of the nature of Pyle's innocence. Only then does Fowler's predicament carry full moral weight. Should innocence be sacrificed?

Fundamentally, Pyle's political intentionality prompts us to consider the disjunction between goodness and outcome, with how it is that innocent intentions can lead to evil and harmful consequences. Innocence takes different forms in the novel.

Phuong's innocence is not a moral innocence. She is ignorant of politics and history, but not of her own interests and advantage. When Pyle and Fowler argue over her love she remains distant, often passively indifferent to both, preoccupied with formal status and possession, with cheap, pictorial images of life in the West. Her fascination with the objects of tourism is innocent, however, and, as such, she is incapable of concealing her motives. Fowler says of her:

I loved her for the innocence of her question. She might lie from politeness, from fear, even for profit, but she would never have the cunning to keep her lie concealed.[11]

Her wants are too transparent for her to be anything but sincere, and her simplicity makes her incapable of recognizing Fowler's lie when he first tells her that his wife in England will consider a divorce. Equally, she is uninterested in Pyle's theorizing about the moral value of marriage and family life, but very aware of the material advantages offered by an American way of life. Phuong's naivety and greed are innocent of duplicity, but it is only Pyle who treats her and her society as a child. Her acceptance of life and uncomplicated self-regard protect her from the battle which is fought around her, and she is insufficiently self-aware to be complacent or dissatisfied.

Phuong does not inspire protection from Fowler but love, and he is willing to lie and cheat to retain it. Her innocence is distinguishable from that of a victim caught up in a personal and political cross-fire. Fowler's wife is innocent of direct involvement in his present life, but her past association makes her vulnerable to further humiliation and suffering and he is led to reflect:

> Unfortunately the innocent are always involved in any conflict . . . How much you pride yourself on being *dégagé*, the reporter, not the leader-writer, and what a mess you make behind the scenes. The other kind of war is more innocent than this. One does less damage with a mortar.[12]

But, as Fowler comes to see, this is not true. When he travels north he sees the suffering of the innocent victims of the war – the canal stuffed with bodies, the Vietnamese mother and child shot in a cross-fire, a sampan strafed by a B.26. The civilians killed and maimed in the bomb explosion are innocent of direct involvement in the war, but theirs is the innocence, not of simplicity or morality, but of accident. They are guilty of nothing except being there in that particular place at that particular time.

The pose which Fowler adopts until the end of the novel is that of a spectator. But his innocent belief in the possibility of living a life which is uninvolved causes pain and suffering to those who know him. Personal and political conflict run parallel with one another. Fowler's objection to commitment lies in the dishonesty which he thinks that it inevitably produces. The liberal insistence that political action be based on a clear conscience is incapable of sustaining itself. Compassion cannot be extended infinitely without dishonesty and contradiction. This has a private and a public dimension. When Pyle and Fowler discuss their relationship with Phuong, Pyle says in a striking political allegory:

'. . . we both have her interests at heart.' . . . I said, 'I don't care that for her interests. You can have her interests. I only want her body. I want her in bed with me. I'd rather ruin her and sleep with her, than, than . . . look after her damned interests.'[13]

It is Pyle's innocent, liberal belief that it is possible to understand others' needs and to protect and provide for their interests which is redolent with the possibilities of patronage and violence. To speak about others in the language of interest is already to violate their autonomy. Fowler's distrust of involvement is not confined to personal motivation. In politics he points to the costs of moral purity:

'I'd rather be an exploiter who fights for what he exploits, and dies with it. Look at the history of Burma. We go and invade the country: the local tribes support us: we are victorious: but like you Americans we weren't colonialists in those days. Oh no, we made peace with the king and we handed him back his province and left our allies to be crucified and sawn in two. They were innocent. They thought we'd stay. But we were liberals and we didn't want a bad conscience.'[14]

Pyle and Fowler discuss communism in South-east Asia, the domino-theory, and liberal alternatives to colonialism. But theirs is not an argument between two rival theories. It cannot be settled by appeal to evidence or reason. It is not an academic debate. The course it takes is that of a human life, not a scholarly conversation. Two opposing dispositions are at work on one another, innocence and experience, but their contact involves subtle and unexpected ironies. Fowler realizes the moral costs of an insistence on acting well. Unlike Pyle he knows what goodness can do. But at this stage his realization has changed his view of personal but not political commitment. To fight for Phuong he is prepared to lie to her as well as to Pyle, but in politics he is not yet fully aware of the vileness of Pyle's virtue.

It is Pyle's innocence which must receive our main attention here. How is it the case that his good intentions in politics turn into catastrophe? There are hints in Greene's novel that the answer has to do with the inevitable imperfection of the political, that in a corrupt world it is impossible to avoid a corrupt act and the innocent will be more dangerous than most. There is a logical purchase for innocence here but not for the specific problem it creates. Equally,

Pyle is a sincere man, prepared to act honourably to Phuong, always concerned to tell the truth to Fowler, and even to save his rival when his life is threatened in an ambush. It would be much easier for us if Pyle's innocence could be reduced to the common currency of deceit. But this is impossible. There is no doubt about the intensity of his protest that Phuong may not find suitable a rather *risqué* display of entertainment at a cabaret. His shame at Granger's sexual crudity is genuine, and Fowler is in no doubt that his innocence requires protection, a reaction he later comes to regret:

> That was my first instinct – to protect him. It never occurred to me that there was greater need to protect myself. Innocence always calls mutely for protection, when we would be so much wiser to guard ourselves against it: innocence is like a dumb leper who has lost his bell, wandering the world, meaning no harm.[15]

When Pyle thinks he is in love with Phuong he tries to do the honourable thing according to his moral understanding. He wants to be fair to Phuong, to give her the freedom to choose, and he doesn't want Fowler to think badly of him. It is the fact that we cannot doubt his integrity that creates the problem.

However, not all moral integrity is innocent, and this is how Pyle's character is repeatedly described in the novel. What are the hallmarks of innocence? In Pyle we do not observe natural purity. His is not the unschooled innocence of Billy Budd. Absorbed in political theory he displays the confident campus integrity of cerebral wisdom. His is a learned innocence. He is described as having read a lot of books, as having given the concepts of democracy, freedom, and nationalism a searching analysis. His wants are moderate, mediated by a polite moral sense. Unselfish and healthy, Pyle is compassionate, concerned, and involved. His character has been formed, however, solely through abstract reflection, uncontaminated by contact with life. Once his examination of ideas has established the truth, that is how the world must be. The Harvard library has provided Pyle with his principles. The danger lies in his determination to make life conform with them. This is the source of Pyle's fanaticism. It appears not as a willingness to give up everything and sacrifice himself for a cause we know is evil but in his conviction that the conclusions of what Greene calls 'that indefatigable young brain'[16] are alone sufficient to rescue the world from political misery and upheaval.

This is Pyle's rationalism and his death is the cost of attempting to put York Harding's ideas into practice. *The Role of the West* is a rationalist political handbook; its author, as Fowler says, 'gets hold of an idea and then alters every situation to fit the idea'.[17] Politics for him is the straightforward application of a moral formula. Alien cultural practices, societies with strange beliefs and different ways of life are not regarded as autonomous, understandable on their own terms, but as inadequate approximations to a universal rational model held to be true *a priori*. Indo-China is the next lucky recipient of liberal aid, the next fortunate subject of Pyle's determination to enact York Harding's theories in the world. Democratic political theory is Pyle's political handbook. It is the ideological substitute for experience, and his innocence resides in his tutored belief that it alone is sufficient to save the world. Pyle's politics is, in Oakeshott's phrase, 'the politics of the book'.[18] It embodies a twentieth-century illusion. Oakeshott writes:

> And, book in hand . . . the politicians of Europe pore over the simmering banquet they are preparing for the future; but, like jumped-up kitchen-porters deputizing for an absent cook, their knowledge does not extend beyond the written word which they read mechanically – it generates ideas in their heads but no tastes in their mouths.[19]

Does it matter if the book is *The Role of the West* or *Mein Kampf*? Pyle's good intentions are a crucial element in the drama. His involvement in the Diolacton plot bears out his belief that it is possible to take a moral short-cut with his principles and emerge morally unscathed. His knowledge is the abstract knowledge of rationalism, and his innocence coexists ironically with the massive technical information at his country's disposal.

The distortions of experience which result from Pyle's ignorance of what he is doing are not accidental. His belief in the political efficacy of good intentions encourages him to negotiate with General Thé, and he is completely unaware both of the risks he is running and how they may be reduced by a cautious withholding of trust. It is innocent moral conviction which prompts him to reply to Fowler:

> 'A man becomes trustworthy when you trust him.' It sounded like a Caodaist maxim. I began to feel the air of Tanyin was too ethical for me to breathe.[20]

It is not coincidence that others have to pay the price for Pyle's morality; the risk he takes is only with his own moral contentment. This is required by his innocence. His moral security must be the centre of the world's attention. This is the depth of Pyle's self-absorption. In his relationship with Phuong, with Fowler, and with Indo-China his concern to act well takes the form of avoidance of blame – an innocent life, a life of benevolence, free from self-reproach, free from the pain of having behaved badly. Fowler says of him, sardonically:

> To him the whole affair would be happier as soon as he didn't feel mean – I would be happier, Phuong would be happier, the whole world would be happier, even the Economic Attaché and the Minister. Spring had come to Indo-China now that Pyle was mean no longer.[21]

After the bomb explosion Pyle's moral simplicity saves him from guilt. The dead he describes as casualties of war; their lives given up for democracy, sacrificed for the right cause. His government is 'looking after the relatives too'.[22]

Pyle embodies the active power of moral innocence. His innocence is too secure and strong a disposition to be corrupted or manipulated. Its significance is positive, and it faces the world not in an attitude of passive submission, awaiting its inevitable loss, but in the posture of crusader, determined to transform it in accordance with its own categories. Pyle shows how politics can be transfigured by moral innocence.

As in *Billy Budd*, inarticulation plays a part in *The Quiet American*. Pyle experiences frequent lapses into speechlessness. There are many situations where he does not know what to say or do. This may be contrasted with the character of Vigot, the sad police-officer who reads Pascal, and who is charged with investigating Pyle's murder. Vigot chooses his words with care, and he understands that Fowler is not as uninvolved as he thinks. He half-knows the part played by Fowler in the murder, but he also appreciates the political dimension involved in identifying those responsible:

> 'As a friend,' Vigot said, 'is there nothing you could tell me in confidence? My report's all tied up. He was murdered by the Communists. Perhaps the beginning of a campaign against American aid. But between you and me . . .'[23]

Half-truths and deliberate misunderstandings are signs in the conversation of the self-aware and the experienced. Vigot and Fowler do not talk to one another in terms of proposition or theory. Neither mode is sufficiently finely tuned to communicate the necessary ironies of political morality. Fowler's moral compromise has fallen short of deliberate duplicity, but it has involved him in a political crime. His motivation is ambivalent, something which is recognized in the coded directions of Vigot's speech. Punctuated by silences and disturbing conjecture, Vigot's remarks are made in the vocabulary of moral awareness. Experienced in betrayal and in the imperfections of private and public life, Vigot is not tempted to reduce justice to compassion. Equally, he knows that justice may not always be served by sticking to the rules. To this extent his disposition is in contrast to that of Vere in *Billy Budd*. But both recognize the mediating formality of the legal and political worlds and both attempt to exercise judgement realistically, taking into account individual justice and the moral facts of the case. Vigot talks as he does because he recognizes in Fowler a man discovering the nature of commitment, a man who is drawn against his will into losing his mask as disengaged reporter. What does such a discovery mean? How does it affect our understanding of political morality?

Fowler's insistence that he is a spectator has an undeniable religious dimension. 'God exists only for leader-writers',[24] he asserts, and in a universe devoid of religious meaning he takes on the role of observer, uncommitted and uninvolved. But he discovers slowly that his picture of himself is an illusion. When his life is threatened during the attack on the watch tower, and when a Vietnamese guard is wounded, his indifference is broken down. Later, when he learns of the non-combatant atrocities which are caused by the bomb-blast in the centre of Saigon, he is no longer able to maintain a position of remoteness. It is, however, the impact of innocence which shakes him out of disengagement and his realization that it is Pyle who has organized the explosion forces him to take sides. Here the impact of innocence in politics is different from *Billy Budd*. Billy's goodness provokes Claggart into destroying that which he can never have. Vere is forced into the moral anomaly of punishing the innocent for the appearance of guilt. Fowler, too, discovers that he must engineer the destruction of innocence but he does not do so out of envy. He is not jealous of Pyle's innocence and, even if Pyle's youth and enthusiasm occasionally remind him of what he is not, he knows that Pyle's death will not re-create these things for him.

Fowler's decision to provide the information which leads to Pyle's murder implicates him in his death, and it is a commitment which he has taken on because of the impact of Pyle's innocence on his life. It is Heng, the Chinese communist, who says to him:

> 'Sooner or later,' Heng said, . . . 'one has to take sides. If one is to remain human.'[25]

Fowler accepts that his god-like withdrawal from life is not sustainable. He explains his new-found commitment as a moral reaction to Pyle:

> What'll he do next, Heng? How many bombs and dead children can you get out of a drum of Diolacton?'[26]

What kind of account can we give of Fowler's commitment? It is certainly different from the way in which someone may get accidentally drawn into politics, involved in situations which rapidly get out of control. His decision to help in the murder of Pyle indicates the extent of Fowler's transformation from spectator to agent, but it is not completely straightforward and encourages him to reflect on the complexity of what it means to take a decision. To an extent such complexity is often neglected in contemporary philosophical discussions of commitment.

For Roger Trigg the concept of commitment involves two distinct logical segments.

> It presupposes certain beliefs and also involves a personal dedication to the actions implied by them. Each element can occur without the other, but if someone is truly committed, both elements will be present. Someone who devotes his life to a cause which he does not believe in cannot be genuinely committed, whatever the reasons for his hypocrisy. Similarly, no-one who holds certain beliefs and fails to make an effort to act on them can be thought in any way committed.[27]

Trigg accepts that propositional belief is not by itself sufficient and that a consistent pattern of action by an individual is needed to establish genuine commitment. A mere statement of belief is not enough to show commitment because it does not exclude the possibility that the agent is lying or deceiving himself. But he insists that the propositional constituent in commitment cannot be removed completely because it then becomes impossible to engage in reasoned arguments about beliefs as distinct from commitments.

If it is part of the logic of commitment that it is directed towards some idea or person, then we must raise the question of the object of Fowler's commitment. Quite clearly this is not Communism. Heng encourages Fowler to act decisively, but Fowler's agreement does not derive from an ideological position or from a newly discovered sympathy for the aims of the movement. In order to finish Pyle, Fowler has to give him to the Communists, but this is very different from saying that Communism is the object of his commitment. So what is his object? A determined hatred of Pyle's disposition is one possible answer. But is hatred for Pyle a belief which anyone could argue about? Trigg seems to say that commitment involves a belief side which is supported by reasons and a dedication side which is supported by strength of will. But this tells us little about how an individual may commit himself to action or how he may think of himself afterwards. Fowler comes to see that it is Pyle's innocence which is dangerous, not any cause he represents. It would be difficult to convert Pyle's disposition into a political cause, even though his simple attachment to democracy is a part of his political character. We may put this point slightly differently. Could Fowler's commitment be stated in terms of a set of beliefs about Pyle? He certainly believes that Pyle's disposition involves harmful consequences in the world. But this is not like the assertions in, say, Marxism or Christianity to which someone may be committed. Fowler's decision involves belief, but not the kind expressed in a structured world-view.

From Trigg's standpoint, it may be difficult to see why Fowler's decision should be regarded as a commitment at all. It does not commit him to Heng, except in the weak sense of keeping his promise to signal Pyle's whereabouts, because he is not a Communist sympathizer. His dislike of Pyle cannot be expressed in reasons or argument detached from the kind of man he is and how he has affected Fowler's life. But equally this does not mean that Fowler is a hypocrite, a liar, or deceiving himself. He realizes the kind of man Pyle is when he notices his reaction to the victims of the bomb explosion expressed in terms of getting funds for the relatives from Washington. This gives him the courage to commit himself to bring about Pyle's death by using the only political means available. It would be possible to describe Fowler's commitment as false if he lied about his motives to others or deceived himself about what his true motives were. The question of motivation is central here because, for Trigg, 'What I am committed to determines the nature of my commitment'.[28] This means, for example, that it is logically impossible to be a committed Marxist if one believes that Marxism is fundamentally mistaken. But why should the belief element in commitment be restricted to propositional assertions? Pyle's innocent threat prompts Fowler to commit himself, but his motives are mixed and not reducible to a distinct number of beliefs. Why should this be a reason for thinking Fowler any less committed to destroying him?

Fowler's commitment cannot be explained in terms of beliefs and dedication, but this does not mean it is nothing more than personal dislike. It might be argued that this commitment is located in the language he uses and the community in which it is spoken. Speaking commits him in various ways to others. Fowler's realization that Pyle's innocent goodness is the cause of devastation commits him to action. The form this takes is that of giving a sign, taking a book to a lighted window to catch the light; a sign, something not fully incorporated in speech, but whose significance would not be missed by those waiting for its communication. Peter Winch, for example, writes:

> The notion of commitment marks the distinction and the
> connection between the following two concepts: *what words mean*
> and *what people mean by words*. People can only say something
> and mean it if they use words that mean something; and it belongs
> to the kind of meaning that words have that they can be used by
> people in statements that they (the people) mean. But this is only
> possible in a society where people are so related that for one
> person to say something is for him to commit himself with others;
> and an important part of such a relation is that there should be a
> common respect for truthfulness.[29]

Fowler's decision expresses his determination to destroy Pyle, but to the assassins who wait for his signal his motivation is irrelevant. It does not matter to them whether it is money or sympathy for their cause. What Fowler's commitment means to them is different from what it means to him. For them, all that matters is that he gives the sign. The signal has a meaning for the sender to which the receiver is indifferent.

Commitment for Fowler marks a sea-change in his life, but this does not take the form of attachment to a cause. He has not experienced conversion, but what it is to act in such a way that the consequences cannot be retrieved. After his decisive involvement in Pyle's death he reflects on it in a spirit of self-reproach:

> Suffering is not increased by numbers: one body can contain all the suffering the world can feel. I had judged like a journalist in terms of quantity and I had betrayed my own principles; I had become as *engagé* as Pyle, and it seemed to me that no decision would ever be simple again.[30]

Vere's decision to sentence Billy Budd to hang arises in the context of his office and his moral commitment to its rules. These considerations are central to his justification and how it is publicly understood. Fowler has no office, and his journalism is simply a neutral reference-point against which his commitment is to be understood. But more important than what is publicly communicable in language is what the change means to him. When he reflects on his transition from spectator to agent he admits that the difference between himself and Pyle is not that great:

> Was I so different from Pyle, I wondered? Must I too have my foot thrust in the mess of life before I saw the pain?[31]

Fowler is led to the brink of religious faith but not beyond. Like Pyle, his decision is borne out of individual outrage. His commitment has a minimum public reference, just enough to satisfy the requirements of communication and ensure that the deed is done. Its true perspective is his own reflection on his life, its relation to Phuong and to Pyle. Prompted by innocence, Fowler's reaction is to make even deeper attempts at self-enquiry and it is this that colours the political character of his acts.

Pyle's Caodaist maxim, 'a man becomes trustworthy when you trust him', half-echoes Henry VI's 'foolish pity'. When Henry sees the political consequences of his sentiments he tries to withdraw. Pyle, on the other hand, is strong where Henry is weak. What for Henry is a defeat is for Pyle a spur to further action. Pyle sees the political world as a subject awaiting his engagement. His sense of the superiority of goodness pulls him towards Billy Budd. His unawareness of the moral cost of his innocence pulls him towards Henry. In all three, innocence alters the lives of those with whom it makes contact. These three literary texts focus on forms of moral engagement in situations of supreme political intensity: of civil war; of war and revolution; of internal upheaval and foreign intervention. They show how morality may enter politics in ways not captured by the conventional expressions of the 'Dirty Hands' view. Henry refuses to employ the tough acts necessary to preserve a state not for reasons of conscience but through moral innocence. Billy Budd's moral disposition is pure not simply because he keeps his hands clean. He is incapable of doing otherwise. It is Pyle's innocence which draws him towards corruption, not a worldly recognition that in politics we have to act badly on occasion to get anything done at all. His goodness preserves him from an awareness of what he has done, and he sees his enemies not as providing a justification for an unjust act in the course of a just war, but as objects for conversion and trust. His liberal rationalism is such that it is entirely appropriate that Fowler should signal his end with a book.

It is the standpoint of the agent which is neglected by conventional views of political morality; as a consequence the specific impact of innocent goodness is missed. They fail to capture the reactions of those who come into contact with such a disposition, and give no explanation beyond failure to grasp political expediency for why moral innocence can have such a catastrophic effect. Innocence can place both individual and community in danger. If it attempts to reform the world after its own likeness the consequences are immense; it can force commitment from those who least expect to give it. Fowler's commitment is not explicable in terms derived from political morality. He does not sacrifice Pyle as a means to Communist revolution, even though this might be the effect. Equally, he does not destroy him simply to retain Phuong, although he would be capable of doing so. Rather, Pyle's innocence has brought about a change in Fowler which would not otherwise have occurred. It is not as if Fowler's commitment represents a new-found willingness to pay any moral price to achieve a political end. On the contrary, it is innocence alone that must be destroyed, and, as with Vere, it is Fowler's moral courage which has to bear the burden. Here innocence, political morality, and commitment come together in ways not contemplated within the framework of theory. Overwhelmingly, however, the problem we are faced with by such examples is the disjunction between intention and outcome, with how it is that innocent goodness can lead to evil and harmful consequences. What accounts have been offered of this connection?

Chapter Ten

INNOCENCE AND EXPERIENCE

... nothing is to be expected from time ... goodness does not suffice ... and benefits ... will not placate envious malignity.
(Machiavelli, *The Discourses*)

But even as we look upon history as an altar on which the happiness of nations, the wisdom of states, and the virtue of individuals are slaughtered, our thoughts inevitably impel us to ask: to whom, or to what ultimate end have these monstrous sacrifices been made?
(Hegel, *Introduction to the Lectures on the Philosophy of World History*)

The contrast between moral innocence and moral goodness may be brought out in the context of political morality. Moral goodness is not, of course, devoid of outcome. The public nature of political action and the fact that moral conduct commits us to others mean that decisions involve ramifications beyond that of private scrutiny. Moral goodness refuses negotiation with evil whatever undesirable consequences follow, but it is precisely the incapacity of moral innocence to recognize the existence of evil at all which marks it off from moral goodness. It is essential to the idea of moral innocence that it is ignorant of the propensity for evil both in the individual and in others. We have located this innocence in highly volatile political circumstances. Henry is unaware of Gloucester's ambition. Billy Budd does not know the depth of evil in Claggart's intentions towards him. Pyle is too innocent to recognize evil in others and to realize the moral enormity latent in his idealism.

From a consequentialist standpoint there is no significant difference between moral innocence and any other serious moral refusal to trade consequences against one another. Both show the political damage which can result from single-minded devotion to principle. But moral innocence is not simply a failure to balance one outcome against another. Ignorant of evil it cannot see the need to judge better against worse or good against bad. Like moral goodness it refuses negotiation with evil, but this is because the possibility of doing so does not arise. So we cannot understand the outcomes of moral innocence in consequentialist terms.

Moral considerations are dangerous because political effectiveness is only possible if we recognize that there will be circumstances where they have to be left aside. As it is in the nature of moral considerations that they cannot be left aside, then political wisdom is diminished and dangerous outcomes made more likely. However, an intrinsic feature of the forms of moral innocence I have discussed is the belief that moral goodness is sufficient for political effectiveness, a belief which arises not merely from naivety, but from the purity of the expectations which it brings to political life. In a different context, such purity may be regarded as entirely appropriate in both expression and result, but in politics this is not so. What is it about the disjunction between innocent goodness and outcome which creates the difficulty?

The discussion is not unique to moral innocence in so far as it applies to all attemps to link moral character and outcome. The relation between pride and the fall which follows it is not just a loose, empirical generalization. We are being told something about what happens to a person who thinks in a certain way about the world and his place in it. Moral innocence, however, is unusual in the sense that it is unreflective not only of the existence of evil but also of its own identity. This makes its relation to outcome difficult to establish. This does not mean that it is of no interest to politics. On the contrary, if the current impasse in thinking about political morality is to be removed then it is essential to chart the relation between moral disposition and political outcome. It is important to realize here that we are discussing not the outcomes of events but human dispositions which resist explication in straightforwardly causal terms. Does Billy Budd intend to strike Claggart dead? Does Pyle intend to harm the civilians caught up in the bomb blast? Moral innocence means that Claggart's death, like the deaths of those in the centre of Saigon, is not simply an unintended consequence. But equally they cannot be described as deliberate. In many significant respects human intentionality is the moral corner-stone of problems in political morality. In the case of moral innocence, do things just happen to turn out as they do?

Machiavelli argues that it is Fortune which controls the relation between agent, action, and outcome, and that moral innocence as compared with heroism and prudence is incapable of mastering events and achieving political glory. The logic of Machiavelli's argument requires that the historical process is largely outside individual control, and whatever our character it is always possible for historical change to render it dangerous or anachronistic. But this seems too deterministic and too general. It is from Machiavelli, too, that we derive the idea that politics is a flawed and imperfect world only fleetingly allowing political greatness when character and circumstances contrive it. The danger of moral innocence, therefore, depends logically on political imperfection. In such a world, it cannot help issuing in outcomes which contradict its disposition. But once again, determinism vitiates the explanation. Why is it the case that in a corrupt world we cannot avoid a corrupt act? If, as it appears, the claim is true by definition we are given no account of how innocence may first manifest itself, and so none regarding its outcomes and how it may be lost.

We might consider the possibility of intervening circumstances of an external or structural kind which exist independent of the agent, and which occur between intention and outcome. They would serve to explain the outcome by showing how it could come about even though it was not intended or hoped for. It is certainly true, for example, in *Henry VI*, that many of the characters act in ignorance of the political events and developments which intimately concern them. But in itself such ignorance is not sufficient for us to postulate a moral or historical 'hidden hand' to provide a rational explanation for the apparent disjunction. This could only get off the logical ground if we had already agreed that there was some pattern to moral existence or history which had been disturbed and which needed restoration. We would then be able to describe the outcome as a temporary aberration, the servant of a deeper purpose, or an unintended consequence which, nevertheless, is actually in accordance with the original scheme of things. None of these applies in the case of moral innocence. We can describe an outcome as a temporary aberration only if we have asserted in advance a general pattern from which it seems to be a deviation. And we have made no such assertion. Equally, we have not proposed a deeper purpose which a 'hidden hand' mechanism is aimed at satisfying. More important, moral innocence seems closer to its outcomes than the description of unintended consequences suggests. They are not unintended because innocent conduct lacks the elements of knowledge and deliberation which intentionality requires. The idea of unintended consequences does not distinguish between remote and adjacent effects. The outcomes of innocence are so intimately connected to its character that we need a stronger account than that offered by action and effect. Finally, the attempt to rescue meaning through structuralism, with its emphasis on intervening circumstances, is rather to see all outcomes as unintended consequences. Henry laments the suffering caused by the civil war, but it is misleading to suggest that as the civil war was the unintended consequence of his actions then his moral character played no part in its occurrence.

'Hidden hand' explanations tend to assume ignorance of the mechanism which determines the course of events. Thus, outcomes which appear indeterminate derive their explanation from the logic of the original mechanism. It can also be argued that political decisions involve consequences of scale which can never be completely incorporated within the language of prediction and forecast. In war, revolution, and the intervention by one state in the affairs of another, for example, political conduct involves an element of risk which can never be removed, and which some political philosophers have attempted to include as part of a normative argument. Sidgwick, for example, writing of the disadvantages of intervention, says:

> There is further a serious danger that if intervention be tolerated, the intervening State or States will take advantage of their neighbour's weakness to secure some unjust gain at its expense; and that this ill-gotten gain will carry with it the seeds of future bitterness and strife. Such intervention, therefore, should generally be viewed with reprobation.[1]

The risk element is built into the argument against intervention in the form of an empirical prediction – that as political conduct like this will result in undesirable consequences then it should be avoided. Risk in this context is seen in the light of unpredictable outcomes. We are ignorant of the results of an action, decision, or policy, and either we are prepared to take the risk or we are not. Sidgwick's arguments against intervention place a moral stress on the dangers of it turning into war and drawing other states into military confrontation. But does ignorance have to be understood solely in the context of predictability and forecast? On this view, ignorance of the future is overcome through prediction by associating events and outcomes in the form of an empirical law or generalization. But this establishes only an external connection between them, and does not explain how such ignorance could be given a moral significance. An inability to recognize the nature of actions and their consequences does not derive its moral sense from false predictions or mistaken forecasts. This leads to the possibility of developing a closer logical connection between character and political outcome.

One writer who has explored this is R. F. Holland and I would like to examine a short section in his *Against Empiricism*.[2] Holland argues against a background of utilitarianism which mistakenly assumes that the basic relation between action and good or evil is that between an action and its outcome. Actions may be described as causal instruments or means and they are to be judged entirely in terms of their efficiency in fulfilling this function. For Holland, utilitarianism fails to account for the relation between action and the disposition or context which precedes it.

> No adequate account is taken of actions as reactions to alterations that have already occurred or (what is not the same thing) as answers to actions already performed, as responses to evil and good encountered or received, and as modes of recognition – especially the recognising of, or the refusal to recognise, a limit.[3]

Against the familiar utilitarian difficulty that it allows the consequences and actions to be in principle separable from each other Holland does not simply urge that actions must sometimes be understood on their own terms. He argues that evil as response, say a response to weakness by taking advantage, involves consequences which are internal to the action and not merely accidental to it. His claim is that evil has evil consequences, and that unless luck intervenes these will follow, and they will do so because they are internal to its nature.

> By an internal consequence I mean one that, life being what it is, is more or less bound to ensue and this is not an accidental matter. For example the child who has been made a butt at school and not

been injured by it is, if he exists, exceptional. Instances of this type of connection are written into our language. Thus brutality brutalizes. Discouragement – I am thinking of what a teacher might do – discourages, that is, leads non-accidentally though not always to discouragement, whereas upholding a high standard sometimes does so incidentally.[4]

Such internal connections do not only exist between words and concepts. They link character and action. They arise from a manner or style and Holland argues that the relation between action and what it expresses is an internal one. Where this is something of moral significance then character, conduct, and outcome are related internally. For Holland, someone like Claggart or Iago, possessed by envy of the good, does not just happen to act badly, and the consequences of their actions do not just happen to be tragic.

There are two dimensions of moral innocence open to Holland's analysis. The first concerns the relation between agent and action, the second between action and outcome. Between innocence and action the internal connection is quite natural. When Dansker in *Billy Budd* speaks of Claggart's 'sweet voice' we know that he refers to a man who is not to be trusted because his true motives are concealed. Dansker talks of Claggart's kindly way of speaking, and Billy replies:

> 'No, not always. But to me he has. I seldom pass him but there comes a pleasant word.'
> 'And that's because he's down upon you, Baby Budd.'
> Such reiteration, along with the manner of it, incomprehensible to a novice, disturbed Billy almost as much as the mystery for which he had sought explanation.[5]

What is to Dansker a warning is to Billy a sign of kindliness and warmth. Billy's response is not an accidental consequence of his character. It flows naturally from it. Equally, Henry VI responds to Gloucester's wickedness with fairness, and his innocence prevents him from seeing what others see, that Gloucester is evil through and through. Similarly, Pyle's willingness to trust the altruism of others derives from his character and is expressed in his actions, for example his journey north to talk to Fowler and his negotiations with General Thé. Such considerations show that action is internally related to moral innocence, and is not to be described as accident, deviation, or mistake. Furthermore, the speech and conduct of innocence in relation to experience is not simply political naivety. It is not as if we are presented with a morality honed by contact with temptation but which finds itself lost in the complex geography of politics. Moral innocence is not like moral principle which enters politics only to find itself ineffective. It is not political but moral simplicity which creates the difficulty.

The second dimension concerns the relation between action and outcome. Utilitarianism allows for the outcome to be detached from the action which precedes it and concentrates on the production of future states of affairs. But it does this in the language of ends and means, and its stress is on the capacity to forecast which means are most effective in achieving specific ends. However, it cannot account for temporal concepts whose logic does not conform to the pattern set by empirical generalization, causal law, or prediction. Here present disposition and action relate to the future not as expectation, which can be grounded well or poorly, or prediction, which can be proved true or false, but as hope or aspiration. Hope relates directly to the moral ideals of the agent. When Billy Budd cries 'God bless Captain Vere!' just prior to his execution, we are made aware that his innocence permeates his vision of the kind of life he thinks Vere will live after his decision to find Billy guilty. Henry VI conducts policy in the light of his hopes for a more peaceful world and his trust that his goodness is sufficient to bring this about. Pyle's hope for a democratic Indo-China is not a forecast but an active expression of his innocent belief in the relation between political principle and practice. By reversing the utilitarian perspective on the relation between agent, action, and outcome, it is possible to see how innocence expresses itself in present conduct and how its hope shapes future events.

In the history of ethics it is a common assertion that human goodness and well-being have to be grounded in knowledge, and that human capacities, ranging from the pursuit of self-interest to the execution of justice, are diminished by ignorance. Human beings cannot be moral agents freely acting in a political world if they are ignorant. Michael Slote writes:

> It is difficult to believe that there could be valid basic principles of moral obligation binding upon mankind of such a sort that no one

241

could ever be committed to their basic validity except through ignorance.[6]

One of Slote's purposes is to attempt a valid connection between morality and prudence.

> if acting out of ignorance is to some degree, other things being equal, against self-interest, then the principle of morality and ignorance, by ruling out basic moral principles that demand that kind of sacrifice of self-interest, establishes a certain connection between valid morality and prudence or self-interest.[7]

In relation to moral innocence Slote's general claim involves a number of difficulties. Ignorance is intrinsic to moral innocence in a manner not shared by all dispositions. We cannot imagine someone who is both innocent and aware of the evil in the world. As long as innocence lasts it carries its ignorance with it like a shell. Moral innocence does not recognize the incidence and location of evil. The morally innocent do not know that their words and actions have more than one meaning and that the individuals and causes they trust and support may be different from the way they appear. In moral and legal thinking the claim that someone did not know what he was doing or saying admits of a variety of meanings. However, in the case of moral innocence its ignorance cannot simply be set aside as a kind of mitigating circumstance. It is essential to its nature. In response to this, it is open to us to deny that innocence is moral, or, at least, not yet moral, and that whatever sacrifices of self-interest it involves are of no moral significance. However, it seems to me that we do regard innocence as exemplifying a unique kind of moral purity. To say that it is pure but of no moral significance seems to miss the point. For those who come in contact with it innocence has an impact which is moral in kind. It is not as if their lives had been touched by a being whose ignorance took the form of unintelligence or poor information.

Stressing the connection between knowledge and well-being means that the outcomes of actions and policies can be subject to a certain degree of control. They are not indeterminate in the sense of being matters of luck or chance. However, the morally innocent are ignorant of evil. Billy Budd's purity prevents him from seeing Claggart for what he is. Further, such ignorance is essential to his goodness. It could not lose it and remain the same. Does such blindness mean that its impact on the world is indeterminate? To argue in this way is to suggest that the political outcomes of innocence are a matter of chance. The morally innocent are ignorant of the motives of others and lack the foresight to realize their own impact on the world. How things turn out, therefore, can only be a question of luck.

In giving consideration to the problem of how things turn out there is an important difference between the relations between events within a narrative and what it is about such relations that philosophy regards as significant. In a novel such as *The Quiet American* the outcomes make sense only within the context of the fictional narrative. Pyle's ignorance of the damage he causes has a place in his relations with other characters and the sequence of events. But for philosophy such fictional relationships and dispositions are of interest if they draw our attention to weaknesses in certain accounts of rational action and outcome: an account of moral innocence may stress the place of luck in morality.

In Bernard Williams' paper, 'Moral luck',[8] he discusses the place of luck in morality and emphasizes the impossibility of its inclusion in any moral theory of a Kantian type. The attempt to generate formal criteria of morality from the notion of rational agency cannot accommodate contingency in the justification it is prepared to allow. Equally, neither a contractualist stress on a framework of moral rules nor a utilitarian concern with consequences will help settle the problems he wishes to examine.

He asks us to consider the role of luck in two dilemmas. The first is Gauguin's choice either to honour his family commitments or to abandon them so as to devote himself to his art. The second is Anna Karenina's recognition that her love for Vronsky can be satisfied only by sacrificing the moral claims of her son. In both cases decisions are justified in a way which involves an appeal to how things will turn out, and this entails an understanding of what would constitute an obstacle to the realization of their hopes. Thus, Williams claims that for Gauguin

> the only thing that will justify his choice will be success itself. If he fails . . . he has no basis for the thought that he was justified in acting as he did. If he succeeds, he does have a basis for that thought.[9]

The moral decisions made by agents in these circumstances involve a necessary element of risk, but not all kinds of risk are morally relevant. Williams argues persuasively that there is a difference between external luck, say where Gauguin is injured en route to Tahiti, and internal luck, where he is placing everything on his faith that he has it in him to become a great painter. If Gauguin's aim fails because of the first consideration this does not matter morally in the same way as it would if it failed because of the second. The luck which is intrinsic to his project depends on whether he can create the great art of which he considers himself capable. It is this that is morally significant. Equally, if Vronsky had been killed accidentally this would have concluded Anna's hopes, but in a way which would not have given moral significance to their non-fulfilment.

Moral decisions of this kind involve a risk, not in the sense of simply taking a chance that things will turn out as hoped, unimpaired by external interference, but in the special sense of risking intrinsic failure. Williams expresses this distinction as follows:

> With an intrinsic failure, the project which generated the decision is revealed as an empty thing incapable of grounding the agent's life. With an extrinsic failure, it is not so revealed, and while he must acknowledge that it has failed, nevertheless it has not been discredited, and may, perhaps in the form of some new aspiration, contribute to making sense of what is left.[10]

Of course, in these dilemmas such decisions do not remove or diminish the moral claims of those who suffer as a result. But for Williams this implies not that the risk taken by such moral agents is outside morality, but rather that it exists in relation to their life and the moral coherence of their hopes.

There is an additional dimension. The dilemmas which interest Williams are not straightforward conflicts between one moral value and another. In Gauguin's commitment to art and Anna's love for Vronsky we are presented with two features of what it means to live a human life. But art and love cannot be satisfied without a conflict with morality. Of course, the dilemma depends on our understanding art and love to be valuable in human existence, but it is not their general significance which is important but the role they have in an individual life. Anna's failure is not just the failure of a programme or an experiment which has gone wrong on this occasion but which can be repeated at a future date. It is complete tragedy for her.

Williams' examples are not comparable in all respects with the

244

cases of moral innocence we have examined. While it is true, for example, that Henry VI does not face a moral dilemma, it remains the case that his innocent disposition and the political requirements of his rule are at odds with one another. To this extent, therefore, his innocence is relevant to how things turn out and this entails the acknowledgement of risk. His actions do not take the form of explicit choices or decisions, at least not in the manner required by the resolution of a specific dilemma, but they do stem from the disposition which characterizes his life. What then creates the risk? Williams' distinction between internal and external luck is instructive here. Clearly, the political chaos of Henry's rule does not derive solely from external misfortune any more than Gauguin's success was dependent on his travelling to Tahiti without injury. Rather it derives from the internal character of his disposition. His 'foolish pity' is not capable of sustaining political rule. The risk is internal to Henry's innocent goodness and not contingently related to the circumstances it has brought about.

As Williams points out, the knowledge involved in seeing why a plan or disposition has succeeded or failed is retrospective in character. It is a discovery which can only come about after things have run their course, after the game has been played to the full, and it may take the form of a recognition that failure is due not simply to external misfortune, but to the intrinsic weakness of the plan and the agent's capacity to carry it out. In this respect, the fact that moral innocence is a disposition rather than a plan is unimportant. What is important, however, is that this discovery is impossible for the morally innocent. It is available to them only after their innocence has been lost. Like Anna's love, innocence is not exchangeable or recoverable. It is not an accident that the moral innocents in all three texts are murdered, executed, or assassinated. This is not to imply that their deaths were untimely. A persistent innocence is unsustainable both as a disposition which involves others and as a mode of political action.

My interest has been with the intrinsic relation between moral innocence, ignorance, and political outcome. I would now like to give a more detailed scrutiny to the ways moral innocence changes the lives of those who encounter it. This may be expressed in terms of impact on an individual's life and of the transformations experienced by the political community. It is the effect innocence can have on the experienced.

Consider Billy Budd who wears his natural goodness unconscious of what it is and how it nourishes Claggart's envy. To Dansker, Billy is a baby in an adult world. To Claggart, Billy's goodness serves only as a contrasting reference point to the moral impoverishment of his own soul. It is Vere, of course, whose personality receives the full force of Billy's moral innocence. His condemnation of Billy was a moral decision arising out of a moral commitment to the rules governing his office. This is not a decision which all members of the court martial would have felt morally capable of making. Does this mean that Vere had Billy's death on his conscience? This is clearly not the interpretation which Melville wishes to convey. Vere's last words are the repetition of Billy's name, but these are not to be understood as his recognition that he had been wrong to decide as he did:

> That these were not the accents of remorse would seem clear from what the attendant said to the *Bellipotent*'s senior officer of marines, who, as the most reluctant to condemn of the members of the drum-head court, too well knew, though here he kept the knowledge to himself, who Billy Budd was.[11]

Vere does not feel remorse for what he did, but on his deathbed he repeats Billy's name. The simplicity of this act contrasts with the ways in which the affair is publicly remembered. The official naval chronicle stresses formal rectitude and relies exclusively on the surface meaning of the characters and the events. In its pages the main actors are abstractions, servants of political rhetoric and legal jargon. What is concealed in the official history is displayed in popular ballad, and Billy's goodness and his manner of death are incorporated into myth and legend. Vere's final words express his awareness of what he has sacrificed, but they do not imply that he was wrong to do so. His primary commitment is to human rules and purposes, frail, tragic, and imperfect though they may turn out to be, but Billy's primitive and unsullied goodness remains, as his final utterance shows, a matter of obsessive concern.

Innocence and experience act out a different dialectical dance in *The Quiet American*. Unlike Vere, there are no rules of office to guide Fowler in his growing awareness of Pyle's threat. Further, in his decision to become involved in Pyle's death he reaches a degree of commitment he did not previously find possible. Newly committed, Fowler discovers the moral costs of engagement. Innocence provides Fowler with a benchmark for reflection on Pyle's life and his own. He has realized the impossibility of remaining uninvolved, and he now knows the moral costs of political action. Vere and Fowler take decisions which affect their lives and which are intelligible only in relation to their encounter with innocence. Of course, these decisions have public outcomes – the execution of Billy Budd, and the assassination of Pyle – but they arise from the effect of innocence on moral character. This means that the relation beween morality and politics is mediated by a change in disposition. Pyle's innocent campaign of improvement is halted not simply by a Communist bullet but by the active complicity of a man who was previously an outsider, an observer. Political action here is dependent on a change of heart, and this means that politics derives from morality construed not as a framework of principle but as an object of personal recognition and acceptance.

The problem which faces Vere does not appear to him as a private individual. Public activity involves the obligations of office which are not reducible to individual duties. It is possible that such obligations can only be fulfilled by conduct which would otherwise be regarded as morally blameworthy. An important aspect of office-holding is that office-holders are trusted regarding the kind of acts they are allowed to perform. To some extent this arises from an element of secrecy present in all political societies. To some extent it arises because the context in which politics is conducted is such that total trust and unconditional openness would defeat even the most laudable political objectives.

Such considerations enable us to see more clearly the political cost of King Henry's goodness. As the legitimate monarch he has a responsibility to the duties of his office. However, rather than protect his realm against internal strife and danger from abroad, his moral character promotes them. His unnatural decision to concede the succession and his withdrawal from politics in the act of abdication together exhaust his limited capacity to control events, and both stem directly from goodness. Henry, dissatisfied with anything less than a total moral transformation of politics, recoils from it in innocent distaste. Those who trust him to act with kingly authority are disappointed by his goodness. Those who wish to challenge his rule find innocence easy prey to their ambition. King Henry has thrown a false net of goodness over political life. The result is insurrection, civil war, and multiplying political crime. Here we have an overlap between moral disposition and the conceptual formalities of politics as a public activity of governing. The personal inclination to be candid and trusting has destroyed the conditions of trust on which rule depends. Henry believes goodness to be sufficient for politics. Such a belief is inconsistent with the political obligations of monarchy.

Moral innocence is a proper disqualification from politics. Unrestrained by experience, it is incapable of decency or deviation. It makes politics impossible. In Conrad's *Heart of Darkness* Marlow returns from his African journey with the knowledge of the kind of man Kurtz has become and the political and moral corruption he represents. On his meeting with the woman Kurtz was to marry he substitutes her name for 'the horror! the horror!' as the final words Kurtz spoke. He has preserved her innocence with a lie. He says:

> I laid the ghost of his gifts at last with a lie.[12]

Marlow has not kept faith with Kurtz's understanding of what he has become and the world he has created. But to do so would destroy the girl's innocence and undermine her belief in the essential goodness of the world. Marlow is a man who would prefer to tell the truth; but he realizes that the truth cannot be told. As Berthoud puts it:

> Her trustfulness earns her the right to be told the truth; yet the only truth there is for him to tell must destroy the basis of that trust.[13]

Marlow chooses the preservation of innocence, but implicit in his choice is the recognition that this can happen only through illusion. It is Marlow who has committed the deeper treachery, not Kurtz. His lie has perpetuated innocence in the only way possible, but in so doing he has created a false idealism, a goodness unsustainable in the world and fatal to politics.

Chapter Eleven

CONCLUSION

How do moral considerations bear on politics? In this book I have stressed the importance of moral disposition. This entails a shift away from formal theory towards an account of the moral standpoint of the agent in political contexts. I have emphasized that certain moral dispositions exclude politics, are deeply incompatible with it, and in fact endanger it. Such an exclusion does not arise from politics. It is not that politics sets the limit to morality. On the contrary, such moral dispositions as innocence in a variety of ways exempt themselves from politics. We are made aware both of the intrinsic limits to morality and of the autonomy of politics. Moral ideas do not filter political proposals, allowing some to pass but not others, a picture which gives morality an exaggerated ascendancy. It is rather that certain moral dispositions disqualify themselves from politics, so establishing a limit which is set from within morality. This book is in praise of politics. Politics has a conceptual identity which need not take second place to morality. And as morality sets its own limits on itself there is no necessity to describe this identity in terms derived from realism.

In his *In Defence of Politics* Bernard Crick discusses what he calls 'true political morality – indeed political greatness'.[1] His reference is to Lincoln's delineation of Republican Party policy for the abolition of slavery, which stressed both its immorality and the difficulty of removing it without coming into conflict with equally powerful constitutional obligations. The realization and expression of this dilemma is, for Crick, a necessary prelude to political understanding and judgement, and he contrasts it with two alternatives. Someone may be tempted to abandon politics

249

for the lead of the benevolent autocrat who will promise the end of slavery tomorrow, or he may simply do nothing because he is not willing to muddy his conscience with such 'terrible compromises' or equivocation.[2]

The use of the term 'conscience' can be misleading if it prevents us from seeing the variety of moral disposition. Crick is right to say that Lincoln genuinely believed slavery to be immoral. But is it correct to argue that 'it is rare good fortune for the leader of a state himself to combine absolute ethics and the ethics of responsibility'?[3] The Weberian language in this passage is not an accident. Crick writes:

> Certainly on an issue such as slavery, some people must keep a pure moral vision alive, but such visions, perhaps held only by 'saints', fanatics, reformers, intellectuals, will be partially fulfilled only when there is an attempt to realise them in terms of public policy.[4]

The rarity of finding someone like Lincoln depends on the sharp division between 'a pure moral vision' and 'public policy'. But is this distinction so clear cut? One answer is in terms of moral disposition, that is, the abolition of slavery might be undertaken for reasons of moral conviction, from personal pride in the achievement, or for the public good.

Crick is right to stress the importance of moral disposition in politics, showing that even where the choice of moral end is agreed, the means to its achievement are dependent on moral disposition and political judgement. However, the blurring of distinctions within pure moral visions and simple references to conscience seem to refer back to a more standard morality/politics dichotomy.

The place of moral disposition in politics is given greater weight by Ronald Beiner, who writes in *Political Judgment*:

> We may perhaps think of judgments of character, judgments of persons and of personal qualities, as a facet of private life, as possessing an intimacy far removed from the abstract impersonality of public life. (The assumption may be that politics concerns the workings of institutions rather than the disclosure of persons.) But in fact judgments of persons and of personal character form a large and essential aspect of political judgment, and anyone who is a poor judge of character or whose judgment of

persons is deficient will be likewise deficient in matters of political judgment.[5]

This emphasis on moral disposition is valuable; what remains is to see exactly how a moral deficiency expresses itself 'likewise' in politics. I have shown what it is about pride and moral innocence which diminishes judgement and the reasons why this has such catastrophic political effect.

Charles Taylor, in the course of some well-aimed criticisms of utilitarianism, shows that an exclusive emphasis on consequences which attends some realist theories of politics completely ignores the moral character of individuals or states from which they are derived. As such, utilitarianism has no means of accounting for crucial moral differences between individuals and states and must be indifferent to moral disposition unless it can be proved to have a significant instrumental value. For Taylor, to make these consequentialist calculations in politics is already to admit moral corruption.

> The wrongness of dropping napalm on a village of noncombatants has not been measured when one has counted the number of dead in order subsequently to balance them against the number of lives saved; something of moral moment already lies in the fact that we are ready and able to calculate in this way over the lives of children, say; we have to be hardened, to be pushed a little closer to the monstrous, to be able to make this calculation and act on it.[6]

Taylor is right to deny that we can make human life the subject of calculation in the same way as we might count the number of apples in a barrel or balance one barrel-load against another. But it is not so clear what of 'moral moment' is involved either when such calculation is entered upon or when it is refused. Once this question is raised, moral disposition is crucial. A rejection of moral arithmetic, of evaluating gain against loss, may be derived from a variety of different moral standpoints. It makes a difference as to what these are. My concern has been to display this diversity in relation to moral innocence.

It is important to see how the production-line morality of consequentialism ignores the deeper perspective of the moral agent. It matters to individuals how they live, how they treat others, and how they see the moral limits on their conduct in a way which cannot be reduced to mutual benefit, advantage, or protection. Moral understanding is not accidentally related to human nature or something which can be tacked on to it after its basic characteristics have been discovered. Peter Geach is mistaken when he suggests that 'Men need virtues as bees need stings'.[7] It makes a difference to human beings how the virtues are brought to bear on a given situation. Whether moral considerations protect or threaten politics depends on the moral disposition involved. There is no common, sting-like function shared by all virtues, and, hence, no obvious explanation when morality enters politics and things go wrong.

I have argued that the standard constructions of the morality/politics relationship have to be supplemented by a sharper recognition of the priority of moral dispositions. This is not to deny the logical importance of offices as opposed to office-holders. It is, however, a necessary prelude to understanding how moral considerations play a part in the way the duties of office are lived up to. It involves a shift in attention from spectator to agent judgements, to how it is that the same actions or policies may issue from different moral dispositions and how an admirable moral disposition produces political disaster. It requires considerable filling-out of moral detail in both personal character and political context, intricacies often found in literature.

Iris Murdoch in *The Sovereignty of Good* asks how moral understanding plays a part in the choice between, for example, staying with one's family or leaving to meet a political commitment.[8] She argues that questions such as this cannot be answered by an appeal to formal ratiocination or a further specification of moral rules. A similar point is made by Bernard Williams in the course of his discussion of Gauguin's choice between his obligations to those close to him and his leaving them to pursue his art. Someone who was concerned to construct a theory of such choices by relating them to a framework of moral rules would have to include a secondary rule reference to which either would or would not enable Gauguin to justify his choice. As Williams rightly says, this could not assert that 'X' must fulfil his obligations unless he is a great artist, without begging the moral question. Equally if the rule is amended so that it reads that 'X' must fulfil his obligations unless he is reasonably convinced that he is a great artist, the problem is simply made worse. As Williams asks:

What is reasonable conviction supposed to be in such a case? Should Gauguin consult professors of art? The absurdity of such riders surely expresses an absurdity in the whole enterprise of trying to find a place for such cases within the rules.[9]

This introduces a distinction which is missed in Crick's reference to 'rare good fortune'. Luck here may refer to the fortunate conjunction of circumstances which allows the disposition to succeed. But it may also refer to the kind of disposition it is. It is this that must be explored when a choice is made of the kind that Murdoch instances or where moral choices are made in volatile political circumstances. Some outcomes derive not from 'rare good fortune' but necessarily from the actions and dispositions of the agent.

To see why this should be requires that we put aside the preconceptions of theory. Murdoch writes:

> Of course virtue is good habit and dutiful action. But the background condition of such habit and such action, in human beings, is a just mode of vision and a good quality of consciousness. It is a *task* to come to see the world as it is. A philosophy which leaves duty without a context and exalts the idea of freedom and power as a separate top level value ignores this task and obscures the relation between virtue and reality.[10]

What Murdoch refers to as 'a good quality of consciousness' may encompass a variety of moral conduct ranging from self-sacrifice to saintliness. It is essential to appreciate this if the bearing of moral disposition on politics is to be properly understood. We can only chart the deep incompatibility between certain moral dispositions and politics from within morality.

It is an important feature of Murdoch's view that the moral standpoint is not regarded as solely one of duty and obligation. It is true, as Heyd comments, that

> Doing good is an ideal which has no definite boundaries, and unlike refraining from evil, it is not always morally required.[11]

But this does not convey the complexity of a standpoint which repays evil with good, which responds to wrong-doing with charity, and which gives politics its trust. The primary difficulty with such universal compassion is that it has no immediate logical resting-place. Unlike forgiveness which is necessarily related to guilt, absolute ethics is unrestrained by desert, merit, or need. But what does it mean to try to live in accordance with such an ideal? I have indicated that this aspiration is consistent with a variety of ways of life, and I have concentrated on moral innocence and its political effect. We have seen the diverse forms of damage which can result to politics from a specific kind of moral purity, and we have noted the impact that excess of virtue can have on the lives of those individuals who are touched by it.

If moral innocence represents such a profound source of danger, what objection is there to removing it? Robert Nozick in *Anarchy, State and Utopia* refers to the difficulties in applying non-aggression principles to innocent threats and to innocent shields of threats.

> Innocent persons strapped onto the front of the tanks of aggressors so that the tanks cannot be hit without also hitting them are innocent shields of threats.[12]

Nozick's problem is whether it is justifiable knowingly to harm an innocent shield, and he rightly emphasizes that this is not only an intellectual difficulty. The decision to site a gun emplacement behind a children's hospital is an example sufficient to highlight the moral and political complexity involved. But there are a number of important respects in which Nozick's problem is not mine. His arises in the context of his libertarian assumptions regarding the priority of individual rights. I have made no such assumptions and I have not been concerned to formulate principles of non-aggression to which such individuals would agree. More important, Nozick regards the innocent threat or shield as a causal agent in the process by which the threat is made which means responsibility cannot in any way be predicated of them. But this is not how moral innocence makes its impact on the world. The relationship between Billy Budd and Vere is not causal in kind. Equally, Vere is aware, as another officer in his position may not be, that Billy's innocence has disqualified him from responsibility for the blow which killed Claggart. This understanding is a necessary feature of Vere's decision to execute Billy, to sacrifice innocence. Nozick's 'ray gun' as the means of disposing of innocent threats exists in the context of his conception of the rights and powers of individuals. Moral innocence cannot be displaced so straightforwardly and, therefore, the grounds for removing the dangers it poses must be correspondingly more complicated.

I have shown that for Vere the impact of innocence on his life has a tragic quality. Unlike Nozick's innocent shield, Billy's goodness does not conceal a further danger. It is itself the challenge to Vere's moral sensibilities, and when Vere decides as he does he knows he has obliterated it and that he must come to terms with such knowledge. Of course, the moral innocence which we have examined is nothing like mere naivety or superficiality. It is a commonplace of politics that with the best of intentions it is always possible to offer a defence of totalitarian rule. Consider one example of innocence as political gullibility. This is Anna Louise Strong, one of a legion of similar liberal pilgrims, describing Stalin's construction of the White Sea Canal, built by 300,000 slave labourers:

> The labour camps have won a high reputation throughout the Soviet Union as places where tens of thousands of men have been reclaimed. So well known and effective is the Soviet method of remaking human beings that criminals occasionally now apply to be readmitted.[13]

Such credulity may be deeply engrained to the point where it cannot be displaced by any appeal to evidence, and it becomes a victim of its own determination to believe.

Political action is commonly thought to create victims of innocence in a different sense. The destruction of Stevie, the child who innocently carries the bomb in Conrad's *The Secret Agent*, is an emblem of all those whose lives have been consumed by mass destruction and genocide. It would be perversity to ignore the way innocence is corrupted or destroyed. Earlier I mentioned Marlow's decision in Conrad's *Heart of Darkness* to protect the innocence of Kurtz's intended by lying to her about his final words. Marlow faces a similar dilemma to Vere's in *Billy Budd*, where the moral issue is the way innocence is lost, whether to maintain innocence through illusion or to sacrifice it in the full knowledge of the moral costs involved. In *Billy Budd* the illusion is the possibility of allowing innocence to go unpunished. In *Heart of Darkness* it is the girl's belief that Kurtz loved her to the end. Marlow's lie shows the power of visionary innocence and the price we may be prepared to pay to retain its hold over us. Berthoud comments:

> The girl's belief in the essential virtue of mankind, as instanced by her faith in her betrothed, is an illusion, for it is contradicted by

the facts; yet it is not unreal, for it is held with all the force of a truly unselfish conviction. It seems to keep alive, in the darkness of Marlow's experience of actuality, the light of visionary purpose.[14]

But what are we to make of 'visionary purpose' if it is founded on ignorance and illusion? It is, of course, true that Marlow's lie is reluctantly told. He is not only a man who believes in truth-telling. He has come to recognize the power and impact of moral innocence and the extent to which it inspires protection. But he releases into the world a vision of others which is comprehensive and pure, innocent of betrayal and totally confident in giving its trust to another because it is ignorant of the possibility of its being misused. This book has examined the moral limits of such a disposition in both moral life and politics, how morality excludes itself from politics. Bernard Williams claims that

> morality makes people think that, without its very special
> obligation, there is only inclination, without its utter
> voluntariness, there is only force; without its ultimately pure
> justice, there is no justice.[15]

In relation to specific moral dispositions I have tried to show how his claim may be rendered persuasive.

It may be true, as Williams has suggested,[16] that the problem of political morality will not admit a solution unless

> one modifies from both ends, allowing both that the good need not
> be as pure as all that, so long as they retain some active sense of
> moral costs and moral limits; and that the society has some
> genuinely settled politics and some expectations of civic
> respectability.[17]

But the process of modification may not be so bland and trouble-free. In this book I have been primarily concerned with how 'the good . . . need be as pure as all that' and how this moral disposition weakens politics. Arendt, too, recognizes this in her assertion that sufferings of scale cannot simply be endured and that their proper forum for consideration is a political one, though this is to modify the problem from the political end and that has not been my concern. Moral innocence, like the 'Godly-man' Bunyan's pilgrims meet on the slopes of Mount Innocence, is incapable of embodiment in the world and therefore can only misconstrue the political injustices which confront it. Hegel's view that innocence 'is merely non-action, like the mere being of a stone, not even that of a child'[18] means that, for him, innocence is not simply philosophical error. Innocence can show itself to the world as the start of a quest for meaning and persist as a broken relationship to others. Nietzsche's scepticism is well-grounded when he remarks that:

> Especially those who call themselves 'the good' I found to be the most poisonous flies: they bite in all innocence, they lie in all innocence; how could they possibly be just to me?[19]

I have shown how this character can be read as a moral exclusion of morality from politics. To undertake a similar exercise from the standpoint of politics is another philosophical problem.

NOTES

CHAPTER 1: INNOCENCE AND POLITICS

1 See the discussions in Kieran Flanagan, 'The experience of innocence as a social construction', *Philosophical Studies*, The National University of Ireland, 28: 104–40, Dublin, 1981; and Herbert Morris, *On Guilt and Innocence, Essays in Legal Philosophy and Moral Psychology*, Berkeley, 1976.

2 David Hume, *A Treatise of Human Nature*, edited by L. A. Selby-Bigge, Oxford, 1888 (1949), p. 479.

3 Philippa Foot, *Virtues and Vices and Other Essays In Moral Philosophy*, Oxford, 1985, pp. 2–3.

4 P. T. Geach, *The Virtues, The Stanton Lectures, 1973–4*, Cambridge, 1977, p. 16.

5 D. Z. Phillips, 'In search of the moral "must": Mrs Foot's Fugitive Thought', *Philosophical Quarterly*, 27, 1977, p. 144.

6 D. Z. Phillips, 'Does it pay to be good?', *Proceedings of the Aristotelian Society*, NS 65, 1964–5, pp. 50–1.

7 ibid., p. 59.

8 Immanuel Kant, *Perpetual Peace*, in *Kant's Political Writings*, edited with an introduction and notes by Hans Reiss, translated by H. B. Nisbet, Cambridge, 1970, p. 112.

9 Immanuel Kant, *Perpetual Peace*, trans. L. W. Beck, New York, 1963, pp. 111–12.

10 Jean-Jacques Rousseau, *The Social Contract*, translated with an introduction by G. D. H. Cole, London, 1963, p. 56.

11 Peter Singer, 'Famine, affluence and morality', *Philosophy and Public Affairs*, 1, 1972, p. 231.

12 See the discussion of this in Dorothea Krook, *Three Traditions of Moral Thought*, Cambridge, 1959, p. 73.

13 In 'Wittgenstein's Lecture on Ethics', *Philosophical Review*, 74, 1965, p. 5.

14 Adam Smith, *The Theory of Moral Sentiments*, edited by D. D. Raphael and A. L. Macfie, Oxford, 1979, vol. I of the Glasgow Edition of the Works and Correspondence of Adam Smith, p. 119.

15 ibid., p. 120.

16 St Matthew's Gospel, 2.16.

17 William Shakespeare, *King Henry VI* (3), V.vi.31–3.
18 Iris Murdoch, *The Bell*, St Albans, 1976, p. 135.
19 J. P. Stern, *On Realism*, London, 1973, p. 96.
20 Michael Slote, *Goods and Virtues*, Oxford, 1983.
21 ibid., p. 49.
22 ibid., p. 50.
23 ibid., p. 50.
24 Michael Oakeshott, *Rationalism in Politics*, London, 1962, pp. 195–6.
25 George Steiner, *Antigones*, Oxford, 1984, p. 35.
26 Peter Winch, *Ethics and Action*, London, 1972, pp. 171–93.
27 ibid., p. 185.
28 Shirley Robin Letwin, *The Gentleman in Trollope: Individuality and Moral Conduct*, London, 1982, p. 72.
29 Winch, op. cit., p. 181.
30 Soren Kierkegaard, *Either/Or*, vol. II, translated by Walter Lowrie, with revisions and a foreword by Howard A. Johnson, Princeton, 1971, p. 232.
31 William Shakespeare, *King Henry VI* (3), op. cit., V.iv.77–80.
32 William Shakespeare, *King Henry VI* (2), III.i.224–5.
33 Morris, op. cit., p. 141.

CHAPTER 2: PUBLIC AND PRIVATE VIRTUE

1 Plato, *Gorgias*, 484C–485B See Plato, *Socratic Dialogues*, translated by W. D. Woodhead, London, 1953, pp. 242–3.
2 Plato, *Apology*, 38A; in *Socratic Dialogues*, op. cit., p. 61.
3 Bernard Williams, *Ethics and the Limits of Philosophy*, London, 1985, p. 21.
4 Terence Irwin, *Plato's Moral Theory*, Oxford, 1977, pp. 90–1.
5 See W. F. R. Hardie, *Aristotle's Ethical Theory*, Oxford, 1968, pp. 258–93.
6 *Gorgias*, 473C, op. cit., p. 224.
7 *Gorgias*, 469B–C, op. cit., p. 218.
8 Herman Melville, *Billy Budd, Sailor and Other Stories*, selected and edited with an introduction by Harold Beaver, Harmondsworth, 1970, p. 363.
9 *Gorgias*, 479A, op. cit., p. 234.
10 *Gorgias*, 478C, op. cit., p. 233.
11 *Gorgias*, 478D; op. cit., p. 234.
12 Plato, *Phaedrus*, 248, in *The Dialogues of Plato*, translated by B. Jowett, vol. I, 3rd edn, Oxford, 1892, pp. 454–5.
13 W. K. C. Guthrie, *A History of Greek Philosophy, vol. III, The Fifth Century Enlightenment*, Cambridge, 1969, p. 413.
14 Herbert Morris, *On Guilt and Innocence*, Berkeley, 1976, p. 158.
15 Soren Kierkegaard, *The Concept of Irony*, translated with an introduction and notes by Lee M. Capel, London, 1966, p. 195.
16 Plato, *Republic*, 495–496, translated by F. M. Cornford, Oxford, 1961, pp. 199–200.
17 ibid., 496, p. 200.
18 ibid., 462, p. 160.
19 ibid., 481–488, pp. 190–1. See J. R. Bambrough, 'Plato's political

---

NOTES TO PAGES 29–51

analogies', in Renford Bambrough (ed.), *Plato, Popper and Politics*, Cambridge, 1967, pp. 152–69.
20 *Republic*, 500–501, op. cit., pp. 204–5.
21 W. B. Yeats, *A Prayer for My Daughter*, in *The Collected Poems*, London, 1963, p. 214.
22 Irwin, op. cit., p. 219.
23 Vinit Haksar, *Equality, Liberty, and Perfectionism*, Oxford, 1979, p. 72.
24 Melville, op. cit., p. 330.
25 Williams, op. cit., p. 36.
26 Aristotle, *Ethica Nicomachea*, 1179b, translated by W. D. Ross, in *Works of Aristotle*, vol. IX, Oxford, 1940.
27 ibid., 1144b.
28 Evelyn Waugh, *Decline and Fall* (London, 1928), Harmondsworth, 1971, p. 146. See also D. S. Savage, 'The innocence of Evelyn Waugh', in B. Rajan (ed.), *The Novelist as Thinker*, London, 1947, pp. 34–46.
29 Aristotle, *Magna Moralia*, 1195a, translated by St George Stock, in *The Works of Aristotle*, vol. IX, Oxford, 1940.
30 ibid., 1195a.
31 ibid., 1190b.
32 Aristotle, *Eudemian Ethics*, 1248a, translated by J. Solomon in *The Works of Aristotle*, vol. IX, Oxford, 1940.
33 Aristotle, *Politics*, 1284a, translated by B. Jowett in *The Works of Aristotle*, vol. X, Oxford, 1946.
34 ibid., 1284b.
35 *Eudemian Ethics*, op. cit., 1241a.
36 ibid., 1243a.
37 Aristotle, *Rhetoric*, Book II, chs 12–15, translated by W. Rhys Roberts in *The Works of Aristotle*, vol. XI, Oxford, 1928. See also Martha C. Nussbaum, *The Fragility of Goodness*, Cambridge, 1986, pp. 337–40.
38 Aristotle, *Rhetoric*, 1389b.
39 ibid., 1390b.
40 Henry James, *The Golden Bowl* (1904), Harmondsworth, 1974, p. 252. See the discussion of innocence in this novel by Martha Craven Nussbaum, 'Flawed crystals: James's The Golden Bowl and literature as moral philosophy', *New Literary History*, Autumn 1983, 15(1):25–50.
41 *Eudemian Ethics*, op. cit., 1248b.
42 *Nicomachean Ethics*, op. cit., 1178b.
43 Immanuel Kant, *Lectures on Ethics*, translated by Louis Infield, Foreword, by Lewis White Beck, Indianapolis, 1963, pp. 212–13.
44 ibid., p. 213.
45 ibid., p. 213.
46 ibid., p. 213.
47 Clement C. J. Webb, *Kant's Philosophy of Religion*, Oxford, 1926, p. 118.
48 Kant, *Lectures*, op. cit., p. 155.
49 Immanuel Kant, *Fundamental Principles of the Metaphysic of Morals*, in Kant, *Critique of Practical Reason and Other Works on the Theory of Ethics*, translated by Thomas Kingsmill Abbott, London, 1959, p. 60.
50 ibid., p. 61.
51 ibid., p. 61.

260

NOTES TO PAGES 51–78

52 ibid., p. 21.
53 Kant, *First Part of the Philosophical Theory of Religion*, in *Critique of Practical Reason*, op. cit., p. 355.
54 Kant, *Groundwork*, in *The Moral Law*, trans. H. J. Paton, London, 1972, p. 65.
55 Kant, *Perpetual Peace*, in *Kant's Political Writings*, edited with an introduction and notes by Hans Reiss, translated by H. B. Nisbet, Cambridge, 1970, p. 116.
56 ibid., p. 125.
57 Kant, *Lectures*, op. cit., p. 193.
58 Kant, *Perpetual Peace*, op. cit., p. 126.
59 Patrick A. E. Hutchings, *Kant On Absolute Value*, London, 1972, p. 143.
60 Ronald Dworkin, *Law's Empire*, London, 1986, p. 404.
61 See John Rawls, 'Kantian constructivism in moral theory', *Journal of Philosophy*, September 1980, 77(9): 515–72; 'The basic structure as subject', in Alvin I. Goldman and Jaegmon Kim (eds), *Values and Morals, Essays in Honor of William Frankena, Charles Stevenson and Richard Brandt*, Dordrecht, 1978, pp. 47–71; and 'Justice as fairness: Political not metaphysical', *Philosophy and Public Affairs*, 1985, 14: 223–51.
62 John Rawls, *A Theory of Justice*, Oxford, 1972, pp. 519–20.
63 ibid., pp. 478–9.
64 ibid., p. 479.
65 David Heyd, *Supererogation, Its Status in Ethical Theory*, Cambridge, 1982, p. 103.
66 Rawls, *A Theory of Justice*, op. cit., pp. 477–8.
67 See Rawls' discussion of this term in his 'Social unity and primary goods', in Amartya Sen and Bernard Williams (eds), *Utilitarianism and Beyond*, Cambridge, 1982, pp. 159–87, esp. 180.

CHAPTER 3: POLITICAL AUTONOMY

1 Harriet Martineau, *Society in America*, edited and abridged by Seymour Martin Lipset, New York, 1962, p. 94.
2 George Orwell, *Writers and Leviathan*, in *Collected Essays*, London, 1961, p. 434.
3 John Donne, *To Sir Henry Wotton*, in *Complete Poetry and Selected Prose*, edited by John Hayward, London, 1936, p. 158.
4 Niccolo Machiavelli, *The Prince*, New York, 1950, p. 56.
5 R. N. Berki, *On Political Realism*, London, 1981, p. 62.
6 Machiavelli, op. cit., p. 528.
7 G. W. F. Hegel, 'The German Constitution', in *Hegel's Political Writings*, translated by T. M. Knox, with an introductory essay by Z. A. Pelczynski, Oxford, 1964, pp. 220–1.
8 Bernard Bosanquet, *The Philosophical Theory of the State*, 4th edn, London, 1923.
9 ibid., p. 304.
10 ibid., p. 303.
11 ibid., p. 305.
12 ibid., p. 304, footnote 1 dated 1919.

13 Michael Oakeshott, *On Human Conduct*, Oxford, 1975, p. 175.
14 ibid., p. 175.
15 Stuart Hampshire (ed.), *Public and Private Morality*, Cambridge, 1978, p. 49.
16 ibid., p. 52.
17 Michael Walzer, 'Political action: The problem of dirty hands', *Philosophy and Public Affairs*, 1973, 2: 160–80; Bernard Williams, 'Politics and moral character', in Stuart Hampshire, op. cit., pp. 55–73; Martin Hollis, 'Dirty hands', *British Journal of Political Science*, 12 October 1982, 19: 385–98. See also, Christopher McMahon, 'Morality and the invisible hand', *Philosophy and Public Affairs*, 1981, 10: 247–77, and Stanley I. Benn, 'Public and private morality: Clean living and dirty hands', in S. I. Benn and G. F. Gauss (eds), *Public and Private in Social Life*, London, 1983, pp. 155–81.
18 In his 'Ruthlessness in public life' in Hampshire, op. cit., pp. 75–91.
19 Walzer, op. cit., p. 164.
20 ibid., p. 165.
21 ibid., p. 166.
22 ibid., p. 168.
23 ibid., p. 162.
24 Nagel, op. cit., p. 83.
25 Williams in Hampshire, op. cit., p. 62.
26 ibid., p. 69.
27 Hollis, op. cit., pp. 385–98.
28 ibid., p. 388.
29 ibid., p. 390.
30 ibid., p. 396.
31 Barrie Paskins and Michael Dockrill, *The Ethics of War*, London, 1979, p. 293.
32 B. Williams, *Ethics and the Limits of Philosophy*, London, 1985, p. 39.
33 Machiavelli, *The Discourses*, I.7.2.4, translated by Leslie J. Walker, 2 vols, London, 1950, vol. I, p. 228.
34 William Shakespeare, *Coriolanus*, II. ii.2–11.
35 ibid., IV.vii.37–42.
36 ibid., V.iii.35–7.
37 ibid., III.i.79–81.
38 David Hume, *A Treatise of Human Nature*, edited by L. A. Selby-Bigge, Oxford, 1888 (1949), p. 599.
39 ibid., p. 599.
40 *Coriolanus* I.iv.30–9.
41 Hume, op. cit., p. 600.
42 G. W. F. Hegel, *Lectures on the History of Philosophy*, translated by E. S. Haldane, London, 1982, vol. 1, p. 92.
43 *Coriolanus*, I.ix.36–40.
44 ibid., III.i.157–9.
45 ibid., III.ii.34–9.
46 ibid., I.i.168–70.
47 ibid., II.iii.93–4.
48 See his 'Study of the first scene of Shakespeare's *Coriolanus*', in *Brecht on*

Theatre, The Development of an Aesthetic, translation and notes by John Willett, London, 1964, p. 264.

49 *Coriolanus*, IV.vii.49–53.
50 ibid., V.iii.118–19.
51 ibid., IV.vi.15–17.
52 ibid., III.ii.46–51.
53 ibid., III.ii.53–7.
54 ibid., III.ii.99–101.
55 ibid., III.iii.131–3.
56 ibid., II.iii.162–3.
57 Simone Weil, *Lectures on Philosophy*, translated by Hugh Price, with an introduction by Peter Winch, Cambridge, 1978, p. 204.
58 *Coriolanus*, V.iii.99–101.
59 ibid., V.iii.142–7.
60 ibid., V.iii.185–9.
61 ibid., III.iii.118–21.
62 ibid., V.v.111–17.
63 Judith Shklar, *Ordinary Vices*, London, 1984, p. 145.

CHAPTER 4: ABSOLUTE VIRTUE AND POLITICS

1 George Orwell, *Reflections on Gandhi*, in *The Collected Essays, Journalism and Letters*, vol. *4, In Front of Your Nose, 1945–50*, Harmondsworth, 1970, p. 527.
2 R. F. Holland, *Against Empiricism, On Education, Epistemology and Value*, Oxford, 1980.
3 ibid., pp. 99–100.
4 Ludwig Wittgenstein, *Tractatus Logico-Philosophicus*, translated by D. F. Pears and B. F. McGuinness, London, 1966, 6.422, p. 147.
5 Holland, op. cit., p. 130.
6 M. H. Weston, 'Willing the good', *Ratio*, 1982, 24(2) p. 107.
7 Iris Murdoch, 'Against dryness', *Encounter*, January 1961, 16, p. 17.
8 David Heyd, *Supererogation, Its Status in Ethical Theory*, Cambridge, 1982 pp. 1–11.
9 ibid., p. 175.
10 See J. O. Urmson, 'Saints and heroes', in Joel Feinberg (ed.), *Moral Concepts*, Oxford, 1969, pp. 60–73.
11 ibid., p. 69.
12 ibid., p. 71.
13 ibid., p. 72.
14 Bernard Williams, *Moral Luck*, Cambridge, 1981, repr. 1985, p. 23.
15 Susan Wolf, 'Moral saints', *Journal of Philosophy*, August 1982, 79(8): 419–39.
16 ibid., p. 419.
17 ibid., p. 421.
18 ibid., p. 419.
19 Owen Flanagan, 'Admirable immorality and admirable imperfection', *Journal of Philosophy* 1986, 83, p. 52.

20 Wolf, op. cit., pp. 426–7.
21 Michael Slote, *Goods and Virtues*, Oxford, 1983, pp. 77–109.
22 ibid., p. 107.
23 John Rawls, *A Theory of Justice*, Oxford, 1972, pp. 129–30.
24 David Hume, *An Enquiry Concerning the Principles of Morals*, edited by L. A. Selby-Bigge, Oxford, 1951, p. 188.
25 John Bunyan, *The Pilgrim's Progress*, London, 1892, p. 215.
26 See Robert Merrihew Adams, 'Saints', *Journal of Philosophy*, 1984, 81: 392–401.
27 See Gary Watson, 'Virtues in excess', *Philosophical Studies*, 1984, 46; 57–74.
28 Elizabeth M. Pybus, 'Saints and heroes', *Philosophy*, 1982, 57: p. 196.
29 A. I. Melden, 'Saints and supererogation', in Ilham Dilman (ed.), *Philosophy and Life, Essays on John Wisdom*, The Hague, 1984, pp. 61–81, p. 70.
30 ibid., p. 75.
31 ibid., p. 79.
32 Holland, op. cit., p. 137.
33 In J. J. C. Smart and Bernard Williams, *Utilitarianism For and Against*, Cambridge, 1973, repr. 1980, pp. 98 ff.
34 Holland, op. cit., p. 139.
35 ibid., p. 141.
36 ibid., p. 142.

CHAPTER 5: THE DISPLACEMENT OF VIRTUE

1 See Philippa Foot, 'Utilitarianism and the virtues', *Mind*, 1985, 94: 196–209.
2 See Jonathan Robinson, *Duty and Hypocrisy in Hegel's Phenomenology of Mind: An Essay in the Real and Ideal*, Toronto, 1977.
3 See H. A. Reyburn, *The Ethical Theory of Hegel*, Oxford, 1921, pp. 191–3.
4 G. W. F. Hegel, *Lectures on the History of Philosophy*, translated by E. S. Haldane, London, 1892, vol. 1, p. 92.
5 See Friedrich Schiller, *On the Aesthetic Education of Man*, edited and translated by Elizabeth M. Wilkinson and L. A. Willoughby, Oxford, 1982, Sixth Letter, esp. p. 41.
6 G. W. F. Hegel, *Lectures on the Philosophy of Religion (1885)*, translated by Rev. E. B. Spiers and J. Burdon Sanderson, 3 vols, London, 1974, vol. 1, p. 273.
7 ibid., p. 279.
8 G. W. F. Hegel, *Aesthetics, Lectures on Fine Art by G. W. F. Hegel*, translated by T. M. Knox, 2 vols, Oxford, 1975, vol. II, p. 1091.
9 ibid., vol. I, p. 197.
10 See Soren Kierkegaard, *Fear and Trembling*, edited and translated by Howard V. Hong and Edna H. Hong, Princeton, 1983, p. 94.
11 Hegel, *Aesthetics*, op. cit., vol. I. p. 259.
12 G. W. F. Hegel, *Lectures on the Philosophy of World History, Introduction:*

Reason in History, translated by H. B. Nisbet, with an introduction by Duncan Forbes, Cambridge, 1975, p. 178.

13 Stanley Rosen, *G. W. F. Hegel, An Introduction to the Science of Wisdom*, New Haven, 1974, p. 216.

14 Hegel, *Phenomenology of Spirit*, translated by A. V. Miller, Oxford, 1979, p. 467.

15 Charles Taylor, *Hegel*, Cambridge, 1975, p. 62.

16 G. W. F. Hegel, *Early Theological Writings*, translated by T. M. Knox, Chicago, 1971, p. 280.

17 ibid., p. 281.

18 G. W. F. Hegel, *Philosophy of Right*, translated with notes by T. M. Knox, Oxford, 1967, p. 261.

19 *Phenomenology*, op. cit., p. 255.

20 Rosen, op. cit., p. 231.

21 *Phenomenology*, op. cit., p. 400.

22 Taylor, op. cit., p. 194.

23 *Philosophy of Right*, op. cit., p. 99.

24 *Phenomenology*, op. cit., p. 232.

25 ibid., p. 231.

26 *Phenomenology*, op. cit., p. 235.

27 *Philosophy of Right*, op. cit., p. 97.

28 George Steiner, *Antigones*, Oxford, 1984, p. 40.

29 ibid., pp. 40-1.

30 Judith Shklar, *Freedom and Independence, A Study of the Political Ideas of Hegel's Phenomenology of Mind*, Cambridge, 1976, p. 115.

31 F. Nietzsche, *Daybreak*, translated by R. J. Hollingdale, Cambridge, 1982, p. 159.

32 F. Nietzsche, *On the Genealogy of Morals*, translated by Walter Kaufman and R. J. Hollingdale, New York, 1969, p. 65.

33 ibid., p. 137.

34 F. Nietzsche, *Ecce Homo*, in *Basic Writings of Nietzsche*, translated by Walter Kaufman, New York, 1968, p. 673.

35 F. Nietzsche, *Beyond Good and Evil*, in *Basic Writings*, ibid., p. 252.

36 *Daybreak*, op. cit., pp. 14-15.

37 ibid., p. 15.

38 F. Nietzsche, *The Twilight of the Idols*, in *The Portable Nietzsche*, edited and translated by Walter Kaufman, Harmondsworth, 1976, p. 491.

39 F. Nietzsche, *The Genealogy of Morals*, in *Basic Writings*, op. cit., p. 456.

40 F. Nietzsche, *Human, All Too Human*, translated by R. J. Hollingdale, Cambridge, 1986, p. 59.

41 See Alexander Nehemas, *Nietzsche, Life as Literature*, Harvard, 1986, pp. 221-8.

42 Max Weber, 'Politics as a vocation', in *From Max Weber*, edited by H. H. Gerth and C. Wright Mills, Oxford, 1958, p. 122.

43 J. P. Stern, *On Realism*, London, 1973, p. 12.

44 Hannah Arendt, *Between Past and Future*, London, 1961, pp. 29-30.

45 Hannah Arendt, *The Human Condition*, Chicago, 1958, p. 77.

46 Hannah Arendt, *On Revolution*, London, 1963, p. 93.

47 As quoted in Elisabeth Young-Bruehl, *Hannah Arendt, For Love of the World*, Yale, 1982, p. 374; see also the useful discussion in George Kateb, *Hannah Arendt, Politics, Conscience, Evil*, Oxford, 1983, pp. 26, 85–115. 85–115.
48 Hannah Arendt, *Lectures on Kant's Political Philosophy*, edited with an Interpretative Essay by Ronald Beiner, Chicago, 1982, p. 50.
49 Arendt *On Revolution*, op. cit., p 82.
50 Quoted in Kateb, op. cit., p. 49.
51 Arendt, *On Revolution*, op. cit., p. 82.
52 ibid., p. 93.
53 ibid., p. 91.
54 Hannah Arendt, *Men in Dark Times*, Harmondsworth, 1973, p. 148.
55 Hannah Arendt, 'Truth in politics', in Peter Laslett and W. G. Runciman (eds), *Philosophy, Politics and Society*, Third Series, Oxford, 1967, p. 112.
56 ibid., p. 127.
57 Arendt, *Between Past and Future*, op. cit., p. 221.
58 ibid., p. 221.
59 Beiner, Interpretive Essay, op. cit., p. 100.
60 Fyodor Dostoevsky, *The Idiot*, translated with an introduction by David Magarshack, Harmondsworth, 1975, p. 494.
61 Bhikhu Parekh, *Hannah Arendt and the Search for a New Political Philosophy*, London, 1981, pp. 184–5.
62 Arendt, 'The crisis in culture', in *Between Past and Future*, op. cit., p. 223.

CHAPTER 6: POLITICAL PHILOSOPHY AND LITERATURE

1 Bhikhu Parekh, *Hannah Arendt and the Search for a New Political Philosophy*, London, 1981, pp. 181–2.
2 C. S. Lewis, *Studies in Words*, Cambridge, 1960, p. 171.
3 John Rawls, 'Kantian constructivism in moral theory', *Journal of Philosophy*, September 1980, 77(9), p. 525.
4 F. H. Bradley, *Ethical Studies* (1876), Oxford, 1959, p. 90n.
5 See L. Wittgenstein, *Philosophical Investigations*, translated by G. E. M. Anscombe, 2nd edn, Oxford, 1958, pp. 48e, 115.
6 T. E. Hulme, *Speculations*, London, 1949, p. 230.
7 Iris Murdoch, 'Vision and choice in morality', *Proceedings of the Aristotelian Society*, Supplementary Volume, 1956, 30, p. 39.
8 ibid., p. 39.
9 W. B. Gallie, *Philosophy and the Historical Understanding*, London, 1964, p. 41.
10 Ronald Beiner, *Political Judgement*, London, 1983, pp. 127–8.
11 George Orwell, *Politics vs Literature*, in his *Collected Essays*, London, 1961, p. 394.
12 Roger Scruton, *The Politics of Culture*, Manchester, 1981, p. 80.
13 Iris Murdoch 'On natural novelists and unnatural philosophers', in *The Listener*, 27 April 1978, p. 533.
14 Liam O'Flaherty, *The Assassin*, London, 1935, pp. 96–7.

15 See the distinctions made by D. D. Raphael, 'Can literature be moral philosophy', *New Literary History*, Autumn 1983, 15(1): 1–12.
16 See John Rawls, *A Theory of Justice*, Oxford, 1972, paperback edn, 1973, p. 432.
17 See D. Z. Phillips, *Some Limits to Moral Endeavour*, Swansea, 1971.
18 Rawls, *A Theory of Justice*, p. 408.
19 Iris Murdoch, 'Against dryness', *Encounter*, January 1961, 16, p. 20.
20 ibid., p. 20.
21 D. Z. Phillips, *Through a Darkening Glass*, Oxford, 1982, p. 62.
22 See Anthony Manser, Review of Phillips, *Through a Darkening Glass*, op. cit., in *Religious Studies*, 19, 1983: 426–8.
23 For a discussion of similar examples see R. W. Beardsmore, 'Learning from a novel', in *Philosophy and the Arts* (Royal Institute of Philosophy Lectures, vol. 6, 1971–2), London, 1973.
24 R. M. Hare, *Freedom and Reason*, Oxford, 1965, p. 183.
25 Renford Bambrough, 'Literature and philosophy', in Renford Bambrough (ed.), *Wisdom, Twelve Essays*, Oxford, 1974, pp. 274–293.
26 ibid., p. 277.
27 See Martha Craven Nussbaum, 'Flawed crystals: James's The Golden Bowl and literature as moral philosophy', *New Literary History*, Autumn 1983, 15(1): 25–50.
28 ibid., p. 31.
29 Hannah Arendt, *On Revolution*, London, 1963, p. 76.
30 J.-J. Rousseau, *Emile*, translated by Barbara Foxley, London, 1911 (1969), p. 193.
31 ibid., p. 193.

CHAPTER 7: POLITICS AND INNOCENT INTENT

1 A. L. Rowse, *All Souls and Appeasement*, London, 1961, p. 117.
2 William Shakespeare, *Henry VI* (3), IV.viii.39–47.
3 ibid., IV.iii.45–6.
4 G. W. F. Hegel, *Early Theological Writings*, translated by T. M. Knox, with an introduction and fragments translated by Richard Kroner, Chicago, 1971, p. 280.
5 *Henry VI* (3), op. cit., V.ii.15–18.
6 See W. H. Greenleaf, *Order, Empiricism and Politics, Two Traditions of English Political Thought, 1500–1700*, London, 1964, esp. p. 119.
7 E. M. W. Tillyard, *The Elizabethan World Picture*, London, 1943.
8 *Henry VI* (1), III.iv.1–12.
9 *Henry VI* (3), IV.iii.34–8.
10 ibid., I.iv.59.
11 ibid., II.ii.62.
12 ibid., III.ii.182.
13 ibid., III.ii.192.
14 ibid., II.ii.130–2.
15 ibid., II.ii.177–8.
16 ibid., II.ii.98–100.

17 ibid., II.vi.51–4.
18 Hegel, *Philosophy of Right*, translated with notes by T. M. Knox, Oxford, 1967, p. 73.
19 *Henry VI (3)*, op. cit., I.iv.77–83.
20 ibid., V.v.63–5.
21 ibid., I.ii.22–4.
22 ibid., III.i.69–71.
23 ibid., III.iii.69–70.
24 ibid., IV.i.35–8.
25 ibid., I.i.110–11.
26 ibid., I.i.112–13.
27 ibid., II.i.169–76.
28 See his introduction to *Henry VI (3)*, The Arden Shakespeare, London, 1964, p. iv.
29 *Henry VI (3)*, II.vi.21–6.
30 ibid., III.i.63–4.
31 ibid., IV.vi.19–25.
32 ibid., IV.vi.40–4.
33 Hannah Arendt, *On Revolution*, London, 1963, p. 82.
34 *Henry VI (3)*, op. cit., V.vi.59–60.

CHAPTER 8: MORAL PURITY AND POLITICS

1 Herman Melville, *Billy Budd, Sailor and Other Stories*, selected and edited by Harold Beaver, Harmondsworth, 1970; all references are to this edition.
2 W. H. Auden, *Collected Poems*, edited by Edward Mendelson, London, 1976, p. 200.
3 Melville, op. cit., p. 328.
4 ibid., p. 331.
5 ibid., p. 363.
6 ibid., pp. 353–4.
7 S. I. Benn, 'Wickedness', *Ethics*, July 1985, 95, p. 809. See also James D. Wallace, *Virtues and Vices*, London, 1978, and Ronald D. Milo, *Immorality*, Princeton, 1984.
8 Melville, op. cit., p. 341.
9 ibid., p. 380.
10 Peter Winch, 'The universalizability of moral judgements', in his *Ethics and Action*, London, 1972, pp. 151–70.
11 ibid., p. 157, quoting Melville, op. cit., p. 387.
12 ibid., p. 157, quoting Melville, op. cit., p. 388.
13 ibid., p. 165.
14 ibid., p. 169.
15 Melville, op. cit., p. 384.
16 ibid., p. 385.
17 ibid., p. 389.
18 ibid., pp. 384–5.

19 ibid., p. 387.
20 ibid., pp. 389–90.
21 Hannah Arendt, *On Violence*, London, 1970, p. 64.
22 Hannah Arendt, *On Revolution*, London, 1963, p. 78.
23 ibid., p. 79.
24 Thomas J. Scorza, 'Technology, philosophy, and political virtue: The case of Billy Budd, Sailor', *Interpretation*, 1975, 5(1): pp. 91–107.
25 Melville, op. cit., p. 336.
26 ibid., p. 336.
27 Scorza, op. cit., p. 104.
28 Melville, op. cit., p. 355.
29 ibid., p. 356.

CHAPTER 9: INNOCENT IDEALISM

1 Preface to Graham Greene, *The Quiet American*, London, 1955.
2 Friedrich Nietzsche, *Daybreak*, translated by R. J. Hollingdale, Cambridge, 1982, 321, p. 159.
3 Greene, op. cit., p. 27.
4 ibid., p. 214.
5 ibid., p. 213.
6 ibid., p. 96.
7 ibid., p. 76.
8 ibid., p. 108.
9 ibid., p. 211.
10 ibid., p. 182.
11 ibid., p. 102.
12 ibid., p. 153.
13 ibid., pp. 70–1.
14 ibid., p. 121.
15 ibid., p. 40.
16 ibid., p. 23.
17 ibid., p. 218.
18 Michael Oakeshott, *Rationalism in Politics*, London, 1962, p. 22.
19 ibid., p. 22.
20 Greene, op. cit., p. 107.
21 ibid., p. 75.
22 ibid., p. 231.
23 ibid., p. 29.
24 ibid., p. 72.
25 ibid., p. 227.
26 ibid., p. 226.
27 See Roger Trigg, *Reason and Commitment*, Cambridge, 1973, pp. 44–5.
28 ibid., p. 45.
29 Peter Winch, *Ethics and Action*, London, 1972, pp. 65–6.
30 Greene, op. cit., pp. 239–40.
31 ibid., p. 243.

CHAPTER 10: INNOCENCE AND EXPERIENCE

1 Henry Sidgwick, *The Elements of Politics* (1891), 4th edn, London, 1919, p. 261.
2 R. F. Holland, *Against Empiricism*, Oxford, 1980, pp. 110–25.
3 ibid., p. 112.
4 ibid., pp. 113–14.
5 Herman Melville, *Billy Budd, Sailor and Other Stories*, selected and edited by Harold Beaver, Harmondsworth, 1970, p. 349.
6 Michael A. Slote, 'Morality and ignorance', *Journal of Philosophy*, December 1977, 74(12), p. 755.
7 ibid., p. 757.
8 Bernard Williams, 'Moral luck', in *Philosophical Papers 1973–80*, Cambridge, 1985, pp. 20–39.
9 ibid., p. 23.
10 ibid., p. 36.
11 Melville, op. cit., p. 406.
12 Joseph Conrad, *Heart of Darkness*, London, 1933, p. 115.
13 Jacques Berthoud, *Joseph Conrad, The Major Phase*, Cambridge, 1978, p. 62.

CHAPTER 11: CONCLUSION

1 Bernard Crick, *In Defence of Politics*, revised edition, Harmondsworth, 1964, p. 155.
2 ibid., p. 155.
3 ibid., pp. 155–6.
4 ibid., p. 155.
5 Ronald Beiner, *Political Judgement*, London, 1983, pp. 164–5.
6 Charles Taylor, 'Ethics and politics', in H. J. Johnson, J. J. Leach, and R. G. Muehlmann (eds), *Revolutions, Systems and Theories, Essays in Political Philosophy*, Dordrecht, 1979, p. 103.
7 Peter Geach, *The Virtues, The Stanton Lectures 1973–4*, Cambridge, 1977, p. 17.
8 Iris Murdoch, *The Sovereignty of Good*, London, 1970, p. 91.
9 Bernard Williams, *Moral Luck*, Cambridge, 1985, p. 24.
10 Murdoch, op. cit., p. 91.
11 David Heyd, *Supererogation, Its Status in Ethical Theory*, Cambridge, 1982, p. 128.
12 Robert Nozick, *Anarchy, State and Utopia*, Oxford, 1974, p. 35.
13 See Paul Hollander, *Political Pilgrims, Travels of Western Intellectuals to the Soviet Union, China, and Cuba 1928–1978*, Oxford, 1981, pp. 145–6.
14 Jacques Berthoud, *Joseph Conrad, The Major Phase*, Cambridge, 1978, p. 63.
15 Bernard Williams, *Ethics and the Limits of Philosophy*, London, 1985, p. 196.

16 Bernard Williams, 'Politics and moral character', in Stuart Hampshire (ed.), *Public and Private Morality*, Cambridge, 1978, pp. 55–73.
17 ibid., p. 69.
18 Hegel's *Phenomenology of Spirit*, translated by A. V. Miller, Oxford, 1979, p. 282.
19 Friedrich Nietzsche, *Thus Spoke Zarathustra*, in *The Portable Nietzsche*, edited and translated by Walter Kaufman, Harmondsworth, 1978, p. 298.

REFERENCES

Adams, Robert Merrihew, 'Saints', *Journal of Philosophy*, 1984, 81: 392–401.

Arendt, Hannah, *On Revolution*, London: Faber & Faber, 1963.

Arendt, Hannah, *The Human Condition*, Chicago: University of Chicago Press, 1958; 2nd impression, 1959.

Arendt, Hannah, *Between Past and Future*, London: Faber & Faber, 1961.

Arendt, Hannah, *Men in Dark Times*, Harmondsworth: Penguin Books, 1973.

Arendt, Hannah, *Lectures on Kant's Political Philosophy*, edited with an Interpretive Essay by Ronald Beiner, Chicago: University of Chicago Press, 1982.

Arendt, Hannah, *On Violence*, London: Allen Lane, 1970.

Arendt, Hannah, 'Truth in politics', in Peter Laslett and W. G. Runciman (eds), *Philosophy, Politics and Society*, Third Series, Oxford: Basil Blackwell, 1967, pp. 104–33.

Aristotle, *Nicomachean Ethics*, translated by W. D. Ross, *The Works of Aristotle*, vol. IX, Oxford: Oxford University Press, 1925; reprinted 1940.

Aristotle, *Magna Moralia*, translated by St George Stock, *The Works of Aristotle*, vol. IX, Oxford: Oxford University Press, 1925; reprinted 1940.

Aristotle, *Eudemian Ethics*, translated by J. Solomon, *The Works of Aristotle*, vol. IX, Oxford: Oxford University Press, 1925; reprinted 1940.

Aristotle, *Politics*, translated by Benjamin Jowett, in *The Works of Aristotle*, vol. X, Oxford: Oxford University Press, 1921; reprinted 1946.

Aristotle, *Rhetoric*, translated by W. Rhys Roberts, in *The Works of Aristotle*, vol. XI, Oxford: Oxford University Press, 1928.

Auden, W. H., *Herman Melville* in *Collected Poems*, edited by Edward Mendelson, London: Faber, 1976.

Bambrough, Renford (ed.), *Plato, Popper and Politics*, Cambridge: Heffer, 1967.

Bambrough, Renford (ed.), *Wisdom: Twelve Essays*, Oxford: Basil Blackwell, 1974.

Beardsmore, R. W., 'Learning from a Novel', Royal Institute of Philosophy Lectures, vol. VI, 1971–2, in *Philosophy and the Arts*, edited by Godfrey Vesey, London: Macmillan, 1973, pp. 23–46.

Beiner, Ronald *Political Judgment*, London: Methuen, 1983.

272

REFERENCES

Benn, Stanley I., 'Public and private morality: Clean living and dirty hands', in S. I. Benn and G. F. Gauss (eds), *Public and Private in Social Life*, London: Croom Helm, 1983, pp. 155–81.

Benn, S. I., 'Wickedness', *Ethics*, July 1985, 95: 795–810.

Berki, R. N., *On Political Realism*, London: Dent, 1981.

Berthoud, Jacques, *Joseph Conrad, The Major Phase*, Cambridge: Cambridge University Press, 1978.

Bosanquet, Bernard, *The Philosophical Theory of the State* (1899); 4th edn 1923; reprinted 1951, London: Macmillan.

Bradley, F. H., *Ethical Studies* (1876); 2nd edn 1927; reprinted 1959, Oxford: Oxford University Press.

Brecht, Berthold, 'Study of the first scene of Shakespeare's *Coriolanus*', in *Brecht on Theatre, the Development of an Aesthetic*, translation and notes by John Willett, London: Methuen, 1964, pp. 252–65.

Bunyan, John, *The Pilgrim's Progress*, London, 1892.

Collingwood, R. G. *Speculum Mentis*, 1924; reprinted 1963, Oxford: Clarendon Press.

Conrad, J., *The Secret Agent* (1907), Harmondsworth: Penguin Books, 1965.

Conrad, J., *Heart of Darkness*, London: Dent, 1933.

Crick, Bernard, *In Defence of Politics*, Harmondsworth: Penguin, 1964.

Donne, John, *To the Countesse of Bedford*, in *Complete Poetry and Selected Prose*, edited by John Hayward, London: The Nonesuch Press, 1929; 4th impression 1936.

Dostoevsky, Fyodor, *Crime and Punishment*, translated by David Magarshack, Harmondsworth: Penguin Books, 1975.

Dostoevsky, Fyodor, *The Idiot*, translated with an introduction by David Magarshack, Harmondsworth: Penguin Books, 1975.

Dworkin, Ronald, *Law's Empire*, London: Fontana, 1986.

Flanagan, Kieran, 'The experience of innocence as a social construction', *Philosophical Studies*, The National University of Ireland, Dublin, 1981. 28: 104–40.

Flanagan, Owen, 'Admirable immorality and admirable imperfection', *Journal of Philosophy*, 1986, 83: 41–60.

Foot, Philippa, *Virtues and Vices and Other Essays in Moral Philosophy*, Oxford: Basil Blackwell, 1978; reprinted 1985.

Foot, Philippa, 'Utilitarianism and the virtues', *Mind*, 1985, 94: 196–209.

Gallie, W. B., *Philosophy and the Historical Understanding*, London: Chatto & Windus, 1964.

Geach, P. T., *The Virtues, The Stanton Lectures 1973–4*, Cambridge: Cambridge University Press, 1977.

Greene, Graham, *The Quiet American*, London: William Heinemann, 1955.

Greenleaf, W. H., *Order, Empiricism and Politics, Two Traditions of English Political Thought, 1500–1700*, Oxford: Oxford University Press, 1964.

Guthrie, W. K. C., *A History of Greek Philosophy, Vol. III, The Fifth-Century Enlightenment*, Cambridge: Cambridge University Press, 1969.

Haksar, Vinit, *Equality, Liberty and Perfectionism*, Oxford: Oxford University Press, 1979.

Hampshire, Stuart (ed.), *Public and Private Morality*, Cambridge: Cambridge University Press, 1978.

Hardie, W. F. R., *Aristotle's Ethical Theory*, Oxford: Clarendon Press, 1968.

Hare, R. M., *Freedom and Reason*, Oxford: Oxford University Press, 1963; reprinted 1965.

Hawthorne, Nathaniel, *The Blithedale Romance*, London, 1901.

Hegel, G. W. F., *Lectures on the Philosophy of Religion*, translated by Rev. E. B. Spiers and J. Burdon Sanderson, 3 vols, London, 1985; reprinted The Humanities Press, 1974.

Hegel, G. W. F., *Aesthetics, Lectures on Fine Art*, translated by T. M. Knox, 2 vols, Oxford: Oxford University Press, 1975.

Hegel, G. W. F., *Lectures on the History of Philosophy*, translated by E. S. Haldane, 3 vols., London: Kegan Paul, Trench and Trübner 1892.

Hegel, G. W. F., *Lectures on the Philosophy of World History, Introduction: Reason in History* translated by H. B. Nisbet, with an introduction by Duncan Forbes, Cambridge: Cambridge University Press, 1975.

Hegel, G. W. F., *Phenomenology of Spirit*, translated by A. V. Miller, Oxford: Oxford University Press, 1977; reprinted 1979.

Hegel, G. W. F., *Early Theological Writings* (1948), translated by T. M. Knox, with an introduction and fragments translated by Richard Kroner, Philadelphia: University of Pennsylvania Press, 1971.

Hegel, G. W. F., *Philosophy of Right* (1952) translated with notes by T. M. Knox, Oxford: Oxford University Press, 1967.

Hegel, G. W. F., *Hegel's Political Writings*, translated by T. M. Knox with an introductory essay by Z. A. Pelczynski, Oxford: Oxford University Press, 1964.

Heyd, David, *Supererogation, Its Status in Ethical Theory*, Cambridge: Cambridge University Press, 1982.

Hill, Geoffrey, *Funeral Music An Essay*, in Jon Silkin (ed.), *Poetry of the Committed Individual*, Harmondsworth: Penguin, 1973.

Holland, R. F., *Against Empiricism, On Education, Epistemology and Value*, Oxford: Basil Blackwell, 1980.

Hollander, P., *Political Pilgrims, Travels of Western Intellectuals to the Soviet Union, China, and Cuba, 1928–1978*, Oxford: Oxford University Press, 1981, pp. 145–6.

Hollis, Martin, 'Dirty hands', *British Journal of Political Science*, 12 October 1982, 19: 385–98.

Hulme, T. E., *Speculations*, London: Routledge & Kegan Paul, 1924; reprinted 1949.

Hume, David, *An Enquiry Concerning the Principles of Morals*, edited by L. A. Selby-Bigge, Oxford: Oxford University Press, 1951.

Hume, David, *A Treatise of Human Nature*, edited by L. A. Selby-Bigge, Oxford, 1888; reprinted 1949.

Hutchings, P. A. E., *Kant on Absolute Value*, London: Allen & Unwin, 1972.

Irwin, Terence, *Plato's Moral Theory, the Early and Middle Dialogues*, Oxford: Clarendon Press, 1977.

James, Henry, *The Golden Bowl*, 1904; Harmondsworth: Penguin Books, 1974.

REFERENCES

Kant, I., *Lectures on Ethics*, translated by Louis Infield, Foreword by Lewis White Beck, Indianapolis: Hackett Publishing Company, 1963.

Kant, I., *Critique of Practical Reason and other Works on the Theory of Ethics*, translated by Thomas Kingsmill Abbott, London: Longman, 1909; reprinted 1959.

Kant, I., *Kant's Political Writings*, edited with an introduction and notes by Hans Reiss, translated by H. B. Nisbet, Cambridge: Cambridge University Press, 1970.

Kateb, George, *Hannah Arendt: Politics, Conscience, Evil*, Oxford: Martin Robertson, 1983.

Kierkegaard, S., *The Concept of Irony*, translated with an introduction and notes by Lee M. Capel, London: Collins, 1966.

Kierkegaard, S., *Either/Or*, vol. II, translated by Walter Lowrie, with revisions and a foreword by Howard A. Johnson, Princeton: Princeton University Press, 1971; reprinted 1974.

Kierkegaard, S., *Fear and Trembling*, edited and translated by Howard V. Hong and Edna J. Hong, Princeton: Princeton University Press, 1983.

Krook, Dorothea, *Three Traditions of Moral Thought*, Cambridge: Cambridge University Press, 1959.

Letwin, Shirley Robin, *The Gentleman in Trollope: Individuality and Moral Conduct*, London: Macmillan, 1982.

Lewis, C. S., *Studies in Words*, Cambridge: Cambridge University Press, 1960.

Machiavelli, N., *The Discourses*, translated by Leslie J. Walker, 2 vols, London: Routledge & Kegan Paul, 1950.

Machiavelli, N., *The Prince*, New York: The Modern Library, 1950

McMahon, Christopher, 'Morality and the invisible hand', *Philosophy and Public Affairs* 1981, 10: 247–77.

Manser, Anthony, Review of D. Z. Phillips, *Through a Darkening Glass*, in *Religious Studies*, 1985, 19: 426–8.

Martineau, Harriet, *Society in America*, edited and abridged by Seymour Martin Lipsett, New York: Anchor Books, 1962.

Melden, A. I., 'Saints and supererogation', in Ilham Dilman (ed.), *Philosophy and Life, Essays on John Wisdom*, The Hague: Martinus Nijhoff 1984, pp. 61–81.

Melville, Herman, *Billy Budd, Sailor and other Stories*, selected and edited by Harold Beaver, Harmondsworth: Penguin Books, 1970.

Milo, Ronald D., *Immorality*, Princeton: Princeton University Press, 1984.

Morris, Herbert, *On Guilt and Innocence, Essays in Legal Philosophy and Moral Psychology*, Berkeley: University of California Press, 1976.

Murdoch, Iris, *The Bell*, St Albans: Triad/Panther, 1976.

Murdoch, Iris, 'Vision and choice in morality', *Proceedings of the Aristotelian Society*, Supplementary Volume 1956, 30: 32–58.

Murdoch, Iris, 'On natural novelists and unnatural philosophers', Interview with Bryan Magee, *The Listener* 27 April 1978, pp. 533–5.

Murdoch, Iris, 'Against dryness', *Encounter*, January 1961, 16: 16–20.

Murdoch, Iris, *The Sovereignty of Good*, London: Routledge & Kegan Paul, 1970.

Nagel, Thomas, 'Ruthlessness in public life', in Stuart Hampshire (ed.), *Public and Private Morality*, Cambridge: Cambridge University Press, 1978, pp. 75–91.

Nehemas, Alexander, *Nietzsche, Life as Literature*, Harvard: Harvard University Press, 1986.

Nietzsche, F., *Thus Spoke Zarathustra*, in *The Portable Nietzsche*, edited and translated by Walter Kaufman, Harmondsworth: Penguin Books, 1976, repr. 1978.

Nietzsche, F., *On the Genealogy of Morals*, translated by Walter Kaufman and R. J. Hollingdale, New York: The Modern Library, Random House, 1969.

Nietzsche, F., *Basic Writings of Nietzsche*, translated by Walker Kaufman, New York: The Modern Library, Random House, 1968.

Nietzsche, F., *Human, All Too Human*, translated by R. J. Hollingdale, Cambridge: Cambridge University Press, 1986.

Nietzsche, F., *Daybreak, Thoughts on the Prejudices of Morality*, translated by R. J. Hollingdale, Cambridge: Cambridge University Press, 1982.

Nozick, Robert, *Anarchy, State and Utopia*, Oxford: Basil Blackwell, 1974.

Nussbaum, Martha Craven, *The Fragility of Goodness*, Cambridge: Cambridge University Press, 1986.

Nussbaum, Martha Craven, 'Flawed crystals: James's The Golden Bowl and literature as moral philosophy', *New Literary History*, Autumn 1983, 15(1): 25–50.

Oakeshott, M., *On Human Conduct*, Oxford: Oxford University Press, 1975.

Oakeshott, M., *Rationalism in Politics*, London: Methuen, 1962.

O'Flaherty, Liam, *The Assassin*, London: Jonathan Cape, 1935.

Orwell, George, *Writers and Leviathan*, in *Collected Essays*, London: Secker & Warburg, 1961, pp. 427–34.

Orwell, George, *Politics vs Literature*, in *Collected Essays*, London: Secker & Warburg, 1961, pp. 377–98.

Orwell, George, *Reflections on Gandhi*, in *The Collected Essays, Journalism and Letters, vol. 4, In Front of Your Nose, 1945–50*, Harmondsworth: Penguin Books, 1970, pp. 523–31.

Parekh, Bhikhu, *Hannah Arendt and the Search for a New Political Philosophy*, London: Macmillan, 1981.

Paskins, B. and Dockrill, Michael, *The Ethics of War*, London: Duckworth, 1979.

Phillips, D. Z., *Some Limits to Moral Endeavour*, Swansea: University College, 1971.

Phillips, D. Z., *Through a Darkening Glass*, Oxford: Basil Blackwell, 1982.

Phillips, D. Z., 'Does it Pay To Be Good'? *Proceedings of the Aristotelian Society*, 1964–5, NS 65: 45–60.

Phillips, D. Z., 'In search of the moral "must": Mrs Foot's fugitive thought', *Philosophical Quarterly*, 1977, 27: 140–57.

Plato, *The Dialogues of Plato*, translated by Benjamin Jowett, vol. I., 3rd edition, Oxford, 1892.

Plato, *Socratic Dialogues*, translated by W. D. Woodhead, London: Nelson, 1953.

REFERENCES

Plato, *The Republic*, translated by F. M. Cornford, Oxford: Oxford University Press, 1961.

Pybus, Elizabeth M., 'Saints and heroes', *Philosophy*, 1982, 57: 193–9.

Raphael, D. D., 'Can literature be moral philosophy', *New Literary History*, Autumn 1983, 15(1): 1–12.

Rawls, John, *A Theory of Justice*, Oxford: Oxford University Press, 1972.

Rawls, John, 'Kantian constructivism in moral theory', *The Journal of Philosophy*, September 1980 77(9): 515–72.

Rawls, John, 'Social unity and primary goods', in Amartya Sen and Bernard Williams (eds), *Utilitarianism and Beyond*, Cambridge: Cambridge University Press, 1982, pp. 159–85.

Rawls, John, 'Justice as fairness: Political not metaphysical', *Philosophy and Public Affairs*, 1985, 14: 223–51.

Rawls, John, 'The basic structure as subject', in Alvin I. Goldman and Jaegmon Kim (eds), *Values and Morals, Essays in Honor of William Frankena, Charles Stevenson and Richard Brandt*, Dordrecht: D. Reidel, 1978, pp. 47–71.

Reyburn, H. A., *The Ethical Theory of Hegel*, Oxford: Oxford University Press, 1921.

Robinson, Jonathan, *Duty and Hypocrisy in Hegel's Phenomenology of Mind, An Essay in the Real and Ideal*, Toronto: University of Toronto Press, 1977.

Rosen, Stanley, *G. W. F. Hegel, An Introduction to the Science of Wisdom*, New Haven: Yale University Press, 1974.

Rousseau J.-J., *Emile*, translated by Barbara Foxley, London: Dent, 1911; reprinted 1969.

Rousseau, J.-J., *The Social Contract and Discourses*, translated by G. D. H. Cole, London: Dent, 1913; reprinted 1963.

Rowse, A. L., *All Souls and Appeasement*, London: Macmillan, 1961.

Savage, D. S., 'The innocence of Evelyn Waugh', in B. Rajan (ed.), *The Novelist as thinker*, London: Dennis Dobson, 1947, pp. 34–46.

Schiller, F., *On The Aesthetic Education of Man*, edited and translated by Elizabeth M. Wilkinson and L. A. Willoughby, Oxford: Oxford University Press, 1982.

Scorza, Thomas J., 'Technology, philosophy and political virtue: The case of Billy Budd, Sailor', *Interpretation*, 1975, 5 (1): 91–107.

Scruton, Roger, *The Politics of Culture*, Manchester: Carcanet Press, 1981.

Shakespeare, W., *The Complete Works*, edited by W. Craig, Oxford: Oxford University Press, 1964.

Shakespeare, W., *Henry VI (3)*, The Arden Shakespeare, introduction by A. S. Cairncross, London: Methuen, 1964.

Shklar, J., *Freedom and Independence, A Study in the Political Ideas of Hegel's Phenomenology of Mind*, Cambridge: Cambridge University Press, 1976.

Shklar, J., *Ordinary Vices*, London: Harvard University Press, 1984.

Sidgwick, H., *The Elements of Politics* (1891), 4th edn, London: Macmillan, 1919.

Singer, Peter, 'Famine, affluence and morality', *Philosophy and Public Affairs*, 1972, 1: 229–43.

Slote, M., *Goods and Virtues*, Oxford: Clarendon Press, 1983.

Slote, M., 'Morality and ignorance', *Journal of Philosophy*, December 1977, 74(12): 745–67.

Smart, J. J. C. and Bernard Williams, *Utilitarianism For and Against*, Cambridge: Cambridge University Press, 1973; reprinted 1980.

Smith, Adam, *The Theory of Moral Sentiments*, edited by D. D. Raphael and A. L. Macfie, The Glasgow Edition of the Works of Adam Smith, vol. 1, Oxford: Clarendon Press, 1976; reprinted 1979.

Sophocles, *Antigone*, in *The Theban Plays*, translated by E. F. Watling, Harmondsworth: Penguin Books, 1956.

Steiner, George, *Antigones*, Oxford: Clarendon Press, 1984.

Stern, J. P., *On Realism*, London: Routledge & Kegan Paul, 1973.

Taylor, Charles, *Hegel*, Cambridge: Cambridge University Press, 1975.

Taylor, Charles, 'Ethics and politics', in H. J. Johnson, J. J. Leach, and R. G. Muehlmann (eds), *Revolutions, Systems and Theories, Essays in Political Philosophy*, Dordrecht: D. Reidel, 1979, pp. 99–111.

Tillyard, E. M. W., *The Elizabethan World Picture*, London: Chatto & Windus, 1943.

Trigg, Roger, *Reason and Commitment*, Cambridge: Cambridge University Press, 1973.

Urmson, J. O., 'Saints and heroes', in Joel Feinberg (ed.), *Moral Concepts*, Oxford: Oxford University Press, 1969, pp. 60–73.

Wallace, James D., *Virtues and Vices*, London: Cornell University Press, 1978.

Walzer, Michael, 'Political action: The problem of dirty hands', *Philosophy and Public Affairs*, 1973, 2: 160–80.

Watson, Gary, 'Virtues in excess', *Philosophical Studies*, 1984, 46: 57–74.

Waugh, Evelyn, *Decline and Fall*, Harmondsworth: Penguin Books, 1971.

Webb, C. C. J., *Kant's Philosophy of Religion*, Oxford: Clarendon Press, 1926.

Weber, Max, *From Max Weber*, edited by H. H. Gerth and C. Wright Mills, Oxford: Oxford University Press, 1958.

Weil, Simone, *Lectures on Philosophy*, translated by Hugh Price, with an introduction by Peter Winch, Cambridge: Cambridge University Press, 1978.

Weston, M. H., 'Willing the good', *Ratio*, 1982, 24(2): 101–9.

Wilde, Oscar, *Plays*, Harmondsworth: Penguin Books, 1963.

Williams, Bernard, *Ethics and the Limits of Philosophy*, London: Fontana, 1985.

Williams, Bernard, 'Moral luck', *Philosophical Papers 1973–80*, Cambridge: Cambridge University Press, 1981; reprinted 1985.

Williams, Bernard, 'Politics and moral character', in Stuart Hampshire (ed.), *Public and Private Morality*, Cambridge: Cambridge University Press, 1978, pp. 55–73.

Winch, Peter., *Ethics and Action*, London: Routledge & Kegan Paul, 1972.

Wisdom, John, *Paradox and Discovery*, Oxford: Basil Blackwell, 1965.

Wittgenstein, L., *Tractatus Logico-Philosophicus*, translated by D. F. Pears and B. F. McGuinness, London: Routledge & Kegan Paul, 1966.

Wittgenstein, L., 'Wittgenstein's Lecture on Ethics', *Philosophical Review*, 1965, 74: 3–12.

REFERENCES

Wittgenstein L., *Philosophical Investigations*, translated by G. E. M. Anscombe, Oxford: Basil Blackwell, 2nd edn, 1958.

Wolf, Susan, 'Moral saints', *Journal of Philosophy*, August 1982, 79(8): 419–39.

Yeats, W. B., *The Collected Poems*, London: Macmillan, 1933; reprinted 1963.

Young-Bruehl, Elisabeth, *Hannah Arendt, For Love of the World*, London: Yale University Press, 1982.

NAME INDEX

Adams, Robert Merrihew 264 n.26
Adeimantus 28
Aeschylus 90
Antiphon 18
Archelaus 22
Arendt, Hannah 126, 150, 153–65, 166–7, 171, 182, 185–6, 209–11, 216, 256; 'The crisis in culture' 164; *Lectures on Kant's Political Philosophy* 254; *Men in Dark Times* 160; *On Revolution* 157, 163, 210; *On Violence* 209
Aristotle 22, 35–47, 86, 141, 175; *Eudemian Ethics* 41; *Rhetoric* 43
Auden, W. H. 199

Bakunin, M. 71
Bambrough, Renford 179, 259 n.19
Beardsmore, R. W. 267 n.23
Beiner, Ronald 250–1; *Political Judgement* 250
Benn, S. I. 202
Berki, R. N. 261 n.5
Berthoud, J. 248, 255–6
Bosanquet, Bernard 76–8; *The Philosophical Theory of the State* 76
Bradley, F. H. 169
Brecht, Bertolt 93–4
Bunyan, John 256; *The Pilgrim's Progress* 116
Burke, E. 175, 214
Byron, Lord 219

Cairncross, A. S. 194
Callicles 18, 19, 20
Camus, A. 172; *The Rebel* 172
Churchill, W. 114
Clough, A. H. 219

Collingwood, R. G. 218; *Speculum Mentis* 218
Conrad, Joseph 13, 178, 180, 219; *Heart of Darkness* 219, 222, 248, 255–6; *The Secret Agent* 178, 180, 255
Crick, Bernard 249–50, 253; *In Defence of Politics* 249

Disraeli, B. 175; *Tancred* 175
Donne, John 18, 70; *To the Countesse of Bedford* 18
Dostoevsky, F. 10, 98, 152; *Crime and Punishment* 98; *The Idiot* 10
Dworkin, Ronald 59–61; *Law's Empire* 59

Eichmann, A. 155

Flanagan, Kieran 258 n.1
Flanagan, Owen 112
Foot, Philippa 2, 4
Forster, E. M. 175; *The Longest Journey* 175

Gallie, W. B. 171
Gandhi, M. 100–2, 105
Gauguin, P. 114, 243–5, 252–3
Geach, Peter 3, 252
Goya, F. 179; *Etchings of War* 179
Greene, Graham: *The Quiet American* 2, 101, 197, 217, 218–34, 243, 246
Greenleaf, W. H. 267 n.6
Guthrie, W. K. C. 25

Haksar, Vinit 32–3
Hampshire, Stuart 78–9
Hardie, W. F. R. 259 n.5
Hardy, Thomas 175; *Jude the Obscure* 175
Hare, R. M. 166, 178; *Freedom and Reason* 166

Hawthorne, Nathaniel 116; *The Blithedale Romance* 116
Hegel, G. W. F. 74–5, 91, 126, 127–45, 153, 156, 165, 172, 185, 190, 257; *Aesthetics* 131; *Lectures on the History of Philosophy* 91, 128; *Lectures on the Philosophy of World History* 133, 235; *Phenomenology* 134, 137–40; *Philosophy of Right* 142, 190
Herod 9
Heyd, David 63, 64, 107–8, 253
Hill, Geoffrey 184; *Funeral Music, An Essay* 184
Hobbes, Thomas 86, 94
Holland, R. F. 102, 103, 104–5, 106, 121–4, 125, 238–41; *Against Empiricism* 102, 121, 125, 238
Hollander, Paul 270 n.13
Hollis, Martin 82–4, 85
Homer 179; *Iliad* 179
Hulme, T. E. 170, 173
Hume, David 2, 88–9, 90, 115–16, 119; *A Treatise of Human Nature* 89
Hutchings, Patrick A. E. 261 n.59

Irwin, Terence 31

James, Henry: *The Golden Bowl* 45–6, 180; *The Princess Casamassima* 180
Jefferies, Richard 178; *The Story of My Heart* 178
Jesus 127, 134, 135, 144, 151, 153, 155
Jowett, B. 6

Kant, I, 4–5, 48–59, 65, 70, 85, 129, 134, 137–8, 140, 161, 202; *Lectures on Ethics* 48; *Perpetual Peace* 54
Kateb, George 266 n.47
Kierkegaard, S. 15, 26, 116, 132
Koestler, A. 172; *Darkness at Noon* 175, 178
Krook, Dorothea 258 n.12

Letwin, Shirley Robin 14–15
Lewis, C. S. 167; *Studies in Words* 167
Lincoln, A. 249–50

Machiavelli, N. 1, 55, 71–5, 82, 86, 94, 127, 141, 143, 146, 153, 154, 185, 188–9, 192, 194, 213, 237; *The Discourses* 71, 74, 86, 159, 235; *The Prince* 1, 71, 72
McMahon, Christopher 262 n.17
Manser, Anthony 267 n.22

Martineau, Harriet 69
Marx, K. 71, 150, 172, 175
Melden, A. I. 119–20
Melville, H.: *Billy Budd, Sailor* 2, 23, 33, 37, 155, 157–8, 162–3, 197, 198–217, 228, 229, 240, 255
Mill, J. S. 175, 178; *Autobiography* 178; *On Liberty* 175
Milo, Ronald D. 268 n.7
Montaigne, M. 203, 213
Morris, Herbert 26, 258 n.1, 259 n.14
Murdoch, Iris 1, 10, 106, 116, 169–70, 173, 174, 176–7, 252–3; 'Against dryness' 176; *The Bell* 1, 10, 116; 'On natural novelists and unnatural philosophers' 166; *The Sovereignty of Good* 252

Nagel, Thomas 79, 81, 83; 'Ruthlessness in public life' 68
Nehemas, Alexander 265 n.41
Nelson, Lord 212
Nietzsche, F. 126, 145–50, 153, 165, 184, 214, 219, 257; *Beyond Good and Evil* 147; *Daybreak* 145; *Ecce Homo* 147; *On the Genealogy of Morals* 149; *Human, All Too Human* 149; *Thus Spoke Zarathustra* 184
Nozick, Robert 100, 101, 254–5; *Anarchy, State and Utopia* 100, 254
Nussbaum, Martha C. 180, 260 n.40, 267 n.27

Oakeshott, Michael 12–13, 71, 78, 218, 227; 'On being conservative' 12–13; *Rationalism in Politics* 218
O'Flaherty, L. 174; *The Assassin* 174
Orwell, George 69, 100–2, 105, 106, 172–3; *Nineteen Eighty-Four* 172; *Politics vs Literature* 172; *Writers and Leviathan* 69

Parekh, Bhikhu 266 n.61, 266 n.1
Pascal, B. 228
Paskins, Barrie 84
Periander 40
Phillips, D. Z. 3, 4, 177
Plato 19, 22, 24, 25, 27–34, 35, 39, 47, 70, 82, 103; *Apology* 27; *Crito* 25; *Gorgias* 19, 22, 24; *Phaedrus* 24; *Republic* 27, 28, 29, 31, 32, 34
Polus 23
Pybus, Elizabeth M. 264 n.28

INDEX

Raphael, D. D. 267 n.15
Rawls, John 61–6, 115, 116, 168–9, 173, 176; *A Theory of Justice* 61
Reyburn, H. A. 264 n.3
Robespierre, M. 158
Robinson, Jonathan 264 n.2
Rosen, Stanley 133–4, 138
Rousseau, Jean-Jacques 5, 9, 71, 77, 140, 157–8, 181–3, 199, 212, 213, 214; *Emile* 182, 198; *The Social Contract* 5, 182
Rowse, A. L. 184; *All Souls and Appeasement* 184

Savage, D. S. 260 n.28
Schiller, F. 129–30
Schlegel, F. 133
Scorza, Thomas J. 211–14
Scruton, R. 173–4
Shakespeare, W.: *Coriolanus* 86–99, 174; *Henry VI* (Part 2) 16; *Henry VI* (Part 3) 2, 9, 16, 101, 185–97, 217, 237; *Julius Caesar* 68
Shklar, Judith 99, 144
Sidgwick, Henry 204–5, 206, 239
Singer, Peter 258 n.11
Slote, Michael 11–12, 15, 113–14, 121, 241–3; *Goods and Virtues* 11–12
Smith, Adam 8, 98; *The Theory of Moral Sentiments* 8, 98
Socrates 18–27, 28, 29, 35, 126, 144, 146, 153, 202
Sophocles 141; *Antigone* 141, 143–5, 198
Steiner, George 13, 143
Stern, J. P. 10, 152

Strong, Anna Louise 255
Swift, J. 172

Taylor, Charles 18, 135, 139, 251; 'Ethics and politics' 18
Thucydides 146, 172, 175
Tillyard, E. M. W. 186, 194
Trigg, Roger 230–3

Urmson, J. O. 109–11, 112, 117, 118

Wallace, James D. 268 n.7
Walzer, Michael 79–81, 84
Watson, Gary 264 n.27
Waugh, Evelyn 38; *Decline and Fall* 38
Webb, C. C. J. 49
Weber, Max 150–1
Weil, Simone 96; *Lectures on Philosophy* 96
Weston, M. H. 105, 106
Wilde, Oscar 100; *The Importance of Being Earnest* 100
Williams, Bernard 36, 81, 82, 86, 111, 122, 243–5, 252, 256; *Ethics and the Limits of Philosophy* 86; 'Moral luck' 243
Williamson, Henry 178; *The Pathway* 178
Winch, Peter 14–15, 204–9, 215, 232
Wisdom, John 125; *Paradox and Discovery* 125
Wittgenstein, L. 6, 103–4, 169; *Tractatus Logico-Philosophicus* 103–4
Wolf, Susan 111–13, 114, 117, 118
Wordsworth, W. 178

Yeats, W. B. 30–1
Young-Bruehl, Elisabeth 266 n.47